THE
REALITY
CLUB

EDITED BY

JOHN BROCKMAN

LYNX BOOKS
New York

Excerpt from *The Dreams of Reason* by Heinz R. Pagels used by permission from Simon & Schuster, Inc.

Library of Congress Cataloging-in-Publication Data

The Reality Club

   1. Philosophy. 2. Reality. 3. Life. I. Brockman,
John, 1941–
B73.R43   1988   100   88-8254
ISBN 1-55802-192-2

THE REALITY CLUB

FIRST PRINTING/OCTOBER 1988

In Memory of

Heinz R. Pagels

(1939–1988)

"Reason dreams of an empire of knowledge, a mansion of the mind. Yet sometimes we end up living in a hovel by its side. Reason has shown us our capacity for power, both to create and to destroy. Yet how we use that power rests on our deeper capacities which lie beyond the reach of reason, beyond our traditions and culture, stretching far back into the depths of the evolutionary process that created our species, a process that ultimately asserts the power of life over death. And, ironically, even death, as part of the process of life, asserts that power. That is how we have come into being and now find ourselves committed to the unrelenting struggle of ordinary human existence.

"We surely stand at the threshold of a great adventure of the human spirit—a new synthesis of knowledge, a potential integration of art and science, a deeper grasp of human psychology, a deepening of the symbolic representations of our existence and feelings as given in religion and culture, the formation of an international order based on cooperation and nonviolent competition. It seems not too much to hope for these things.

"The future, as always, belongs to the dreamers."

Heinz R. Pagels

The Dreams of Reason

ACKNOWLEDGMENTS

Kevin Kelley, editor of *The Whole Earth Review*, first suggested a publication about ideas and themes represented during Reality Club meetings. The resulting Reality Club issue of *WER* (summer, 1987) inspired this book. Michael Fine, president of Lynx Communications, Inc., has been a good friend and supportive publisher in all aspects of launching this project. A number of members have read and commented on the contributions. They include Gerald Feinberg, William Calvin, Steven Levy, Mark Mirsky, and Richard Rabkin. Several of the themes begun in an interview between me and Steven Levy in the Reality Club issue of *WER* have been elaborated upon in the introduction to this book, and I wish to thank Stewart Brand for his supportive feedback and for first elucidating the metaphor of intellectual life as The Reality Club.

I wish to thank Janet Byrne for her useful editorial suggestions. Katinka Matson, literary agent for *The Reality Club* and associate editor, has worked closely with me on every phase of this project.

Finally, I wish to acknowledge the many contributions of the late Heinz Pagels who played a major role in running the Reality Club over the past two years and was one of its founding members. Heinz died on July 23, 1988 in a mountaineering accident while climbing Pyramid Peak, a 14,000-foot summit near his summer home in Aspen, Colorado. Heinz was actively involved in all aspects of The Reality Club and was a great source of interesting ideas and constructive criticism regarding this book. We have all benefited from his intelligence, erudition, and energizing presence. We shall miss him.

CONTENTS

THE
REALITY
CLUB

JOHN BROCKMAN

The motto of The Reality Club is "to arrive at the edge of the world's knowledge, seek out the most complex and sophisticated minds, put them in a room together, and have them ask each other the questions they are asking themselves."

Since 1981 The Reality Club has held free-for-all meetings once or twice a month, usually in New York. The evening consists of a one-hour talk or presentation by a speaker to Reality Club members. The talk is followed by lively, challenging, and often impolite discussion. We charge the speakers to represent an idea of reality by describing their creative work, their lives, and the questions they are asking themselves. We also want them to share with us the boundaries of their knowledge and experience.

In selecting speakers we look for people whose exceptional creative work has expanded our notion of who and what we are. In addition to the fourteen contributors to *The Reality Club 1,* the more than one hundred speakers have included psychologist Rollo May, Zen master Richard Baker-Roshi, political activist Abbie Hoffman, poet Michael McClure, mathematician Benoit Mandelbrot, cultural historian William Irwin Thompson, essayist Annie Dillard, physicist Freeman Dyson, poet Gerd Stern, energy experts Amory and Hunter Lovins, actor Ellen Burstyn, feminist Betty Friedan, computer scientist Edward Feigenbaum, plant physiologist Rupert Sheldrake, physicist Fritjof Capra, religious historian Elaine Pagels, physicist Heinz Pagels, anthropologist-shaman Michael Harner, director Richard Foreman, sociologist Sherry Turkle, and editor Stewart Brand. (See page 319 for a list of Reality Club talks.)

The ideas behind the creation of The Reality Club began

to germinate in my mind in the 1960s. Conceptual artist James Lee Byars and I used to spend a part of every day walking and talking in Central Park. He had a theory that reality was something you "took off the tongue." I was intrigued with the similar idea that reality is a process of decreation. It is what people say it is. Reality is invention—human invention—an invention taken off the tongues of a finite number of individuals.

The format of the meetings was inspired by a series of weekly meetings with the composer John Cage to which I was invited in the mid-1960s by Dick Higgins of Something Else Press. Cage was interested in meeting young, creative people in New York. The agenda had Cage leading a discussion. Everyone in the room was erudite, filled with intellectual hunger and the desire to exchange ideas. Most of them went on to brilliant careers in the arts.

The sessions were held at Higgins's town house in Chelsea. Cage would throw out some thoughts and the talk would go around the room. He had a theory, that there is *one mind*—the one we all share. An idea would bounce back and forth across the room without ownership and yet have a life of its own and an evolution in and of itself.

Simultaneously, I was grappling with certain issues and ideas that were changing my own way of thinking. Marshall McLuhan got me excited about the ideas of biologist J. Z. Young. Young's idea was that man creates tools and then molds himself in their image. To me, this indicated that reality is man-made. The universe is an invention, a metaphor.

Soon after, I began assembling my own evenings of artists, writers, sculptors, and poets. We met in an unscheduled, haphazard way at my apartment. No agenda, except to be in the presence of one another's intelligence. I had realized that in New York, there are very few opportunities to sit down with people and discuss ideas in a rigorous manner. Most interactions are either social or business, and it is a rare occasion and special treat to be able to sit down with people who are your equals and seriously discuss what you have been thinking about. My vision for the club was formalized in 1981 to the point of naming it The Reality Club. I was on a long car trip with Katinka Matson, and I described to her what I thought was a witty idea for a club for the bright people I knew—most of whom were unable, because of their brains, to get into any kind of club, fraternity, or sorority in school. This club would have its own club jacket, motto, and exclusive membership. The name, The Reality Club, was, of course, a pun. Anyone who has read my books understands that my goal was to pose a challenge to contemporary ideas of language, thought, and reality. But the joke was on me. People took it very seriously and still do. Facts smirk.

Membership in The Reality Club is informal and by invitation only. If you are invited to talk before the club, you become a member. Speaker selection is a word-of-mouth enterprise. Quite often it simply comes down to people who interest me. Or members will suggest someone they are interested in hearing. There is no selection committee. Very few of our speakers are best-selling authors or famous in the mass culture. I am much more eager to hear ideas that have not been generally exposed, and I am particularly drawn to people who can tell me I'm wrong. Most individuals, by the time they are thirty, know almost as much as they are ever going to know, and the most important thing that they can get from another person is a sense of awkwardness, confusion, and contradiction. How do you live on the edge of the most sophisticated awareness that exists? Play the fool.

I recall a talk given by Paul Ryan, our resident cyberneticist and a former Passionist monk. Even now, I have no idea what he was talking about. But listening to him, verbally assaulting his positions and in turn being decimated by his gentle and Jesuitical intellectual Tai Chi, ranks as one of life's memorable experiences.

Another evening, I attempted to ask Lynn Margulis what the point was of talking about events that supposedly happened three billion years ago. How can the human mind even comprehend the idea of three billion years? That was the last word I got in.

It is not uncommon for a speaker to leave a meeting feeling like chopped liver, although the spirit of the meetings is good-natured and fun. One speaker, who had been working on a paper for two years, met with a barrage of highly critical and yet well-founded comments. He had put six years of his life into his new theories, and I was worried about how he would handle the negative response. The next day he called to tell me that the evening was a very useful experience as he had been working in intellectual isolation and was grateful for the opportunity to test his ideas out on a peer group. People with a deep knowledge of his field had wanted to set him right.

Speakers seldom get away with loose claims. Maybe a challenging question will come from a member who knows an alternative theory that really threatens what the speaker had to say. Or a member might come up with a great idea, totally out of left field, that only someone outside the speaker's field could come up with. This creates a very interesting dynamic.

The most challenging evenings are when the speakers present the questions they are asking themselves. This is in contrast to evenings during which the speakers discuss questions they have already answered. In communications theory information is not defined as data or input but rather as "a difference that makes a difference." It is this level I hope the speakers will achieve. I want speakers who are willing to take their ideas into the bull ring. As Heinz Pagels said, "We are interested in 'thinking smart,' versus the anesthesiology of 'wisdom.' "

The Reality Club encourages people who can take the materials of the culture in the arts, literature, and science and put them together in their own way. We live in a mass-produced culture where many people, even many established cultural arbiters, limit themselves to secondhand ideas, thoughts, and opinions. The Reality Club consists of individuals who create their own reality and do not accept an ersatz, appropriated reality. Our members are out there doing it rather than talking about and analyzing the people who are doing it.

In the spring of 1986 I accepted an invitation from *The Whole Earth Review* to be the guest editor of a "Reality Club Issue" of their publication. The strong response to that summer 1987 issue has inspired this first issue of *The Reality Club*, a semiannual publication. The essays presented here are representative of Reality Club talks, and in some cases, they are adaptations of talks.

The Reality Club is different from The Algonquin, The Apostles, The Bloomsbury Group, or The Club, but it offers the same quality of intellectual adventure. The Reality Club is not just a group of people. I see it as the constant shifting of metaphors, the advancement of ideas, the agreement on, and the invention of, reality. Intellectual life is The Reality Club.

John Brockman
New York City

THE TWO FACES OF CREATIVITY

▼

MORRIS BERMAN

. . . modern creative work has a strong addictive or compulsive component to it; the artist is expected to outdo himself or herself with each succeeding product. It is here that we see the schismogenic character of modern creativity most clearly. The structure is one of "upping the ante," in other words; work is often "unfinished" because it is done in the pursuit of an inaccessible ideal. It must depart from tradition, must create a new genre, and it gets difficult to keep on doing this. As a result, modern creativity tends to have high psychic costs.

There is one aspect of Western creativity that has been commented upon by sociologists and cultural historians alike, and that is its peculiar tendency to burn out or destroy the artist, often at a relatively young age. Why this should be so remains unclear, but the "tortured artist syndrome," represented by figures as diverse as James Dean and John Keats, does seem to be a persistent feature of modern Western life. Thus Elliott Jaques, some years ago, provided ample statistics to show a recurrent pattern of mid-life crisis, frequently leading to death, among creative people, while Katinka Matson, in *Short Lives*, gives the reader a series of extremely interesting vignettes that reveal artistic self-destructive tendencies all too clearly. In a similar vein, A. Alvarez, in his study of suicide, argues that modern creativity is "provisional, dissatisfied, restless." All of this, as the cultural anthropologist Gregory Bateson would have said, comes under the heading of "schismogenesis"—the tendency to move toward climax or breakdown; and in this sense, modern Western creativity is a reflection of the culture in which it is embedded. There are exceptions, of course, but the cliché of the driven (and, frequently, alcoholic) artist is not only common, but actually a kind of cultural ideal—a "good thing," as it were; or at least, something we have come to expect.[1]

That creativity has to be self-destructive or schismogenic is, accordingly, taken as a given. Genius continues to be regarded as akin to madness, and creative individuals are somehow seen as members of a separate species, inhabiting worlds that most of us will never see or even understand. The problem with this way of viewing human creativity is that it is ahistorical. It assumes that the mainsprings of the creative impulse are somehow archetypal, true for all time; that in effect, there is only one way to "do it." As a result, we have thousands of histories of art, music, science, architecture, and so on, but apparently nothing on the history of creativity itself. Of course, if the creative act is fixed for all time, then there is nothing to write. But suppose this were not so? Suppose the creative process itself has evolved over the centuries, or millennia? This would mean that there *is* more than one way to do it, and that future creativity might be a very different animal from the one it is now. My guess is that the creative process can be understood both historically and psychodynamically, in terms of a typology, and that such a typology can lay bare not only the nature(s) of creativity itself, but also of the wider culture(s) of which it is a part. Both in art and in society, schismogenesis leading to breakdown might not be the only option we have. What follows is thus an investigation into the varieties of creative experience as well as an attempt to explore what the alternatives to the schismogenic model are or might be.

One of the best treatments of the subject occurs, surprisingly enough, in an extraordinarily bad piece of historical writing published by Sigmund Freud in 1910, viz. his study of the life and work of Leonardo da Vinci.[2] As an historical argument, the essay is a complete failure, a mass of unsubstantiated conjecture and speculation. Yet in a few short pages, Freud generates a typology of the creative process that strikes me as being immensely suggestive, and it is one that stayed in my mind long after I forgot the discussion of Leonardo per se. Freud's typology is too stark, and it is also incomplete; yet given the available alternatives, it is not a bad place to start. Freud was specifically interested in intellectual activity, and its relationship to sexuality; but I believe that if we are willing to broaden this and talk in terms of sensual experience of the world in general—an experience that includes curiosity and exploration as major components—his analysis can be extended to all forms of creative work. Let me, therefore, take a bit of poetic license with Freud's exposition, modifying it in certain ways, and see whether it can be helpful to the inquiry at hand.

Freud begins his discussion by noting that there is a certain type of person who pursues creative activity "with the same passionate devotion that another would give to his love. . . ." The crucial event, says Freud, is the fate of what he calls the "period of infantile sexual researches," or, more generally, the pleasure the child takes in the sensual exploration of its surroundings. This may include curiosity about the birth process, but the larger expression is a tactile-erotic one, and this total lack of inhibition tends to make the parents nervous. Unconsciously, they are stirred to remember when they, too, were like this, and how this openness toward the world got quashed. Disturbed by this unconscious awareness, they do the same thing to their own children. The impulse then gets thwarted and repressed, and this, says Freud, has three possible outcomes. In the first and overwhelmingly typical case, the child's curiosity gets shut down. The child learns that such openness, such creative expression, is risky business. The result, says Freud, is that creative expression "may be limited for the whole of the subject's lifetime." In the second case, the child's development is sufficiently strong to resist the repression to some degree. The repressed sensuality then returns from the unconscious "in the form of compulsive brooding, naturally in a distorted and unfree form, but sufficiently powerful to sexualize thinking itself and to color [creative or artistic] operations with the pleasure and anxiety that belong to the sexual processes proper." The brooding never ends; eros is transferred to the creative activity and the latter becomes a substitute for it. In the third case, says Freud, "the libido evades the fate of repression by being sublimated from the very beginning." The transition is smooth, the quality of neurosis absent; the instinct operates freely in the service of creative activity.

In general, Freud's schema (modified) might look something like this:

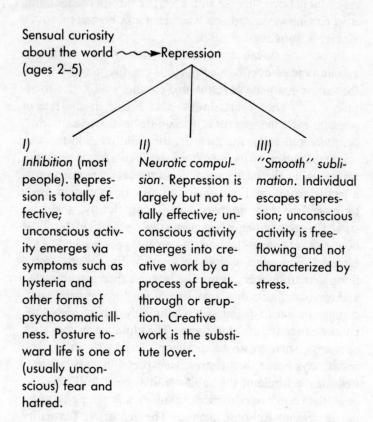

Sensual curiosity
about the world ~~~→Repression
(ages 2–5)

I)
Inhibition (most people). Repression is totally effective; unconscious activity emerges via symptoms such as hysteria and other forms of psychosomatic illness. Posture toward life is one of (usually unconscious) fear and hatred.

II)
Neurotic compulsion. Repression is largely but not totally effective; unconscious activity emerges into creative work by a process of breakthrough or eruption. Creative work is the substitute lover.

III)
"Smooth" sublimation. Individual escapes repression; unconscious activity is free-flowing and not characterized by stress.

There is not much to say about Type I creativity, since it is the counter-example, the decision to give up on creativity (and really on life) altogether. The repression is so effective that all creative expression is blocked forever. Most people mask this early defeat with substitute activity, but it shows up somatically, or psychosomatically, when they are caught off guard. Type II, the neurotic model, was—as far as Freud was concerned—typical of most creative work. As we have said, in this case the person fights back, for the spirit is not completely extinguished. But the result of this partial repression is a situation soaking in ambivalent emotions. The creative work has an obsessive quality to it; one is "married" to one's work, as the saying goes. Tension and passion are the characteristic modes of expression here.

Type III is the least familiar case. The repression is very slight, and the translation of sensual energy or exploring spirit into creative work is carried out with a minimum of trauma. Such work has a relaxed, spontaneous feel to it. In the early pages of the da Vinci biography, Freud puts Leonardo into this category; but by the end of the book, he is forced to conclude, based on his own evidence, that the Italian master was a Type II. As a result, Creativity III emerges as an empty category. It is an intriguing possibility, and Freud's insight here is intuitively brilliant; but it would seem to be a category without content, hanging in the middle of nowhere.

One possible candidate for Creativity III might be children's art. I saw such artwork myself many years ago when I worked in a Montessori nursery for three-year-olds, who had not as yet been hit by too much repression. As aides or counselors, we were instructed never to put the children on the spot by asking them what it was they were painting or constructing, and indeed, they exhibited virtually no performance anxiety whatsoever. It was a pleasure to watch their glee as they immersed themselves in their "work." Looking back, I wouldn't call it great art, but it certainly was not compulsive or conflict-ridden. For better or worse, there were no van Goghs in that nursery. The problem is that if that is all that can be put in this category, then it is not very interesting. What I wish to argue is that Creativity III constitutes a mode of expression that includes most medieval art, the art of non-Western cultures, and the art of traditional societies. It approximates what we call craft, as opposed to art as such. As a result, it throws the creativity of the Western, post-Renaissance world into sharp relief, for it involves a psychodynamic entirely different from that of Creativity II. Modern creativity, or Creativity II, should be seen for what it is: a local and, in fact, fairly recent phenomenon that organizes bodily energy in a particular way. In doing so, it produces a mode of expression that is very powerful and focused, but extremely draining, both for the individual and for the culture at large. In its most extreme and perhaps most talented form, it tends to have the effect we have already mentioned—that of taking the lives of its representatives at a fairly early age.

When I first began thinking about this subject, and specifically about how creativity manifested itself in my own life, there was no avoiding the fact that I fell into the second category. I conformed very well to the popular image of the writer who stayed up all night fueling himself with coffee and tobacco, pacing the floor in frustration as ideas refused to come, and sitting down and writing things out in white heat when they finally surfaced. The pattern was clearly addictive/obsessive; neurotic, in short.

Yet as I thought about it more, I began to see that these were the surface manifestations of a deeper drama. The most creative work I had done resulted from a psychic crisis that ran very deep, and which, once triggered, I was powerless to control. The French psychiatrist Jacques Lacan said that we state our problems on the symbolic level before proceeding to solve them, and something like this had happened to me. It began with the speculation that if worldviews were artifacts, the magical worldview that antedated modern science must have real validity. The more I began to follow that train of thought, the more archaic consciousness began to take me over. Finally, I was in deep trouble. How does the line from *Faust* go? "Two souls reside within my breast." I was both a modern and an ancient, a scientist and an alchemist, and neither side would release its grip. It was a rocky ride, but I had no choice except to live out those contradictions. Once the traditional/modern gap opened up within my psyche, my fate was sealed: I had to heal that split or die. And this, I believe, is the number-one characteristic of Creativity II:

It is a contemporary form of exorcism. (I am not talking here about *productivity*, which has *no* psychic energy behind it, and which merely involves turning out work in a mechanical fashion.) In Creativity II, you are possessed by an internal conflict, and the work is undertaken to resolve it. You create from pain; or as John Fowles put it in one of his novels, you create from what you lack, not from what you have. It is this that gives modern poetry, for example, what Robert Bly has called a "leaping" structure. Chaucer, by way of contrast, derives his power from the beautifully crafted language of the narrative. *The Canterbury Tales* are not soaking in unconscious power; they do not "leap," as do, say, many of Bly's own poems.[3]

The second characteristic follows from this: You create yourself out of your work; the work is characterized by "self-expression." In the modern period, art and self-expression (something Chaucer was *not* after) have practically become synonymous. Creative work must bear a personal signature or style, whereas in the Middle Ages it tended to be anonymous. Medieval artists typically did not sign their work. Cennino Cennini's essay of 1400, *Il Libro dell' Arte*, announced the artist's intention to break with this tradition, and the book is usually regarded as a turning point, marking the end of the craft tradition and the call for modern artistic creativity. Once again, John Fowles is relevant here. "Romantic and post-Romantic art," he writes, "is all pervaded by . . . the flight of the individual from whatever threatens his individuality." Modern creativity, he essentially argues, is heavily fueled by the desire to prove that one exists.[4]

A third characteristic, which tends to follow from the first two, is that the creative insight is seen to break through, or erupt from, the unconscious. It is this eruption that generates the psychic split that demands to be healed, and that alters the personality structure so that the work of integration becomes self-expression. Traditional creativity would have to be different, since traditional societies tend, in varying degrees, to be swimming in the unconscious already. Hence, there is nothing, or at least much less, to erupt.

Fourth, modern creative work has a strong addictive or compulsive component to it; the artist is expected to outdo him- or herself with each succeeding product. ("I work as my father drank," George Bernard Shaw once remarked.[5]) It is here that we see the schismogenic character of modern creativity most clearly. The structure is one of "upping the ante," in other words; work is often "unfinished" because it is done in the pursuit of an inaccessible ideal. It must depart from tradition, must create a new genre, and it gets difficult to keep on doing this. As a result, modern creativity tends to have high psychic costs. The examples of an intense, sustained burst of creative work followed by suicide are legion: Vincent van Gogh, Dylan Thomas (suicide by alcohol), Janis Joplin (suicide by drugs), Jimi Hendrix, Sylvia Plath, Anne Sexton, and on and on. The work ineluctably moves toward breakdown. It is for this reason that so many creative people stop doing what they are doing in their late thirties: They know where it is all leading.[6] This also explains, in part, why the public loses interest in writers such as Norman Mailer. Mailer's first work, *The Naked and the Dead*, remains his best. From the standpoint of modern creativity, the artist is expected to set up and leap over increasingly higher hurdles. This is the structure of an ever-expanding economy; it is not steady-state. Mailer's career was over almost before it began. The modern Western public is trained to expect novelty from its creative sector; it quickly loses interest in artists who have nothing "new" to offer.

Finally, modern creativity often involves, as Freud said, the sexualization, or at least eroticization, of the activity. One's work becomes one's lover—one's central, and obsessive, relationship. All the dramas that are typically played out in such a relationship get played out here: the initial romantic rush, the subsequent tapering off, jealousy and possessiveness, and finally disillusion and the search for a new love. There is a heavy overlap of Oedipal energy here: Male artists are notorious mama's boys, "heroes" winning battles for the mother.

And they do this precisely by innovating, by rupturing tradition—*i.e.*, by slaying the father.[7]

We have, in the West, many images that glorify the notion of creativity as being a triumph over adversity. We speak of "the shit that fertilizes roses," or the grain of sand in the oyster that leads to the generation of a pearl. This is the stuff of *Reader's Digest* stories and Ann Landers columns. And these images do capture a truth, though they mask a larger one. The truth they capture is that creative work can and often does emerge out of conflict; the truth they mask is that other psychodynamic patterns of the creative process are possible, and that, historically, the conflict model may actually represent an aberration. My goal in this essay, however, is not to condemn modern Western creativity as "bad" and to enshrine Eastern or pre-modern creativity as "good." It is, rather, to argue that there are different somatic or energetic processes involved in each case. There is a way, given my own upbringing, that no Indian raga will ever move me as much as Mozart, no Japanese landscape painting resonate for me as deeply as Cézanne's evocative scenes of the Midi. In fact, modern Western art has a brilliance that no medieval icon or Eastern painting can ever approximate, in my view. But my point here is that it takes a particular energetic configuration to create such an effect, and if Freud is right about Creativity II, it actually requires early somatic damage that leads to a distrust of the body, and a corresponding shunting of that bodily energy upward, toward the head. The center of gravity is too high, so to speak; there is a way in which the very brilliance of Western creativity depends on its instability, its extremely high level of tension and stress.

Yet the conflict model of creativity, as Freud realized (though he wasn't able to prove it), does not exhaust the entire subject. Psychologists from Otto Rank to Rollo May have insisted on the necessity of stress or tension for the creative act, without realizing that this is a formula for only one type of creative expression.[8] In *Caliban Reborn*, Wilfred Mellers addresses himself to the issue of conflict and self-expression, and emphasizes how specific it is in time and place:

> While this conception of art is our birthright and has gone to make the world we live in, we have to realize that in the context of history the notion is both newfangled and restricted. It is relevant to only about the last five hundred years of Europe's history. . . .

The difference between music as magic (traditional music) and music as expression, he says, is that the former lacks the element of harmonic tension. Such music, he adds, has a strong corporeal component:

> In the music of primitive cultures . . . the rhythm is usually corporeal and the music is never self-expression but rather a communal act of work or play which may have magic[al] as well as social significance.

Mellers goes on to say that "the compositional principles inherent in European music before the Renaissance are not radically distinct from those of Oriental music." In both Gregorian chant and the Indian raga, rhythms such as breath or heartbeat constitute the creative source. The invention of harmony—something of which traditional and Oriental cultures were aware, but which (says Mellers) they never chose to emphasize—ruptured this pattern. That is, it shifted music from a Creativity III to a Creativity II structure.[9]

Many years ago, living near New York City, I used to play a kind of game, experimenting with the shift between Creativity III and Creativity II energy patterns, without really knowing what I was doing or why. In upper Manhattan, I would go to the Cloisters, which is the medieval section of the Metropolitan Museum of Art, and then, having spent several hours there, would go directly downtown to the Museum of Modern Art. I would recommend this experiment to anybody. If you stay tuned to your physical reactions, the effect is quite remarkable. The immersion in a "craft" environment, complete with tapestries, carved wooden doors, stained glass, and illuminated manuscripts, creates a very soothing sensation. The body lets go, as it were, and time seems to stand still. The sensation of silence and tranquility is particularly striking. To follow this up with an immersion in twentieth-century art is to give yourself a real shock. The sensation here is one of excitement and anxiety; the dreamy and magnetic sense of wholeness, or union, is replaced by a chaos and dramatic brilliance that explodes on the canvas, or from the sculptures. As in the case of van Gogh (see below), it is as if the breakdown of the psyche resulted in the breakthrough of art. Two hours in such a place as this leaves one both exhilarated and emotionally spent. This simple experiment conveys only a fraction (I suspect) of what it means to live in one culture as opposed to the other, and how very different the psychic and emotional pattern that lies at the root of Creativity II is from that which underlies Creativity III.

In December 1986 I unintentionally repeated this experiment, but in reverse. The Metropolitan Museum had mounted an exhibit of van Gogh's last eighteen months—"Van Gogh at Saint-Rémy and Auvers"—and I took the opportunity to see it. I had originally planned to stay several hours; as it turned out, I was totally exhausted in ninety minutes by the intensity of color and emotion that escalated in van Gogh's painting in direct proportion to his increasing madness. Whether it was accidental or deliberately planned by the exhibition's organizers, I do not know, but the show exited onto a very different sort of exhibition, entitled "Individuality and Tradition in Seventeenth-Century Chinese Art." The impact was enormous; I felt a sudden "whoosh" as my entire energy returned to ground level. As I sat and looked at the lovely, relaxed prints of mountains and landscapes, a great feeling of peace came over me. I felt a bodily sense of centering, coming home. I realized that I loved van Gogh, but that I couldn't live with him hanging on my living room walls. The intensity was simply too great; and his creative pattern—which is very typical of Type II creativity—reflected this. In the final seventy days of his life, living under the care of Dr. Gachet at Auvers-sur-Oise, van Gogh turned out no fewer than forty paintings. By contrast, Kung Hsian, one of the seventeenth-century Chinese painters displayed at the Met, turned out comparatively few; and his comments on this are all of a piece with the Creativity III style. "Little by little is better than more and more," wrote Kung Hsian; "this is the advanced stage of a painter." He wrote: "When you are afraid of producing too much painting, you will make a good painting." He explained: "Being clever is not as good as being dull. The uses of cleverness can be grasped at a glance, while apparent dullness may embody limitless flavor." These are sentiments that would never have occurred to van Gogh; nor do they occur to most of us.[10]

My goal here, again, is not to make a judgment, but rather to point out a very significant cultural contrast. The first four elements I identified as being characteristic of Creativity II—healing a split, self-expression, eruption from the unconscious, and an addictive (escalating) pattern—all add up to the schismogenic structure discussed above. Add to this the fifth factor of sexual and Oedipal or erotic tension, and you have a situation that cannot help but be as brittle as it is brilliant, as neurotic as it is rich. It is thus not that Creativity II is "wrong," but that in the late twentieth century, this mode of expression has been pushed to the breaking point. In an evolutionary sense, it cannot extend its trajectory any further. As a result, what we are witnessing in a whole variety of fields is not merely the creation of yet another style or genre, but the transformation of the creative act itself into something else. If creativity has a past, it also has a future, though it is not easy to predict at this stage what it will be. I shall return to this question later on; for now, it might be valuable to try to obtain a deeper understanding of the psychological basis of schismogenic creativity.

The schismogenic nature of Western creativity was first (indirectly) recognized by the Jungian writer Erich Neumann in *The Origins and History of Consciousness*.[11] The essential argument of the book is that the consciousness of the individual passes through the same stages as that of the human race at large, and that mythology is the map of that evolution. The first myths, says Neumann, are creation myths: The earth is submerged, or nonexistent, and is precipitated out of a watery chaos. This is certainly the drama described, for example, in the opening chapter of Genesis. The second set of myths are hero myths, and these record the process of differentiation. The symbols of the first category are water, or the egg, or the ourobouros, reflecting a unitary consciousness or the absence of consciousness: no tension, no opposites, no differentiation. The symbols of the second category are the sun—the entry of light into darkness—and also journeys and conquests. The *Odyssey*, for example, can be read as a psychic journey involving the hero's differentiation from the unconscious, and, in general, from the archetype of the Great Mother. It is the drama of ego vs. unconscious, light vs. dark, male energy vs. female energy, that makes the archetypal journey so fascinating, even to the modern reader. Again and again, Odysseus experiences the enormous pull of that great, unconscious, undifferentiated female power, the desire to melt or merge back into it, to go unconscious, as he once was as a very young infant or a fetus. But what makes him a hero is that he refuses that option. He is not interested in the dark energy of the unconscious, and his "victory" over this is symbolized by the blinding of the cyclops, whose eye is the "third eye" of intuitive understanding.[12] With the birth of the hero, which is really the birth of the ego (or, perhaps, of a certain type of ego), the world becomes ambivalent. It gets split into masculine and feminine, black and white, left and right, God and the devil, ego and unconscious, and this becomes the great drama that all cultures have to deal with, at root. In the Far East, the solution has been characterized as Taoistic—i.e., "both/and"; yin and yang are seen as transformable, interpenetrating, and as I shall discuss shortly, this has given Eastern creativity a particular style. In the West, and especially since the Renaissance, the solution has been Manichaean—i.e., "either/or"; the two poles are mortal enemies, locked in combat to the death. And in the West or Near East, in particular, this has given rise to a third type of myth that tends to combine the first two: the myth of Set and Osiris, or the twin brothers. In this myth, two brothers emerge from the Void (Primal Unity), or the womb, or the Great Mother, viz. the Hero and the Great Mother Representative. The Hero urges separation from the Great Mother; the Representative wants to merge back into her. And so there is a tension that is never resolved.[13]

This is, of course, a mythological struggle, played out in the Western psyche. The twin brothers' conflict is intermediate between hero and creation myths. A defiant ego has emerged, but it is fearful of complete separation. Set and Osiris, or Cain and Abel, are really two parts of the same person. We hear these conflicting voices particularly at those moments when we are about to give in to an addiction: taking a cigarette, smoking a joint, drinking a martini, eating a slab of cheesecake. The body wants merger; the mind says: Resist (or is it the reverse?). This is, in fact, the theme of *Dr. Jekyll and Mr. Hyde*, which is nothing less than a twin brothers' war. Robert Louis Stevenson wrote:

I thus drew steadily nearer to that truth, by whose partial discovery I have been doomed to such a dreadful shipwreck: that man is not truly one, but truly two. . . . I saw that, of the two natures that contended in the field of my consciousness, even if I could rightly be said to be either, it was only because I was radically both; and from an early date, even before the course of my scientific discoveries had begun to suggest the most naked possibility of such a miracle, I had learned to dwell with pleasure, as a beloved daydream, on the thought of the separation of these elements. If each, I told myself, could be housed in separate identities, life would be relieved of all that was unbearable. . . . It was the curse of mankind that these incongruous faggots were thus bound together—that in the agonized womb of consciousness, these polar twins should be continuously struggling.[14]

What does all this have to do with creativity? The point is that creativity—or at least Creativity II—is the *product* of this internal tension. As Neumann puts it, "[this] tension is what we call culture"; and in this I think he may have been mistaken. Being a Jungian, he saw this dynamic as universal and archetypal, and perhaps to varying degrees, it is; but different cultures express it differently and deal with it differently, and this may be the crucial point. Nevertheless, Neumann's formulation of twin brothers arguing over the Abyss is an especially important clue as to what goes on in modern creativity. The "game" is to let the whole drama play itself out on the terrain of the psyche, and channel the resulting energy into art, poetry, or whatever. It is precisely here that we find the mechanism that underlies the brilliance of modern Western creativity, giving it its keen edge and also its tragic aspect. For in order for his or her work to be increasingly brilliant, the artist has to generate greater and greater twin-brother splits, or encounters with the Void, from which to recover. Finally, as in the case of Dylan Thomas or Janis Joplin or so many others, the gap becomes too great. The chasm widens beyond their heroic powers, and they cannot manage to get back. Modern creativity is a battlefield of psychic, and often physical, corpses.

A good study of this turbulent or tormented phenomenon in modern art occurs in a work by James Lord called *A Giacometti Portrait*, which is a study of the great sculptor, Alberto Giacometti, at work. It very clearly embodies the first four themes of modern creativity that I have noted. Giacometti is never satisfied with his work; it is never, in his eyes, really finished; he sees his Self totally on the line every time he sits down before an easel or a piece of clay, and so on. Lord writes how he once found Giacometti at a nearby café on a coffee break, his hollow eyes gazing into nowhere, ''staring into a void from which no solace could come.''[15] Any healing that is engendered tends to be short-lived. You are constantly challenged to create *yourself*, and this process never ends. ''I work in a state of passion and compulsion,'' said the artist Joan Miró in 1959.

> When I begin a canvas, I obey a physical impulse, a need to act. . . . It's a struggle between me and what I am doing, between me and the canvas, between me and my distress.[16]

The problem with this struggle is that it often ends in death or madness.

There are numerous examples of Western creativity one can take as illustrations of Type II, and as I indicated earlier, much of this is well documented. The classic example of the tortured-genius syndrome, and one that has been worked over in great detail, is Vincent van Gogh, whose art was so clearly ''a cry of anguish,'' an attempt to merge with life, a substitute for intimacy. ''The more I am spent, ill, a broken pitcher,'' he wrote, ''by so much more am I an artist—a creative artist. . . .''[17] This is one of the paradoxes of modern creativity—that the search for self-expression actually winds up depleting the Self. The artist of the Type II category is like a broken doll, an *imitatio Christi*, exhausting himself or herself for art's sake, which is ''all.'' In this case, however, you are the agent of your own crucifixion: You make something greater than yourself, seek the unattainable, become a flawed vessel, ultimately emptied or destroyed. For van Gogh and many others, acute depression is somehow welcome, a source of creative drama and energy.

A more complex and interesting example of the Creativity II pattern is Wolfgang Amadeus Mozart, about whom so much has been written in recent years. Exactly what happened in Mozart's infancy we shall never know; but there is evidence to suggest the presence of repressed antagonism toward his father, Leopold, for nearly twenty-five years.[18] Very early on, Leopold Mozart, himself a musician, realized he had a prodigy on his hands, and proceeded to take on the role of impresario, abandoning his own career and dedicating his life to that of his son. He made Wolfgang totally dependent on him, stage-managing virtually every step of Mozart's rise to fame. As a child, Wolfgang was fond of saying, "Next to God comes Papa"; and if antagonism was present, it must have been very deeply buried. Mozart's letters home during this period—about twenty years—were filled with an ostensible love and appreciation of Leopold, and his music during this time was childlike, exuberant, spontaneous. Operas and concerti literally poured from his pen. There is simply no evidence of conflict here, and the style of work reflects this.

All of this gradually began to change in the late 1770s. Wolfgang began to realize that his father had effectively kept him a child all his life, and that Leopold still, after all his (Wolfgang's) achievements, was disappointed with him. He began to realize also that he feared and resented Leopold, and by 1781 the resulting anger began to surface in some of their correspondence. Yet there was only so much Mozart could say, for Leopold was by now an old man, and Mozart did not want to hurt him. But the conflict that had been so deeply buried finally surfaced, with even more needing to come out; and all of this got channeled into his work. Wolfgang Hildesheimer, one of Mozart's more recent biographers, notes that the four years from 1784 to the end of 1787 were Wolfgang's most prolific and creative ones, and that this was also the period of his greatest experimentation and discovery. Mozart's interest in destroying old genres and creating new ones was at its height during this time. As Hildesheimer writes, "The revolutionary Mozart is the Mozart of his last eight years." Repressed Oedipal rebellion surfaces in his two most brilliant operas. In *The Marriage of Figaro* (1786), which was based on a play by Beaumarchais that had long been banned in Vienna, Figaro, the servant of a member of the nobility, Count Almaviva, thwarts the latter

in an amorous adventure and emerges the victor. As Hildesheimer tells us, Mozart

> . . . knew [that] Figaro was no fairy tale. His theme yielded
> a model for his own behavior; an unconscious drive, prob-
> ably long latent, came to the surface and tempted him to
> stop living according to the rules imposed on him from
> outside. He began to "let himself go."

It was this opera, which so antagonized precisely the class
that Leopold had toadied to, so as to grease the wheels of
his son's career, that marked the beginning of the end of
that career: the descent into poverty and, by the end, relative obscurity.

The theme of the upper-class Don Juan character, whose
sexual conflicts are so great as to drive him to seduce virtually every woman he meets, and who comes off rather
badly for it, is repeated and greatly magnified in Mozart's
opera *Don Giovanni*, which appeared the very next year,
in 1787, only five months after Leopold's death. It is surely
one of the greatest operas of all time; and it is interesting
to note that Freud once remarked that it was the only opera
that interested him. We need hardly wonder why: One of
Mozart's own additions to the libretto was the reappearance
of the slain father as an accusing ghost (the statue). Critics
said he stole the theme from *Hamlet*, but they hardly had
to look that far afield. What we find in Mozart's work, from
this point on, with its obvious attack on the aristocracy, its
Oedipal themes, and its smashing of traditional genres, is
the working out of powerful internal conflicts through the
creative act itself. Mozart was not necessarily suffering
here; indeed, Hildesheimer claims he was getting high off
all this conflict. But my point is that the later Mozart is a
classic Type II, and that the energy was coming from a
place of anger and frustration. This energy—and it had
twenty-five years of repression behind it—was clearly phe-
nomenal. Between *Figaro* and *Don Giovanni* (eighteen
months), Mozart wrote thirty-five separate works; between

Don Giovanni and *Così fan tutte* (thirteen months), sixty-three more compositions. These were followed, in 1791, by a mass of chamber music, cantatas, and court dances, plus two more operas, one of which was *The Magic Flute*. And in *The Magic Flute*, the Oedipal conflict is revealed as finally resolved: Sarastro, the obvious father figure, is the priest of universal love. As Peter Shaffer has Mozart's arch-rival, Antonio Salieri, say in the play *Amadeus*, when Salieri attended the premiere of the opera and saw the silhouette of Sarastro against the sun: "And in this sun—behold—I saw his *father*! No more an accusing figure but forgiving!—the highest priest of the Order—his hand extended to the world in love! Wolfgang feared Leopold no longer: A final legend had been made!"[19]

The catharsis was apparently successful. As Hildesheimer notes, the spontaneous, childlike effect of Mozart's earlier years, absent since 1778, reappears now in the music for the first time in thirteen years; and significantly, *The Magic Flute* would seem to lack the power and brilliance of *Figaro* and *Don Giovanni*. It was, in any event, too late. Believing that someone had poisoned him, Mozart began, in 1791, to write his own requiem, the "Requiem Mass," which was never completed. He died at age thirty-five, for reasons that remain obscure to this day.[20]

I wish to return, finally, to what I have called traditional creativity, or Creativity III. There are endless examples of this, of course, and I could easily furnish at this point texts of Japanese haiku, photographs of ancient Greek or Egyptian vases, or Hopi or Celtic designs, in addition to the seventeenth-century Chinese landscape painting mentioned earlier. Let me, however, refer to only one classic painting, which is, because of its immense popularity, probably familiar to many readers—namely, the famous ink drawing of six persimmons attributed to Mu ch'i, an artist who lived in Szechuan province (central China) in the late thirteenth and early fourteenth centuries. The drawing has been reproduced in many art books and histories of art, and it shows six persimmons, two white, two gray, and two that are black. The simplicity and elegance of the drawing make it one of the most beautiful works of Eastern art ever to have appeared. Here is the commentary of one modern student of Chinese art, Chang Chung-yuan:

> This picture of six persimmons is one of the best works ever produced by Chinese artists. Before Mu ch'i picked up his brush, his mind was in a state of no-thought. Thus, we have in this painting a manifestation of the primary indeterminacy of the uncarved block. What his mind reflected at that moment his brush would put down. First two deep black contours and then to their left two gray contours. To the extreme left and right he placed two plain white contours. The ink wash of the two first contours is pitch black without any shading at all, and the two contours at the left are all gray with only a light touch. The two outside contours are pure white. The shades of the ink wash from dark to gray and from gray to white correspond to the inner process going on in the painter. When he was still in the depth of the preconscious, the density of his creative night found expression in two dark contours. With the awakening of his consciousness, the inner darkness loses its density and manifests in two gray contours. As he awakens fully, his creative innocence is entirely unveiled. So the white contours are its expression. What is expressed in the picture corresponds to what happened in his mind. Through his brush-work, the various states of his mind can be traced from the primary indeterminacy of the uncarved block to transparency.[21]

The first thing that strikes me about this work, and indeed, about the whole Creativity III genre, is the absence of what might be called a "Freudian layer." There is seemingly no pent-up sensual or sexual struggle in this material. Eros and internal conflict do not play much of a role. What Chang describes is a fairly smooth descent *into* the unconscious, not an eruption from it. Hence, it is clear that the dark persimmons would come first, in a state of meditative trance, and the lighter ones after, as the artist comes back to more conscious awareness. The state of "no-mind" familiar to Eastern thought is largely foreign to the modern West (van Gogh was *out* of his mind, not in no-mind). For no-mind is a state of detachment or wholeness, and this indicates that the healing takes place *before* the work begins. This material does not reflect the *search* for unity; it is, rather, an artistic expression of psychic unity *previously attained*. To invert John Fowles, you create from what you have, not from what you lack.

Second, there is no "self-expression" here. It is not a particular person or healing journey being depicted. If there is a twin-brothers' tension here, it is fairly muted. The *unity* is what is being expressed, and that is seen as being universal. As already noted, traditional artists, and Western artists prior to the Renaissance, typically did not sign their work. It is all anonymous because it bears the "mark of God," so to speak; a theme pursued by the great French philosopher and mystic Simone Weil. Weil's idea of creative work was what she called "decreation"—you "de-create" yourself in order to create the world. It would be more accurate to say that you don't create the work, but rather that you step out of the way and let it happen. In this way, it is significant that so much Oriental art and poetry is about nature, about the physical world, not about the Self and its dilemmas.[22]

Third, there is no schismogenic or Manichaean structure here. The work is spontaneous and regarded as finished. It is also part of a craft tradition—i.e., the idea is to stay *within* a genre, not to have to invent a new one constantly. And as with craft, all of this is part of daily life: pouring tea, carving wood, cooking persimmons—all activities are considered worthy of craftsmanship. You don't have a special place called a "gallery" to which beauty is assigned for storage and display, nor do you have a special heroic category in society reserved for creative people (the Balinese are an excellent example of a society permeated by art, rather than having art and artists regarded as exceptional). As Ananda Coomaraswamy once put it, "The artist is not a special kind of person; rather, each person is a special kind of artist."[23] And this necessarily means the absence of an addictive or schismogenic structure. This kind of art is continuous with life; it doesn't attempt to "outdo" life by means of psychic acrobatics.

All of this falls into category III, it seems to me, but it is hardly child art. Creativity III, in fact, can be subdivided into two categories: III(a), child art; and III(b), which is the art of an adult who is training himself or herself to be *childlike*—open, immediate, and spontaneous. The difference here is what the Zen master Shunryu Suzuki labeled as Zen mind vs. beginner's mind. The early Mozart was possessed of beginner's mind. He began composing at age five. When he finally became aware of his conflicts, he switched from III(a) to II. This is not surprising; what else would one expect? It is just that the Eastern pattern, or pre-modern one, is so different. The goal is not to go unconscious, or be a three-year-old at a Montessori school, but to pull back enough "yang" energy so that yin and yang can balance out. It is spontaneity of a different sort.

To complicate things further, it seems to me that Creativity II can also be subdivided into two categories:

II(a)—This is what I have described thus far as Creativity II: The healing of the split takes place by playing the struggle out in the work itself. The "exorcism" is, in other words, indirect, or unconscious.

II(b)—This represents a slight shift away from II(a), in that the exorcism is direct. One stays fully conscious of the neurotic dramas that have led one to the particular artistic or creative issue at hand, and one goes directly for the liberation from those dramas, through therapy or one's own internal work. In other words, one moves into one's fears. This releases the energy that is tied up in obsessional patterns, which is then

available for creative work, and which starts to come
out in a more free-flowing way.

The major difference between II(a) and II(b), then, is
that II(b) is on the road to Creativity III, so to speak (Creativity III begins when one is finally done with obsessions), whereas II(a) is not. In fact, in II(a) the artist *fears*
the loss of obsessions, because s/he believes that this would
mean the end of her or his career. "Life" and "obsession"
are seen as being pretty much identical; the heroic ego
whispers in the ear of this person, "Lose me and you'll
never create again." And the voice is sincere, because it
honestly cannot conceive of a different form of creativity.

The fact that our categories have now developed subcat-
egories, and that these may even overlap, is possibly an important clue to where our culture is going. Creativity II may
be our (Western) path to Creativity III, at least in its II(b)
form; it is not all II(a), not all a dead end, and this suggests
that within the evolution of Western creativity itself lies a
tendency toward genuine cultural liberation. This is no small
point: The way in which our private and cultural neurotic
configuration is framed, or dealt with, may actually be the
key in the lock. Those who choose to work through their fears
and repressions in the service of creative work may (if they
do it before they die) break through to a liberating kind of
creativity, and in so doing recode the culture along non-
schismogenic lines. This is an earthshaking possibility.

If we look around at the artistic and literary scene today,
especially in the U.S., we do find some radical departures
from the II(a) model, if only in an attempt to express a
unitary type of consciousness. This may be premature;
Western culture may have to push through II(b) before it
can experiment with III(b) in a truly unselfconscious way.
But the alternative attempts are important, nonetheless.
Wallace Stevens' work displays obvious "decreative" tendencies in the field of poetry; Henry Moore's work does
the same in the area of sculpture. Post-modern minimalist
music is clearly in the Creativity III category. This music,

as exemplified by composers such as Philip Glass, Steve Reich, and Terry Riley, has so completely eliminated the tension/resolution structure typical of Western music since the late Middle Ages that the new form has a curious similarity to Gregorian chant. Reich has stated in public interviews that the study of yoga, cabala, African and Balinese music, and classical breathing exercises, all of which are aspects of traditional cultures, has had a tremendous impact on his work.[24]

It is not clear what all this means, especially since it can be argued that it represents a retrogression, an attempt to return to an earlier cultural period. For various reasons, I think that unlikely; and we should also keep in mind that a major part of the Renaissance involved a revival of antiquity, or what the English potter Bernard Leach called "revitalization," the going backward in order to go forward. The modern potter, said Leach, takes Sung (twelfth-century Chinese) pottery as a model; not for imitation, as an end in itself, but as a way of revitalizing contemporary techniques.[25] It seems obvious that the limits of Creativity II have been reached, and that beyond the tendencies I have described as Creativity II(b), we are searching for completely different modes of cultural and creative expression, in the arts as well as the sciences. As in the case of Creativity II(b), this is a hopeful sign; it suggests that there are somatic forces at work in our culture that are anti-schismogenic; that are working, perhaps unconsciously, to reverse what appears to me, in a general way, to be a destructive trajectory. We are engaged in turning a corner as significant as that which was turned in Western Europe roughly four centuries ago. We can still listen to Gregorian chant, of course, but most of us don't do it very often. In two centuries, Mozart may be in the same category, and the tension/resolution structure of music may be puzzling to our ears.

Beyond the form that creativity will take during the next historical epoch is the question of the human personality structure, the energetic experience that will underlie it, and the nature of Western culture as a whole. Who can say what these will be? There is obviously no way to know. But the following lines from Mary Caroline Richards's book *The Crossing Point* sounds what to me is the most hopeful, and at the same time most realistic, note possible. She writes:

> Eventually the soul asks to be born again into a world of the same order as itself—a second coming into innocence, not through a glass darkly, but face to face, in consciousness . . . We pass through cruel ordeals on the way. Estrangement, coldness, despair. Death.
>
> By going through the experience faithfully, we may come through on the other side of the crossing point, and find that our faithfulness has borne a new quality into the world.[26]

A new quality . . . a new history . . . a creativity that can be shared by everyone. Let's hope it is still possible.

NOTES

[1] Elliott Jaques, *Work, Creativity, and Social Justice* (London: Heinemann, 1970), Chapter 3, ("Death and Mid-Life Crisis"); Katinka Matson, *Short Lives: Portraits in Creativity and Self-Destruction* (New York: William Morrow, 1980); A. Alvarez, *The Savage God* (New York: Bantam Books, 1973), especially pp. 227–52; Gregory Bateson, *Naven* (2nd ed.; Stanford: University Press, 1958), and also various essays in *Steps to an Ecology of Mind* (London: Paladin, 1973).

[2] Sigmund Freud, *Leonardo da Vinci and a Memory of His Childhood*, translated by Alan Tyson (New York: W. W. Norton, 1964). See especially pp. 27–30 for the discussion that follows.

[3] On "leaping" see, for example, Bly's essay "Spanish Leaping," in his journal *The Seventies* 1 (spring 1972), pp. 16–21.

[4] John Fowles, *The Aristos* (rev. ed.; London: Pan Books, 1969), pp. 52–53.

[5] Quoted in Erik H. Erikson, *Young Man Luther* (New York: W. W. Norton, 1962), p. 45.

[6] On this especially see the works by Jaques and Alvarez cited in note 1.

[7] Matthew Besdine, in "The Jocasta Complex, Mothering and Genius," *The Psychoanalytic Review* 55 (1968), pp. 259–77 and 574–600, identifies a whole number of individuals for whom over-mothering seems to have been an important factor in their creativity. The list includes Michelangelo, Poe, Dylan Thomas, Proust, van Gogh, Goethe, Einstein, Shakespeare, Freud, Balzac, and Sartre.

[8] Esther Menaker, "The Concept of Will in the Thinking of Otto Rank and Its Consequences for Clinical Practice," *The Psychoanalytic Review* 72 (1985), pp. 254–64; Rollo May, *The Courage to Create* (New York: W. W. Norton, 1975). Similar studies that see creativity only in terms of the conflict model include classics such as Arthur Koestler, *The Act of Creation* (London: Hutchinson, 1964), and Nicolas Berdyaev, *The Meaning of the Creative Act*, translated by Donald A. Lowrie (London: Gollancz, 1955; orig. Russian ed. 1914). See also the more recent work by Albert Rothenberg, *The Emerging Goddess* (Chicago: Chicago University Press, 1979). It seems to me that Freud must be credited, at so early a date, with seeing that an alternative to Creativity II was at least conceivable.

[9] Wilfred Mellers, *Caliban Reborn: Renewal in Twentieth Century Music* (New York: Harper & Row, 1967), Chapter 1.

[10] Quotations from Kung Hsian are taken from translations of texts that were displayed as part of the exhibition at the Metropolitan Museum of Art during 1986–87.

[11] On the following see Erich Neumann, *The Origins and History of Consciousness*, translated by R.F.C. Hull (Princeton: Princeton University Press, 1979; orig. German ed. 1949), Introduction, pp. 5–41, and 88–127.

[12] I am very grateful to Michael Crisp for this very imaginative, and I think accurate, interpretation.

[13] The splitting of the Great Mother is discussed by Neumann (see note 11, above) on pp. 96–97. The terminology "Great

Mother Representative'' is my own; Neumann's own phrase, which strikes me as being a loaded one, is "destructive male consort.''

14 Robert Louis Stevenson, *Dr. Jekyll and Mr. Hyde* (New York: Bantam Books, 1981; orig. publ. 1886), pp. 79–80.

15 James Lord, *A Giacometti Portrait* (New York: Museum of Modern Art, 1965), p. 38. See also Lord's more recent study, *Giacometti, a Biography* (New York: Farrar, Straus and Giroux, 1985).

16 Miró died in 1984; this quotation appeared in several obituaries that ran in a number of North American newspapers.

17 Quoted in Albert J. Lubin, *Stranger on the Earth* (New York: Holt, Rinehart and Winston, 1972), pp. 3 and 16. See also Matson, *Short Lives*, pp. 363–74.

18 The following discussion is based on Charlotte Haldane, *Mozart* (New York: Oxford University Press, 1960), and Wolfgang Hildesheimer, *Mozart*, translated by Marion Faber (London: Dent, 1983), esp. pp. 131, 138, 175, 180–85, 235, 351, and 357.

19 Peter Shaffer, *Amadeus* (New York: Harper & Row, 1980), p. 83.

20 According to Hildesheimer (see note 18, above), p. 375, Mozart believed someone had given him aqua tofana, a slow-working arsenic poison common enough in the eighteenth century. Shaffer's play *Amadeus* is built around the possibility that Salieri was the villain, and it is certainly curious that Salieri *denied* poisoning Mozart on his (Salieri's) deathbed (Haldane, *Mozart*, p. 129). An inquest on Mozart's death held in London in May 1983 concluded that he could have been poisoned, not by Salieri, but by a married woman with whom he was having an affair. (This was reported on the BBC.) Dr. Peter J. Davies argued against the possibility of poisoning in a two-part article published in the British journal *Musical Times*, in 1984; see also Donald Henahan, "Rest in Peace, Salieri, No One Killed Mozart,'' *The New York Times*, November 11, 1984, Section H. The issue will probably never be resolved.

21 Chang Chung-yuan, *Creativity and Taoism* (New York: Harper & Row, 1970), page facing Plate 4. Mu ch'i's drawing is reproduced on the front cover of this work, as well as on

the front cover of Shin'ichi Hisamatsu, *Zen and the Fine Arts*, translated by Gishin Tokiwa (Tokyo: Kodansha International Ltd., 1971).

22 Weil's essay "Decreation" can be found in *Gravity and Grace*, translated by Emma Craufurd (London: Routledge and Kegan Paul, 1952; orig. French ed. 1947). Matson discusses Weil in *Short Lives*, pp. 375–88. There is of course a large literature on Simone Weil, including studies by Simone Pétrement and John Hellman, among others. T. S. Eliot had already approached the theme of personality vs. non-personality in creative work in his essay "Tradition and the Individual Talent," in *Points of View* (London: Faber and Faber, 1941), pp. 23–24.

23 I have substituted the word "person" for "man," which appears in the original. See Ananda Coomaraswamy, "Meister Eckhart's View of Art," in *The Transformation of Nature in Art* (New York: Dover Publications, 1956; orig. publ. 1934), 2nd ed., p. 64.

24 On minimal art, see Gregory Battcock (ed.), *Minimal Art: A Critical Anthology* (New York: E. P. Dutton, 1968). Philip Glass is perhaps best known for his opera *Einstein on the Beach*, and for composing the soundtrack for Godfrey Reggio's films *Koyaanisqatsi* (1983) and *Powaggatsi* (1987). Terry Riley's most famous work (Steve Reich worked on it as well) is probably "In C"; for an interesting interview with Riley see Jon Pareles, "Terry Riley's Music Moves to Improvisation," *The New York Times*, September 24, 1982. Reich discussed his sources and his own musical development in an interview/performance at the Exploratorium, San Francisco, December 15, 1982; see also the excellent article by Ingram Marshall in *Stagebill* (San Franciso) (December 1982), vol. 2, no. 4, and the interview with Reich in *Parabola* (May 1980), vol. 5, no. 2, pp. 60–72.

25 Bernard Leach, *A Potter's Book*, 2nd ed. (London: Faber and Faber, 1945), p. 42.

26 M.C. Richards, *The Crossing Point* (Middletown, CT: Wesleyan University Press, 1973), pp. 63–64.

SPECULATION
ON
SPECULATION

LYNN MARGULIS

The crucial ancient beginnings of
the human brain lie in the dancing
of bacteria: the intricate mechanisms of cell motility. How do cells
locomote? The answer to this puzzle is the beginning of enlightenment for the origins of mind/brain.

Whereas in science *theory* is lauded, *speculation* is ridiculed. A biologist accused in print of "speculation" is branded for the tenure of his career. This biologist finds herself like a ballet dancer imitating a pigeon-toed hunchback: All of the intellectual training to keep my toes turned out emotionally backfires with a request to speculate freely. What else, though, does John Brockman ask his Reality Club members when he says: "We charge the speakers to represent an idea of reality by describing their creative work, life, and the questions they're asking themselves. We also want them to share with us the boundaries of their knowledge and experience"?

Only a direct response to Brockman's request permits me the luxury of speculation. Never before would I dare mention out loud the questions I am continually asking myself. Without the Reality Club prod, no speculation on speculation would be possible. In a manuscript lacking data, field and laboratory observations, descriptions of equipment and their correlated methodologies, and deficient in references, I feel a huge restraint as I attempt to comply with John's request to slacken the bonds of professionalism and turn my toes in. My well-seasoned inhibitions are nevertheless titillated by the joys of this Brockman-opportunity to really tell you about the hypothesis that I am always testing, that which I am always questioning: my developing worldview of mind. Asking your patience and indulgence to see beyond the inevitable barriers of language, at least I can try to articulate the unmentioned and hitherto unmentionable.

We have an intuitive grasp of the reality to which these terms refer: *perception, awareness, speculation, thought, memory, knowledge,* and *consciousness.* Most of us would claim that these qualities of mind have been listed more or less in evolutionary order. It is obvious that bacteria perceive sugars and algae perceive light. Dogs are aware; whether deciding to chase a ball or not, they seem to be "speculating." Thought and memory are clearly present in nonhuman animals such as *Aplysia,* the huge, shell-less marine snail that can be taught association. *Aplysia,* the sea hare, can be trained to anticipate; it will flee from potential electric shock as soon as a light is flashed. Knowledge, some admit, can be displayed by whales, bears, bats, and other vertebrates, including birds. But conventional wisdom tells us that consciousness is limited to people and our immediate ancestors. Many scientists believe that "mind"—whatever it is—will never be known by any combination of neurophysiology, neuroanatomy, genetics, neuropharmacology, or any other materialistic science. *Brain* may be knowable by the -ologies but *mind* can never be.

I disagree with many versions of this common myth. I believe brain is mind and mind is brain and that science, broadly conceived, is an effective method for learning about both. The results of the -ologies just listed, as well as of many other sciences, can tell us clearly about ourselves and what is inside our heads. Furthermore, humans have no monopoly whatever on any of these mental processes. As long as we indicate consciousness of *what,* I can point to conscious, actively communicating, pond-water microscopic life (and even extremely unconscious bureaucrats). The processes of perception, awareness, speculation, and the like evolved in the microcosm: the subvisible world of our bacterial ancestors. Movement itself is an ancestral bacterial trait, and thought, I am suggesting, is a kind of cell movement.

We admit that computers have precedents: electricity, electronic circuits, silica semiconductors, screws, nuts, and bolts. The miracle of the computer is the way in which its parts are put together. So, too, human minds have precedents; the uniqueness is in the recombination and interaction of the elements that comprise the mind/brain. My contention is that hundreds of biologists, psychologists, philosophers, and others making inquiries of mind/brain have failed to identify even the analogs of electricity, electronic circuits, silica semiconductors, screws, nuts, and bolts. In the absence of knowing what the parts are and how they came together, we can never know the human mind/brain. Only the very recent history of the human brain is illuminated by comparative studies of amphibian and reptilian brains. The crucial ancient beginnings of the human brain lie in the dancing of bacteria: the intricate mechanisms of cell motility. How do cells locomote? The answer to this puzzle is the beginning of enlightenment for the origins of mind/brain.

I cherish a specific, testable, scientific theory. The means for testing it are biochemical, genetic, and molecular-biological. The facilities for the testing are available in New York City. A conclusive proof would require generosity on the part of at least two hugely successful and highly talented scientists and their laboratory assistants, a Columbia University biochemist and a Rockefeller University geneticist. Dr. Charles Cantor, of Columbia University Medical School, has developed new techniques to purify genes (DNA) gently. The purification holds the biological material on agar blocks (a gelatin-like substance) in such a manner that the structures in which the genes reside, the chromosomes, are extracted in their natural long, skinny form. Groups of genes (linkage groups) can be identified. Chromosome counts, difficult to determine microscopically, can be made biochemically.

And Dr. David Luck, an active geneticist at The Rockefeller University for over a quarter of a century, has recently discovered a new type of genetic system. He has found a special set of genes that determines the development of structures, bodies called kinetosomes that are present in thousands of very different kinds of motile cells: those of green algae, sperm, ciliates, oviducts, and trachea, for example. These structures, which I think of as assembly systems for nearly universal cell motors, may be determined by a unique set of genes separate from those of the nuclei and other components of cells. These genes, inferred from genetic studies of Luck and his colleagues, may be exactly the spirochetal remnant genes I predicted still must be inside all motile cells that contain kinetosomes.

Although no exorbitant amount of money would be needed, because testing my theory would be limited by the requirement for time and energy of very busy people, it would be expensive. Furthermore, the results of my testing, even if they are ideal, would cure no disease, stop no war, limit no radioactivity, save no tropical forest, or produce no marketable product. At least in the beginning there would be no immediate profit coming from the work. The very concrete results would simply help us reconstruct the origin of our mind/brains from their bacterial ancestors.

What is the central idea to be tested? I hypothesize that all these phenomena of mind, from perception to consciousness, originated from an unholy microscopic alliance between hungry killer bacteria and their potential archaebacterial victims. The hungry killers were extraordinarily fast-swimming, skinny bacteria called spirochetes. These active bacteria are relatives of the spirochetes of today that are associated with the venereal disease that, in prolonged and serious cases, infects the brain: the treponemes of syphilis. The fatter, slow-moving potential victims, the second kind of bacteria called archaebacteria, were quite different from the spirochetes. By resisting death the archaebacteria incorporated their would-be, fast-moving killers into their bodies. The archaebacteria survived, continuing to be infected by the spirochetes. The odd couple lived together; the archaebacteria were changed by but not killed by their attackers; the victims did not entirely succumb. (There are precedents for this: Plants are green because their intended victims, the chloroplasts that began as oxygen-producing cyanobacteria, resisted death by ingestion.)

Our cells, including our nerve cells, may be products of such mergers. The thin, transparent bodies of the spirochete enemies sneakily incorporated inextricably and forever. The wily fast movement, the hunger, the sensory ability of the survivor's enemies all were put to good use by the evolving partnership. Cultural analogues of such mergers exist: cases in which two very different warring peoples form new identities after the truce, identities, for example, in which unique domesticated plants of one culture become firmly incorporated in that of the second. The presence of Indian corn, tomatoes, and potatoes in Europe is due to the near annihilation of indigenous American Indians. I see our cell movement, including the movements leading to thought, as the spoils of ancient microbial battles.

My speculations, two thousand million years later, may be the creative outcome of an ancient uneasy peace. If this reckoning is true, then the spirochetal remnants may be struggling to exist in our brains attempting to swim, grow, feed, connect with their fellows, and reproduce. The interactions between these subvisible actors, now full member-components of our nerve cells, are sensitive to the experience we bring them. *Perception, thought, speculation, memory,* of course, are all active processes; I speculate that these are the large-scale manifestations of the small-scale community ecology of the former spirochetes and archaebacteria that comprise our brains.

Arcana Naturae Detecta is the name of Anton van Leeuwenhoek's seventeenth-century book revealing the microcosm beneath his single-lens microscope illuminated by a gas lamp. The visible became explicable to him by the machinations of the subvisible. Leeuwenhoek and his followers made clear that "decay," "spoiling," and "rotting food" are all healthy bacterial and fungal growth. In baking, "rising dough" is respiring yeast; in tropical disease, malarial fevers are apicomplexan protists bursting our red blood cells. Fertility is owed in part to semen or "male seed" containing millions of tailed sperm in sugar solution. The disease of Mimi, the heroine of *La Bohème*, is "consumption." From its point of view, "consumption" is the healthy growth of *Mycobacterium* in the warm, moist lungs of the lovely young woman. Speculation, I claim, is legacy of the itching enmities of unsteady truce. Speculation is the mutual stimulation of the restrained microbial inhabitants that, entirely inside their former archaebacterial enemies, have strongly interacted with them for hundreds of millions of years. Our nerve cells are the outcome of an ancient, nearly immortal marriage of two archenemies who have managed to coexist: the former spirochetes and former archaebacteria that now comprise our brains.

Like animated vermicelli married and in perpetual copulatory stance with their would-be archaebacterial victims, these former free-living bacteria are inextricably united. They probably have been united for more than one thousand million years. The fastidiously described speculation is indistinguishable from the theory. I continually play with an idea: The origin of thought and consciousness is cellular, owing its beginnings to the first courtship between unlikely bacterial bedfellows who became ancestors to our mind/brains.

My goal in the rest of this essay is to explain what I mean and why I make such a bizarre assertion.

What needs to be explained? My basic speculation is that mind/brain processes are nutrition, physiology, sexuality, reproduction, and microbial community ecology of the microbes that comprise us. The microbes are not just metaphors; their remnants inhabit our brain, their needs and habits, histories and health status help determine our behavior. If we feel possessed and of several minds, if we feel overwhelmed by complexity, it is because we are inhabited by and comprised of complexities.

The detailed consequences of the theory of spirochete origin of microtubules of brain cells do not belong in an essay about speculation for *The Reality Club*. Indeed, it is unlikely that such a statement would even be considered for publication in the *Proceedings of the National Academy of Sciences*. Rather, I ask only that the unmentionable become discussable over mulled wine and friendship so that the consequences of the hypothesis may be speculated upon. Could thought, speculation, and awareness really have evolved from fast-moving bacteria and their interactions, their hungers, their activities, their satiations, their associations with their fellows, both like and unlike, and their waste-removal processes? Is it possible that we are as entirely unaware of the microbial inhabitants that comprise us as a huge ship tossing in the waves is unaware that her responses are determined by the hunger, thirst, and eyesight of the captain at the helm and his communications with the crew?

What might be the implications for mind/brains if this bacterial origin of speculation is correct? Let us list a few. They all may be incorrect, but they are all testable within the rigors of the scientific tradition.

1. Nerve impulses and the firing of nerves

These become explicable as our motile spirochetes trying to swim; as Betsey Dyer (assistant professor of biology, Wheaton College, Norton, MA) says, captive former spirochetes are spinning their wheels unable to move forward. They have become uncoupled motors going around and around. This quasi-movement is the nerve impulse. It occurs because small, positively charged ions (*e.g.*, sodium, potassium, calcium) are accumulated and released across what is now our nerve cell membrane. These ions, their protein and membrane interactions, derive from the membranes of the original spirochetes.

2. Sweet memories

Two different kinds of memory systems exist: short-term (seconds to minutes) and long-term (indefinitely). The storage of memories is markedly enhanced by adrenaline and other substances that lead directly to increased availability of sugar to the brain cells.[1] Sugar, like anything penetrating the blood-brain barrier—that is, entering the brain from the blood—is very carefully monitored and controlled.

Short-term memory arises every time from casual encounters between the sticking-out parts of former spirochetes and their friends. These interactions begin in seconds; it probably takes a few minutes at most while two or more neurons née spirochetes interact. The casual encounters occur by small-ion interactions with proteins on the surfaces of what used to be spirochete membranes (now they are our nerve cell membranes). In brief, short-term memories derive from the physiology of spirochetal remnants in the brain. We know that the pictorial short-term memory, for the recognition of fractal designs, for example, "is coded by temporary activation of an ensemble of neurons in the region of the association cortex that processes visual information."[2] Presumably the short-term memory is stored when visual information is processed and not in special compartments for short-term memory. The "temporary activation," if I am correct, will be directly homologous to spirochete behavioral interaction—not analogous to it or to computer software manipulation.

Long-term memory is stable; it depends on new protein synthesis. Long-term memory works because it stores the short-term. What were repeated casual encounters between former spirochetal remnants become stabilized attachment sites. Synapse, if I am correct, is the neurophysiologist's term for the well-developed spirochetal remnant attachment site. In brief, long-term memories derive from the growth of spirochetal remnants, including their attachment sites, in the brain.

Sugar enhances memory processes because it feeds preferentially the spirochetal remnants so that they can interact healthily and form new attachment sites. Sugar has been the food of spirochetes since they squiggled in the mud.

As Edelman (1985) has pointed out, no two monkeys, no two identical twins, are identical at the level of fine structure of their neuronal connections. "There must be a generator of diversity during the development of neural circuits, capable of constructing definite patterns of groups but also generating great individual variation. Variation must occur at the level of cell-to-cell recognition by a molecular process. Second, there must be evidence from group selection and competition in brain maps and re-entrant circuits. This must occur not in the circuitry but in the efficacy of preformed connections or synapses."[3] I believe Edelman is discovering the actively growing latter-day populations of microbes that comprise every brain. Edelman's "populations" are nerve cells and their connections. I interpret Edelman's populations literally as remnants of ancestral microbial masses. The spirochetal remnants, either poised or ready to grow, attach and interact depending on how they are treated during a human's crucial stages (fetal development, infancy, and early childhood). Neural Darwinism, differential growth by selection of spirochete associations, determines the way in which the brain develops.

Mental health is, in part, how we feed the normal spirochetal remnants that make up our brain. Learning becomes a function of the number and quality of new connections—attachment sites—that these wily apobeings forge. The spirochetal remnants grow faster, dissolving temporary points of contact while consolidating firm connections that are our nerve cell endings during our infancy and childhood. More potential changes occur early—in infancy and adolescence—relative to those of adulthood. The growth patterns of nerve cells née spirochetes are sensitive to the food, such as essential fatty acids, that the rest of our body provides for them; experience is always active, always participatory and, if registered in long-term memory, unforgotten. Our memories are their physical networks. Our crises and climaxes are their "blooms," their population explosions. Senility is spirochetal-remnant atrophy. It is no coincidence that salt ions and psychoactive drugs, including anesthetics, have strong effects on spirochetal movement of the free-living mud-bound cousin spirochetes.

Clearly these enormous contemplative issues cannot be solved here alone by me. All I ask is that we compare consciousness with spirochete microbial ecology. We may be vessels, large ships, unwitting sanctuaries to the thriving communities comprising us. When they are starved, cramped, or stimulated we have inchoate feelings. Perhaps we should get to know ourselves better. We might then recognize our speculations as the dance networks of ancient restless tiny beings that connect our parts.

NOTES

[1] Paul E. Gold, "Sweet Memories," *American Scientist*, 1987, vol. 75, pp. 151–55.

[2] Y. Miyashita and H. S. Chang, "Neuronal Correlate of Pictorial Short-Term Memory in the Primate Temporal Cortex," *Nature*, 1988, vol. 331, pp. 68–70.

[3] Gerald M. Edelman, "Neural Darwinism: Population Thinking and Higher Brain Function," 1985. In *How We Know, Nobel Conference XX*, ed. Michael Shafto, Gustavus Adolphus College, St. Peter, Minnesota, pp. 1–30.

A FLOWING SENTENCE, A TRAIN OF CONSCIOUSNESS, A RIPPLING ARPEGGIO: THE TRILOGY OF *HOMO SERIATUM*

WILLIAM CALVIN

We must face the fact that humans have a better claim on the title "Homo seriatim" than on "Homo sapiens"—we're more consistently serial than wise.

Three centuries ago, Leibnitz propounded what might now be called the *physiologist's premise*: "Everything that happens in man's body is as mechanical as what happens in a watch."

Does that apply to the mind, too? Most people initially think it unlikely. But perhaps Spinoza suspected as much when he said: "The order and connection of ideas is the same as the order and connection of things." Earlier in the seventeenth century, Descartes was bold enough to conceive of a completely self-sufficient nervous mechanism able to perform complicated and apparently intelligent acts. Unfortunately, he still had a conceptual problem regarding followers-and-leaders and so mired us even deeper in the dualistic body-and-soul metaphors of an earlier age.

But by the late nineteenth century, Thomas Henry Huxley had prophesied that: "We shall, sooner or later, arrive at a mechanical equivalent of consciousness"; and this is manifestly the premise of my fellow neurophysiologists. Huxley reflected not only the biologists' mood in the wake of Darwin's revolution; the physicist Ernst Mach summarized in 1895 what many psychologists and philosophers had also begun to say, about how mental mechanisms could use the potent variation-and-selection combination:

> [From] the teeming, swelling host of fancies which a free
> and high-flown imagination calls forth, suddenly that

> particular form arises to the light which harmonizes per-
> fectly with the ruling idea, mood, or design. Then it is
> that which has resulted slowly as the result of a gradual
> selection, [that] appears as if it were the outcome of a
> deliberate act of creation. Thus are to be explained the
> statements of Newton, Mozart, Richard Wagner, and
> others, when they say that thoughts, melodies, and har-
> monies had poured in upon them, and that they had
> simply retained the right ones.[1]

And after this last century of spectacular progress in the
brain sciences and evolutionary biology, we have arrived
at the threshold of fulfilling Huxley's prophecy: *We are
probably within a decade or two of creating consciousness.*

Our creations probably won't be full-fledged human
mimics complete with our primate-style emotions and their
overlay of Ice Age modifications. And undoubtedly not everyone will agree that they are "truly conscious" (we'll
surely see escalating definitions, analogous to those of
"true language," when animal studies started to turn up
interesting abilities).

But our creations will be distinctive individuals *in silico*
who can think much like our metaphorical "little person
inside the head"—that which contemplates the past and
forecasts the future, makes decisions about relative worth,
plans what to do tomorrow, feels dismay when seeing a
tragedy unfold, and narrates our life story as it unfolds.
They will almost intuitively "speak our language." Because of that, conversations with such a "robot" (for lack
of a better word) will be far more interesting than those
we've attempted with our other animals—at least, once
these robotic individuals have a few years' experience observing the world and interacting with a potpourri of teachers. Most people will probably concede that they're
conscious, and ethical considerations will arise (can one
"pull the plug" on such an individual?).

What will make this possible? Two things, to my way of
thinking: a mechanistic understanding of how brains chain

things together, and a technological offshoot of massively parallel computers, which I call "massively serial computers" (which will be totally unlike today's rule-bound serial computers, more formally known as von Neumann Machines). I propose to call the product of this marriage a Darwin Machine. It uses some emergent properties of the Law of Large Numbers—but basically, just think of it as mimicking biological evolution on a greatly accelerated time scale, creating new thoughts rather than new species.

Mach's list of trial-and-error achievements, one notes, mostly involves Spinoza's "order and connection of ideas." We are always stringing things together: phonemes into words, words into sentences, concepts into scenarios, notes into melodies—and then fussing about getting them in the right order.

Chaining is most obvious for language: Our brain uses word-order rules to create a language with an infinite number of novel messages, rather than the several dozen standard interpretations associated with the several dozen cries and grunts in the repertoire of any other primate species. But we, too, only use a few dozen basic speech sounds: Though inflection rules may augment them, it isn't our mellifluous voices that constitute a significant advance but rather our arrangement rules, the meaningful order in which we chain our utterances. "Dick called Jane" means something very different from "Jane called Dick."

And talking-to-ourselves consciousness is, among other things, particularly concerned with creating scenarios, trying to chain together memory schemata to explain the past and forecast the future. As Peter Brooks recently observed in *Reading for the Plot:*

> Our lives are ceaselessly intertwined with narrative, with the stories we tell and hear told, those we dream or imagine or would like to tell, all of which are reworked in that story of our own lives that we narrate to ourselves in an episodic, sometimes semiconscious, but vir-

tually uninterrupted monologue. We live immersed in narrative, recounting and reassessing the meaning of our past actions, anticipating the outcome of our future projects, situating ourselves at the intersection of several stories not yet completed.[2]

It is our ability to choose between such alternative scenarios that constitutes our free will—though, of course, our choices are only as good as our imagination in constructing a wide range of candidate scenarios.

Logical reasoning also seems dependent on the rules of reliable sequencing to create statements where one thing entails another. Our sophisticated projection abilities are very sequential: A chess master, for example, tends to see each board configuration not just after the next move but a half dozen moves ahead, as several alternative scenarios.

Chaining things together isn't everything. Much of our imagination is pictorial; certainly our emotional judgments are similarly "right-brain," and we would be strikingly impoverished without them. But such "left-brain" sequential abilities are obviously a key development in post-ape brain evolution. Language, scenario-spinning consciousness, and music constitute a trilogy of sequential abilities for which we seek a better understanding. We must face the fact that humans have a better claim on the title *Homo seriatim* than on *Homo sapiens*—we're more consistently serial than wise.

And we do a lot of selecting from among choices we create and chain together—as if there were many planning tracks in the brain, something like the candelabra-shaped railroad marshaling yard where many trains are assembled but only one let loose on the "main track" of speech and consciousness. If we can understand such a process—how trains randomly vary, how their order is compared to memories of successful sequences of the past, what constitutes a "good enough" plan on which to act—we will have achieved an important step in understanding ourselves.

One can already envisage a class of possible computers which I call "Darwin Machines," so named because they work like a greatly speeded-up version of biological evolution. They shape up new thoughts in milliseconds rather than new species in millennia, using innocuous remembered environments rather than the real-life noxious ones, but in much the same way as Darwin's natural selection repeatedly edits the random genetic sequence variations to order to shape new body styles.

They, or something like them, may provide our second-generation mechanistic explanation of consciousness—the first generation belonging to the Darwin enthusiasts of the late nineteenth century, and their many predecessors who overcame the seemingly natural tendency to treat mind as irretrievably different. As massively parallel computers develop, we will be able to better simulate such marshaling-yard arrangements—and such a massive serial computer may allow us our first conversations with an intelligent form of artificial life.

How we think is nowhere as clear as what we think about. Suppose, however, that we were to achieve such a general understanding of the mechanisms whereby we think—the way in which we analyze the world around us, arrive at new ideas and judge their usefulness, and so guide our actions? We might achieve some control over patholog- ical thinking—*worry*, for example, is the unproductive rep- etition of a bothersome thought that prevents new ideas or concerns from rising to consciousness. How do we avoid "getting stuck"?

And an advanced understanding might create the poten- tial for many of us to think in the creative ways that only a few geniuses now achieve. Personally, I'd like to be able to compose symphonies in my head, hear the combined instruments of the orchestra playing, and then write down the music, in the way that Mozart was reportedly able to do. I'd like to be able to think in four- or six-dimensional space, the way some mathematicians can do. I'd like to be able to recall something that I read somewhere, complete with the sentences that preceded and followed it. I'd like to be able to run through in my head the next ten ploys of a labor negotiation or an important conversation, so as to better choose a good course of action.

Maybe, if we come to understand how the brain does such serial order things, our children will be able to shape our education to match actual mental processes (rather than the Procrustean bed of guesswork education theories). And we will be able to craft artificial aids such as computers that will approximately match up with the mental processes inside our heads, provide a natural fit (rather than fitting someone's glorified idea of how logical rules structure the brain).

Our conception of what goes on inside our heads is central to the next step in evolution. That our present concepts are faulty can be seen by how awkwardly we wear the clothes crafted by the people who think our minds are some logical, rule-governed machine. The Artificial Intelligentsia have produced machines that do well what we naturally do poorly—such as solving mathematical theorems—but which are incredibly awkward at doing things that we do easily, such as navigating through a strange room or jumping to a correct conclusion on the basis of limited data. It is almost as if they were trying to appreciate things from the wrong viewpoint. Finding the right viewpoint can often effect an enormous simplification—remember what Copernicus's heliocentric vision did to Ptolemy's complicated epicycles?

No research areas are more troubled by the lack of a reliable viewpoint than psychology, cognitive sciences, AI, and neurobiology. Though criticized for a century or more, most of us still fall back (albeit uncomfortably) on the lay view of what is inside the head. Most people, if questioned about what goes on inside their head, will talk as if there were a little person inside the head receiving reports from the eyes and ears and skin, and issuing the commands that run the muscles. We imagine an executive issuing orders to subservient departments; with the advent of computers and of the recognition of the importance of serial ordering, the executive became a "programmer" of equal omnipotence.

This old notion of hierarchies inside the brain led inevitably to the concept that somewhere there was a highest center, able to command all subservient centers. And we've actually found some. In fish, you can find two "command" neurons in the brain stem: if the right-hand Mauthner cell fires a single impulse, all of the muscles on the fish's left side twitch violently. This massive tail-flip is used to get the fish away from something that is starting to nibble on it. If one of those cells chooses to speak, it overrides all ordinary reflexes and the fish flips. Humans don't have Mauthner cells, but there are some single neurons that seem very important, that can get your attention so compellingly that all else seems irrelevant.

Where are they—perhaps in the pineal, where Descartes suggested the soul might reside? Or maybe in our all-important frontal lobes? (No. As romantics have postulated, this most important center is not even inside the brain; indeed, provided that you keep your head bowed, it is closer to the heart. These command neurons are in your teeth. A barrage of impulses from a few small nerve fibers inside a single tooth is quite sufficient to ruin your day. All other centers in the brain are seemingly rendered subservient to that tooth, when it chooses to speak.)

The ability to command is characteristic of the lowest, fire alarm-like mechanisms in our nervous systems—but not, it seems, of the highest mental processes. The obligatory response is handy for military commands, but in seeking the basis of higher mental processes, we are looking for something more like policy-making and diplomacy, with a lot of give and take, consensus as an arbiter. We shall have to be concerned with creativity—where we get our ideas. And choice—how we evaluate candidates and judge if any one of them is good enough to try implementing.

Yes, even mentioning the "little person inside the head"

sometimes promotes a fallacy—that there is a "seat of the soul," a cave somewhere inside the brain where "the *real me*" homunculus resides as a voyeur and puppeteer, watching our senses and pulling our strings. And yes, we need to explain why that is an oversimplification with a lot of excess baggage from body-and-soul days. But we need not throw out our "enfant terrible" with the bathwater: the narrator of our conscious experience can emerge from a committee of brain regions just as the pattern of a snowflake emerges from a cooling committee of water molecules. It doesn't even require a snowflakelike center to form: The unity of consciousness can result from a virtual center, just as physicists can treat all of the molecules constituting the Earth as if they were all concentrated in the center of the Earth when computing gravitational attractions. Virtual centers are much handier conceptually and computationally, and it is not surprising that our brains often make use of a virtual center as we decide what to do next.

Understanding thought is not without its hazards. I suppose that there is always the danger of someone's inventing a human version of the hog-tie: Cowboys have a way of trussing up a cow or a pugnacious bronco that fixes the brute so that it can neither move nor think (someone would argue that religious and political leaders invented the human hog-tie long ago).

But I don't share Gregory Bateson's apprehension; he argued in *Angels Fear* that "if we were aware of the processes whereby we form mental images, we would no longer be able to trust them as a basis for action. They say the centipede always knew how to walk until somebody asked it which leg it would move first."[3] Getting stuck, whether from incessant worry or Hamletlike indecision, is always a potential problem—but for many people, an understanding of how to utilize more effectively the mental processes would be liberating rather than hazardous. While motivations affect the biases and so the judgments (I do worry about a super-cocaine being concocted as we better understand the neurochemistry of motivational systems), what we are talking about here is thought itself: in particular, the mechanisms by which we generate new ideas, compare them to past experience, and then choose between them.

Even there, we can see some potential problems. I have come to suspect that some of the multiple meanings of the word *consciousness* are grounded in fear; that there is intentional obfuscation as well as befuddlement. We use *conscious* for one extreme of a sleep-wakefulness spectrum, as in *unconscious*. We often use it as a synonym for awareness, as when we say, "I was *conscious of* a breeze touching my face." As Ralph Barton Perry said in 1904:

> There is no term [consciousness] at once so popular and so devoid of standard meaning. How can a term mean anything when it is employed to connote anything and everything, including its own negation? One hears of the object of consciousness and the subject of consciousness, and the union of the two in self-consciousness; of the private consciousness, the social consciousness, and the transcendental consciousness; the inner and the outer, the higher and the lower, the temporal and the eternal consciousness; the activity and the state of consciousness. Then there is consciousness-stuff, and unconscious consciousness. . . . The list is not complete, but sufficiently amazing. Consciousness comprises everything that is, and indefinitely much more. It is small wonder that the definition of it is little attempted.[4]

With such a list (and it has only expanded during the present century), we must ask whether consciousness confusion is not being intentionally compounded, whether fear of understanding has dominated curiosity. Julian Jaynes usefully pruned down this laundry list in the introduction to his 1976 book *The Origin of Consciousness in the Breakdown of the Bicameral Mind* and tried to refocus attention on the narrator of our conscious experience as the most important of the many things we call consciousness. Though I see little reason to accept Jaynes's conclusion that this narrator emerged in evolution as recently as three thousand years ago, I do agree with Jaynes that the narrator is the name of the game. And that it is one of the most interesting games in town. We must not only answer "when?" questions but mechanistic "how?" questions and evolutionary "what for?" questions about narrator-dominated consciousness.

Yet we must not forget the many other aspects of consciousness when focusing on the narrator issues, just because they are less susceptible to a mechanistic analysis—though, for the present purposes, I am indeed setting them aside temporarily. I am not redefining consciousness to mean exactly what I want it to mean, neither more nor less (shades of *Alice in Wonderland*), but rather exploiting one handle on a multifaceted problem, casting about trying to find a Copernican improvement in viewpoint.

Consciousness is undeniably useful. Again we find the most succinct statement coming from the late nineteenth century, this time from the physicist Heinrich Hertz: "The most important problem which our conscious knowledge should enable us to solve is the anticipation of future events, so that we may arrange our present affairs in accordance with such anticipation."

Richard Alexander expanded on this in *The Biology of Moral Systems*:

Consciousness and related aspects of the human psyche (self-awareness, self-reflection, foresight, planning, purpose, conscience, free will, etc.) . . . represent a system for competing with other humans for status, resources, and eventually reproductive success. [They are] a means of seeing ourselves and our life situations as others see us . . . so as to outguess, outmaneuver, outdo those others—most particularly in ways that will cause . . .

them to continue to interact with us in fashions that will benefit us and seem to benefit them. Consciousness, then, is a game of life in which the participants are trying to comprehend what is in one another's minds before, and more effectively than, it can be done in reverse.[5]

This illuminates one of the potential hazards of understanding how we think (as opposed to understanding motivation per se): As Alexander points out, if others understand how we think, they might somehow take advantage of it. Of course, one could say that modern pseudo-scientific advertising has already done this, and that charlatans have traditionally done it. But Alexander also points out one cure: "I have suggested that consciousness is a way of making our social behavior so unpredictable as to allow us to outmaneuver others. . . ." By creating lots of choices, we have so many avenues open to us that we are hard to predict, too wily to trap. And an understanding of how to generate even more of Mach's "teeming, swelling host of fancies" can only make each of us more unique, not more predictable and manipulatable.

But why sequencing? And how did an elaborated sequencing committee arise in evolution? While often useful, command queues for detailed preplanning are seldom essential: Goal-plus-feedback usually suffices, as when raising a cup to one's lips and getting progress reports from the joints and muscles, using them to adjust the path.

Where planned chains become essential, and thus likely to evolve rapidly, is where feedback becomes impossible, yet a linked series of moves must be precisely executed. Reaction time becomes a problem for brief ballistic movements such as hammering, throwing, clubbing, or kicking: for example, a dart throw takes 119 milliseconds until the fingers let loose the dart, but the round-trip reaction time from arm to spinal cord and back to arm takes 110 milliseconds. The progress reports will mostly arrive too late for path corrections to be made. For organisms that need to be both large (meters of conduction distance) and fast, one often needs the neural equivalent of an old-fashioned roll for a player piano. We carefully plan during "get set" to act without feedback.

Humans often hunt with projectiles; faster and farther throws are always better, provided accuracy can be maintained. My 1983 biophysical model for throwing emphasized the need for submillisecond timing precision in letting loose the projectile. Such timing precision is far in excess of what one can expect from even the best of neurons (they are always pretty jittery, not merely after too many cups of coffee), and the jitter remains troublesome when many are chained together in a single command buffer. This suggests that the precision of the release of a projectile must arise from the Law of Large Numbers (the same rationale as why, in order to halve a standard deviation, one averages four times as much data).

Thus there must be many sequencers that, at least temporarily, can be ganged in parallel (imagine multiple columns of horses pulling a single wagon) during the occasions demanding peak performance in one-shot timing. To reliably hit a rabbit-sized target from twice the distance requires that the jitter in rock release time be narrowed by a factor of 8, and the only known way of accomplishing this feat is, as one gets set to throw each time, to assign 64 times as many noisy neurons to the task and then average their recommendations for the release time. To triple throwing distance requires a 729-fold increase in neurons assigned to the task. "Concentrating" as we get set to throw probably involves recruiting a lot of nervous neighbors to help out, all "pushing" together—not unlike when a dozen bystanders heave together to push an automobile out of a ditch. But it's not just a dozen, in the case of neurons—since faster and farther throws are always better, throwing has a prodigious appetite for more and more sequencing neurons.

This gives one a very different perspective of randomness. Technology treats noise as an unwanted impediment, Darwinism as a means of exploring new avenues, but here we see it as a stimulus to evolve redundant machinery— whose secondary uses may be revolutionary. I have proposed (in *The Throwing Madonna* and more elaborately in *The River That Flows Uphill*) that hand movements may have a lot to do with the evolution of our brain's greatly improved abilities to handle sequence. As Jacob Bronowski said: "The hand is a cutting edge of the mind." And, indeed, various cognitive scientists have suggested that the hand shapes up our conceptual abilities via tool-making.

But I am suggesting something that is mechanistically rather different from the proposal of the cognitive cognoscenti, proposing instead that the brain's sequencer machinery can be used for shaping up sentences, scenarios, and listening to arpeggios when not required for planning a complicated hand movement. This says that spare-time "co-opting" may have been all-important. So even if evolution shaped up our sequencing machinery via our success in rock throwing, we would get some "free" improvements in other chaining-dependent abilities such as language and planning—at least, during the times when we were not busy getting set to throw.

Darwin Machines aren't just some future class of massively serial computers that simulate Darwinism: Darwin machines can be biological as well. Where in the brain does our Darwin Machine live? It may involve much of the left cerebral hemisphere in mammals. This is not to say that the right brain is uninvolved, only that even in monkeys, the left hemisphere is best at deciphering rapid sound sequences—and so it apparently became a natural home for many language-related abilities.

Indeed, the core of human language cortex is a sequencing area for both incoming sounds and outgoing movements, just what grammar needs. Comparison of grammars shows that the typical subject-verb-object word order of an English sentence is not biologically determined: Japanese syntax uses subject-object-verb, while classical Arabic puts the verb first. What the biology may provide is the serial buffer to hold the phrase while it is analyzed according to the learned rules (though more subtle grammatical linkages are perhaps constrained by buffer branchings, corresponding to Chomsky's deep structure). There are some suggestions that the capacity of one important serial buffer is about a half dozen items, judging from phenomena such as chunking of memory.

Precisely timed hand movements are probably controlled out of the cerebral cortex, mostly the frontal lobe's motor strip, about an inch above your ear. But, along with the cerebellum, most of the rest of the frontal lobe gets in the act, too. Just in front of the motor strip is the so-called premotor cortex (a term that here includes the supplementary motor area), and it has a reputation for chaining together fluent sequences of action, such as you might use to insert a key into a lock, turn a doorknob, and push open a door. When we practice playing a musical instrument, we are likely tuning up the premotor cortex; injuries to it do not result in weakness or paralysis (as do injuries to the motor strip) but merely diminish one's ability to quickly carry out a chained series of motions, what the neuropsychologist Aleksandr Romanovitch Luria liked to call a kinetic melody.

And the rest of the frontal lobe, that which is in front of both the motor strip and the premotor cortex (and known as the "prefrontal cortex"), has a lot to do with planning a novel sequence. A patient with a prefrontal tumor can raise his arm on command if the arm is lying atop the bedcovers—but might get stuck if asked to raise his arm if he first has to extract it from under the covers and then raise it. If you ask the patient to remove his arm from under the covers, he can do it. If he is then asked to raise it, he can. But he may not be able to plan out this novel sequence and then execute it.

Detailed knowledge of movement programs is still a goal rather than an accomplishment; I would share the assessment of J. Z. Young: "I must stress how little is yet known about the programs of the brain. The code has not yet been properly broken; but we begin to see the units of it. . . . We can see that the code is somehow a matter of sequences of neural activities, providing expectancies of what to do next."[6]

So large areas of the frontal lobe are involved in sequencing, and also the temporal and parietal lobe areas associated with language. But they might not have arisen for their usefulness in talking and planning—sequencing machinery might have grown extensive simply because so much of it is occasionally needed for accurate throwing. It's a very different view of our origins from the usual bigger-is-smarter-is-better notions. As I said in *The River That Flows Uphill:*

> From such an evolutionary ratchet jacking up brain size, there arose unbidden our own brain of unbounded potential. From basketball to tennis, this mosaic brain expresses its ancient pleasure in precisely timing a sequence. Transcending its origins, our brain can now create novel sequences using grammar and music. Blind to our foundations, we nonetheless created poetry and reason; with a clearer footing, we can perhaps contemplate how our enlarged consciousness evolved and is evolving.[7]

Musical forms may yet have much to teach us about our brains. Not only do we string muscle commands together to make unique movements, words together to make never-heard-before sentences, and concepts together to make innovative scenarios—but we make melodies as well. The folk singer Bill Crowfoot observes that children in many cultures, speaking many languages, still all use the musical form known as a "minor third" to harass their siblings: *Na-na na na na na.* The more elaborate forms of the *Magnificat* may not be as universal—but, still, they resonate. Why?

If we come to understand why Bach's brain still speaks so compellingly to our brains today, we will have bridged the gap between primary evolutionary adaptations and the magnificent secondary uses that can be made of the same brain machinery. Music is an emergent property, unless someone can figure out how a lilting aria and a choral fugue and a rippling arpeggio were shaped up by survival-sensitive adaptations. Senza Sordino's notes for the *Mass in F* and the *Magnificat* demonstrate some of the musical features that tickle our brains:

> . . . the final "kyrie eleison" is composed as a counter-fugue—that is, each thematic entry is answered by its inversion. In the further course of the movement, Bach makes use of the contrapuntal techniques of stretto, parallel voice-leading, and mirror inversions of themes.
>
> As the fugal chorus builds to a climax, each voice enters one note higher than its predecessor; and the repetition of this device gives the impression of an endless succession of voices. . . .
>
> The phrase *mente cordis sui* calls forth an astounding harmonic progression, suggesting, in the course of some nine measures, D-major, F-sharp-minor, F-sharp-major, B-minor, D-minor, and, finally, D-major, the first trumpet bringing everyone back to the home key with a descending scale passage and trill that haunts the dreams of every trumpeter.

What is it about our brains that so disposes them to the minor third and the trill, despite the lack of evolutionary adaptations for such musical patterns? Natural selection conceivably might have shaped up our response to the drumbeat—but hardly four-part harmony.

Though this question is seldom asked, I am sure that the standard answer would be the tie with language: both are sequences of sound where recognizing patterns is all-important. And so natural selection for language abilities would, *pari passu*, gain us musical abilities as a secondary use of the same neural machinery. Maybe so. But the many parallel planning tracks as the key element of "get set" in ballistic movements suggests that both language and music are potentially secondary uses of the neural machinery for ballistic skills, that music might have more to do with modern-day baseball than modern-day prose. Sordino's notes end with:

> *Gloria Patri, gloria Filio, gloria et Spiritui sancto! Sicut erat in principio et nunc et semper in saeculorum. Amen.* ("Glory to the Father, and to the Son, and to the Holy Ghost! As it was in the beginning, is now and ever shall be, world without end. Amen.")
> . . . Bach cannot resist the musical symbolism of triplets in the three invocations, to represent the tripartite nature of the Trinity, and a return of the opening music at the end, taking his cue from, "As it was in the beginning . . ." But the musical return serves aesthetics as well as theology, making a perfectly satisfying close to one of the most perfect and satisfying works of the choral literature.

There are many aspects of human brains that would vie for a trilogy if anyone tried to pick the three focal *mechanistic* aspects of our humanity. Surely if one's criteria were traits whose improvements would help us survive the next century, the mental machinery controlling *cooperation*, *conflict resolution*, and *family size* would undoubtedly rank high (all are likely to be strongly shared with our primate cousins—yet researchers in those areas operate on shoestring budgets). But if we focus on the three primary traits via which we differ from the apes in an order-of-magnitude way, we can wind up with a curious trio: *language*, *scenario-spinning consciousness*, and *music*—three aspects of sequential patterns in our brains. Their beginnings are still dimly seen but in their elaboration may lie the higher humanity. And possibly the artificial humanity.

NOTES

[1] T. H. Huxley, *Methods and Results* (Appleton, New York, 1897), p. 191.

[2] P. Brooks, *Reading for the Plot* (Knopf, New York, 1984), p. 3.

[3] Gregory Bateson and Mary Catherine Bateson, *Angels Fear* (Macmillan, 1987), p. 88.

[4] Ralph Barton Perry, "Conceptions and Misconceptions of Consciousness," *Psychological Review*, 1904, vol. 11, pp. 282–96.

[5] Richard D. Alexander, *The Biology of Moral Systems* (New York: Aldine de Gruyter, 1987), pp. 112–13.

[6] J. Z. Young, *Philosophy and the Brain* (Oxford University Press, 1987).

[7] W. H. Calvin, *The River That Flows Uphill: A Journey from the Big Bang to the Big Brain* (Macmillan, 1986), p. 365.

REALITY AND THE BRAIN: THE BEGINNINGS AND ENDINGS OF THE HUMAN BEING

JULIUS KOREIN, M.D.

> Being conservative, we could estimate the onset of the life of a human being—as reflected by the organizational structure of the critical system of the brain and its incipient function—to be after twenty weeks; a person begins to emerge.

We may philosophize about reality and discuss its relative or absolute nature—the underlying invariance or the limitations and distortions of our sensory neural apparatus—but when faced with an individual in extreme pain or one who is bleeding massively, reality becomes a very simple, immediate problem. In the emergency situation one does not contemplate the brain as the organ that perceives itself and naïve reality predominates. When we study the brain through psycho-physiological experiments or consider experiments of nature such as patients with strokes, seizures, or dementia, we begin to learn about structural and functional aspects of what the brain does and how it works. Sophistication in experimental paradigms and advances in a variety of technologies allow us to delve deeper into what the brain does and how it does it. Although we are far from a solution that clarifies brain function in a succinct and total manner, enough knowledge has been amassed so that the brain has a fairly good idea of what the brain does. Certainly, we know enough to make a diagnosis of brain dysfunction with good localization of the abnormality and its probable cause. Complex tests may be performed to gain information about multiple levels of structure and function; these include tests relating to behavioral responses, electrophysiology, and imaging techniques that reveal biochemical and physical architecture of the brain. Ultimately, when an autopsy is performed on a patient who dies with central nervous system disease, the gelatinous brain is placed in a fixative such as Formalin to allow hardening for subsequent microscopic examination. Many other structural and chemical tests and examinations may be performed on the tissue. By correlating the pathology found with the clinical and laboratory evaluations performed on the patient, one confirms or refutes the diagnosis and gains further insight into how the brain perceives reality.

However, the reality discussed in this essay relates to the functioning of the human organism as a whole—as a person and as an individual entity. This approach is, or should be, that of the physician in his interaction with the patient.

The patient may be considered as an information generator describing his complaints and symptoms to the physician, who receives and processes the information. The patient is then examined, and more information is obtained. Based on his previous knowledge and experience, the physician attempts to categorize the clinical findings and formulates a differential diagnosis. This set of localizations and probable causes is a hypothesis to explain the patient's problem. This may then be confirmed by further tests. In this manner medicine appears to be a science. Thus, if a forty-two-year-old man has a sudden onset of headache followed by some weakness of his right face and upper extremity and difficulty with speech comprehension confirmed by examination, a neurologist would include in his differential diagnosis localization of the dysfunction to the left cerebral hemisphere, since the functions of speech and right-sided motor activity reside in the left hemisphere. A second part of his diagnosis would suggest a cause or etiology, which, because of sudden onset of the headache, might be a small hemorrhage, possibly from an aneurysm. In order to substantiate or refute the diagnosis, computerized axial tomography might be performed, which might show a hemorrhage. Further tests might reveal the aneurysm. Of course, all medicine is not so straightforward.

Let us contrast this patient with one suffering intermittent severe pulsating headaches occasionally preceded by minor visual disturbances. The headache may be described in greater detail as to its characteristics, onset, duration, locus, intensity, and periodicity. Physical examination and laboratory findings are negative. It is not uncommon for a physician to come to a primary diagnosis of atypical migraine—the patient does not have the scintillating aura, nausea, or vomiting often associated with classical migraine. Here we clearly see a problem in definition of the disease state depending on how one defines migraine. It may be a narrow filter through which only patients with a highly specific set of findings can be classified, or it may be broadened to include a huge percentage of headache syndromes. The diagnosis, therefore, depends upon the definitions as well as observations, and subsequently on the therapeutic response. There is no clear-cut observation that may be used to refute the diagnosis, since the fuzziness of the concept is related to imprecise definitions. The field of psychiatry and mental illness is a prime example. Thus, a diagnosis is not identical to a hypothesis. We attempt to diagnose specific clinical states of the human being, but these may be imprecise, preventing the performance of tests that will confirm or refute a diagnosis.

We may imagine a multidimensional space of n variables, each representing the value of a clinical observation at a given time. Every individual can be represented at a given moment in time in this n-space by n-coordinates. As time passes the variables may change. The trajectory of "normal" states will be a path that would be well defined with some blurring at the edges. As different patients become ill, the trajectories will deviate from normal but will vary from one another depending on the illness—a brain tumor would go in one "direction," while patients with multiple sclerosis will traverse another path. Similar diagnostic entities would cluster in grouped trajectories. The trajectory of patients with a diagnosis of intracerebral hemorrhage would be well delineated, while that of schizophrenia will be much less clearly demarcated. Diagnoses can be considered a symbol or shorthand for the complex of findings that deviate from the normal. If the patient improves, he will tend to return to the normal group.[1]

In the above-described multidimensional space there will be terminations of trajectories depending on how the patient dies, but all will die and ultimately collect in one invariant group. Similarly, we may expect these variables to have some specific onset or beginning. It is toward these diagnostic states involving the onset and termination of the human being that we will address ourselves.

The problem of seeing the world in terms of a naïve reality (accepting the world at the face value of our "senses") is that this does not permit one to take into account changes, and their deeper consequences. Modern technology has been applied to medicine with a vengeance. The advent of resuscitative and life-support systems in the intensive-care unit are only modest innovations heralding an age exemplified by chemotherapy, organ transplantation, artificial organs, *in vitro* fertilization, storage and implantation of embryos, and genetic engineering, among others. The thrust in this direction of improving medical care has been backed by enormous effort, time, and money.

Consider the deep reasons for this effort—certainly, the quest for truth and the betterment of mankind and many other noble ideals may be invoked. On a more primitive level, a large segment of the population of Western civilization equates death with evil, and people have given the government the mandate to push the barriers of death as far away as possible. A "life at any price" ethic has saturated medicine from the noblest cause. This does not say that all modern technology is monstrous or misused, but it does set the stage for misuse at levels heretofore unimagined. The dilemma of the physician is to curb himself and respond appropriately to the demands of the variety of groups in our culture. The technological response to the reality of disease must be tempered with parallel behavior that considers the reality of the individual's dignity, feelings, and overall well-being. A particular set of practical and ethical problems arising from the new technology relates to brain death and "brain life."

Traditionally, in medicine, death has been defined as irreversible cessation of cardio-respiratory function. We will start from this classical definition and essentially ignore any definitions pertaining to loss of the soul or other concepts related to religion or myth. Practically, when the physician makes the diagnosis of death he can test the state of the patient by checking pulse, blood pressure, respiration, responsivity, spontaneous movements, and the like. If the diagnosis is not obvious, further examination may include cutting a blood vessel to see if pulsatile bleeding occurs; or, laboratory tests such as an electrocardiogram may be formed to verify absence of cardiac activity. It has been said in the more ancient literature that the only unequivocal finding in death is putrefaction. But considering the state of some patients when they arrive at, say, Bellevue Hospital, this is not entirely reliable. Errors have been made despite precautions, and patients have been pronounced dead under a variety of circumstances when they are in fact comatose and still alive. This occurs rarely in the patient's home and virtually never in a hospital setting. Many physicians have anecdotal stories of a patient who is pronounced dead and wakes up in the morgue. The patient is then sent to the hospital, usually to be pronounced dead again within a relatively short period of time. Even Vesalius had the misfortune to attempt to dissect a cadaver that proved to be alive, ultimately resulting in the patient's death and the dissector's inquisition.[2] Consider that the real purpose of modern embalming techniques is to prevent patients from being buried alive. Yet the possibility of this happening is extremely slight with any degree of sound medical judgment on the part of the physician.

In 1957[3] a group of anesthesiologists presented to Pope Pius XII the question whether it was appropriate to keep the corpus or body "alive" when irreparable destruction of the brain was present. The response was a papal allocution entitled "The Prolongation of Life," from which two relevant pronouncements will be stressed. The first was that the pronouncement of death was not the province of the Church but the responsibility of the physician: "It remains for the doctor . . . to give a clear and precise definition of 'death' and the 'moment of death' of a patient who passes away in a state of unconsciousness." The second point was that there came a time in the course of a patient's disease where the situation was hopeless and death should not be opposed by extraordinary means. The definitions of the words *hopeless* and *extraordinary* were not precisely stated in medical terminology, but it was clear that in hopeless cases resuscitative measures could be discontinued and death be unopposed. This papal allocution historically may be considered the point of departure for the reevaluation of death in terms of brain death.

In 1959 three groups of French physiologists did clinical studies on patients in the deepest state of unresponsive coma who were being maintained on a respirator.[4] They had no spontaneous respiration, movement, or responsiveness, and electrodes placed deep in their brains showed no evidence of electrical activity. The condition was described as *coma de'passè,* literally translated as "beyond coma" or "ultra coma." Later it was demonstrated that these patients had no intercranial blood flow. This situation remained a clinical idiosyncrasy associated with the intensive-care unit until the need for organ donors began to increase with the inexorable advance of technology. The initial impetus for redefining death was clearly present prior to the era of organ transplantation. But once organ transplants became therapeutically reliable, the pressure to redefine death in relation to irreversible brain dysfunction increased exponentially. During the period from 1968 to 1981 there was a marked increase in research and studies at an international level to redefine death appropriately. The definition became inextricably intertwined with the ever-increasing demands for kidneys, livers, hearts, and other organs for purposes of transplantation. For example, the treatment of choice for permanent renal failure is transplantation, and dialysis was considered as a temporizing treatment that would be used until the patient could be matched for a kidney.

The Harvard Criteria are most quoted and were published in 1968.[5] The terminology was imprecise, but the diagnosis of brain death was considered established if the patient had none of the following: cerebral responsiveness, movements, respirations (respirator-dependent), and reflexes. Additionally, there was to be no evidence of drug intoxication or hypothermia (reversible conditions), the presence of a flat EEG, and persistence of the entire clinical state for twenty-four hours. During the same year at a medical meeting the Declaration of Sydney was made. This statement reaffirmed death as a process rather than an event and, more important, indicated that the pronouncement of death should involve two physicians unrelated to any transplant procedure. Variations, refinement, and greater precision in the definition and diagnosis of death were developed over the next decade by research performed in Scandinavia, Japan, and the United States. The conclusions of these studies may be summarized as follows:

A prerequisite required establishment of a diagnosis with the performance of all appropriate diagnostic and therapeutic procedures.

Criteria after the onset of apnea and coma included coma with cerebral unresponsivity, absolute apnea (specific test for respirator dependence), absent cephalic (brain-stem) reflexes with fixed dilated pupils, and EEG with electrocerebral silence. The duration of the findings was to be at least six hours from the onset.

Confirmatory test for absence of intracranial circulation, if required.

The redefinition of death, despite the pressures of secondary gain via organ transplantation, has a rational basis. Classical cardiorespiratory death resulted in the diagnosed brain state. This may be looked upon as a causal coinci-

dence in that in the human organism the cessation of respiration and circulation results in central nervous system
destruction. It may be argued that it is only with the destruction of *the critical system of the human organism* that
death of the individual occurs. We may define the critical
system as that system which cannot be replaced by any
biological, chemical, or electromechanical device. The
critical system must subserve the essential behavioral characteristics of the individual human being. Virtually all organ systems are replaceable in humans, with the exception
of the brain. The heart can be replaced by a pump, the
kidneys by an appropriate dialysis unit, the endocrine
glands by hormonal replacement therapy, and so on. A
limb may be artificial, but when it comes to the neuronal
cells that comprise the central nervous system, soon after
birth an individual has a set of these elements that does not
reproduce or regenerate. A neuron may grow by increasing
its dendritic tree and interconnections with changes in the
production of neurotransmitters. The soma may support
growth of a crushed axon, but if the soma is destroyed, the
process is irreversible. The brain depends on the neurons
for its function, and the organism depends on the brain. If
the brain is destroyed, or becomes irreversibly nonfunctional, the critical system is destroyed, and despite all other
systems being maintained by any manner whatsoever, the
human organism as an individual functioning entity can no
longer be considered to exist. Neuronal "brain" transplants may alter brain function but do not replace the entire
critical system. If the brain as a whole or the head could
be transplanted, the *donor* would be the *recipient*. The basis of the individual organism—the person who is the member of the human species—resides in his or her brain. Brain
death, then, is death. This is not to be construed as two
definitions of death, since both the classic definition and
brain-death criteria are based on irreversible cessation of
brain function. The argument may be illustrated both ex-
perimentally and clinically. If a dog's head is experimen-
tally severed from the body and kept alive by an appropriate

life-support system and the same is done to the dog's body, the essence of the animal's "personality" is in the head, not the corpus. The head in such an experiment will eat, salivate, blink, sleep, and respond to stimuli to which it has previously been conditioned—for example, when its name is called. The body can also be kept "alive," but it in no way has the dog's essential being. If a human is quadriplegic because of a cervical spinal cord transection but has a normal brain, he or she may be kept alive by a life-support system; unquestionably, he or she is a person who is aware and responds meaningfully to external stimuli. However, if a person's cerebral hemisphere were destroyed by a shotgun blast, with subsequent deterioration of the brain stem, the temporary maintenance of the body by modern scientific methods does not mean that a human life is being maintained. To press the analogy to an extreme, we may culture skin cells from a person and keep them growing in artificial media for months. If we destroy these cultured cells, however, this does not constitute the killing of a person, although we are obliterating DNA molecules that potentially may be used to construct a human organism. The pitfall of considering words such as *potential* or *imminent* is that they result in ambiguity and confusion—*e.g.*, potential death is not death. The critical system of the human organism is composed of the cerebral hemispheres, deep structures, the brain stem, and cerebellum. It does not include the spinal cord. The functions subserved by the cerebrum are sentience, cognitive behavior, awareness, learning, memory, voluntary movement, speech, ideation, reasoning, and mentation, as well as emotional and goal-directed activity. In contrast, functions subserving the brain-stem mechanisms include complex, stereotyped reflex patterns, respiration, and extraocular movements. The stem also contributes by means of the ascending reticular formation to aspects of consciousness. The cerebellum is involved with coordination and movement patterns. It is the irreversible dysfunction of all these structures that must occur in order to diagnose the death of the human being.

If we accept the definition that death of the human being can be diagnosed when the brain, as the critical system, is dead, we must establish appropriate tests to determine when the brain is irreversibly nonfunctional. These tests must be completely reliable insofar as an error in diagnosis is only permissible in calling a dead person live. One must never under any circumstances diagnose a living person as dead.

Studies and research efforts carried out after 1968 to establish an appropriate battery of clinical and laboratory tests, then, have been concerned with evaluating and codifying those observations and tests required to diagnose unequivocally brain death. In 1981 the President's Commission for the Study of Ethical Problems in Medicine and Biomedical and Behavioral Research established guidelines for a uniform determination-of-death act, defined as follows:

An individual who has sustained either (1) irreversible cessation of circulatory and respiratory functions or (2) irreversible cessation of all functions of the entire brain, including the brain stem, is dead. A determination of death must be made in accordance with accepted medical standards.[6]

In essence, this statement gives parity to the determination of death by either irreversible cessation of circulation and respiration or irreversible cessation of brain function. One should reiterate that condition 1 is actually based on condition 2; both diagnoses devolve on brain death. Clinical observations and tests must unequivocally establish the cessation of all brain function and the irreversibility of that cessation. History and clinical examination of laboratory studies are all considered, and while no specific tests are excluded, it will become evident that clinical judgment is required to determine the extent and duration of tests performed. We will illustrate the application of these tests in two clinical examples.

The first patient is a thirty-seven-year-old man who was involved in an automobile accident and sustained head trauma. He is stuporous, with blood trickling from his left ear. The patient is found to be responsive to painful stimuli with some spontaneous movement and spontaneous respiration. Cephalic reflexes reveal some disconjugate eye movements and sluggish response of the pupils to light. Radiological imaging by computerized tomography (CT scan) reveals an intracranial hemorrhage involving both cerebral hemispheres. Within several hours the patient's condition deteriorates. He is in unresponsive coma. Respirations cease, and he has to be maintained by artificial ventilation. All brain-stem (cephalic) reflexes are absent, including pupillary response to light, and eye movements. Pupils are fixed and dilated. There are no spontaneous movements. However, deep tendon reflexes are elicited from the lower extremities. Tests reveal the absence of toxic agents, and the patient is appropriately evaluated to ensure that he is, in fact, respirator-dependent. If it is observed by repeated examinations that the patient remains in this condition for six hours he will fulfill the *clinical* criteria for brain death despite normal heartbeat and blood pressure. However, the clinical judgment of the physician requires that he determine unequivocally that the patient is, in fact, brain dead, and an electroencephalogram (EEG) is performed, which is isoelectric—no activity even with maximal amplification and interelectrode distances. A second physician evaluates the patient. The clinical findings, their duration, and the EEG results are confirmed. This leads to the diagnosis of brain death—which is death—of this patient. The diagnosis and the time it is made are documented.

Subsequently, relatives donate the patient's kidneys, which were removed prior to discontinuation of the respirator. The moment of death occurred at the time the tests were completed and the diagnosis was established. The time of removal of the respirator and kidneys is irrelevant.

The second patient is a twenty-eight-year-old woman who was found in her bed with an empty bottle of sleeping pills (barbiturates) and a suicide note on the night table. She is brought into the hospital by ambulance and is found to be in deep coma, unresponsive, with shallow respirations. She is areflexive, with small, equal, unreactive pupils and no cephalic reflexes. Respirations cease soon after admission and she requires a respirator. Barbiturate level is markedly elevated in the blood, and tests indicate absolute respirator dependence. EEG is isoelectric. CT scan is normal. The patient does not meet the clinical criteria of brain death since the probable cause of her condition is barbiturate intoxication, which is known to be reversible despite the isoelectric EEG. Dialysis is instituted for a period of thirty-six hours, after which the patient has return of spontaneous movements, cephalic reflexes, pupillary activity, and EEG activity. Her barbiturate level has decreased significantly. Patient recovers uneventfully, she is cleared by psychiatry, and on the day she is to be discharged she hangs herself in the bathroom. She is discovered, cut down, and found to be in deep coma, unresponsive to painful stimulation, with absent cephalic reflexes. Respiration has ceased, and the patient is immediately placed on artificial ventilation. Cardiac arrest occurs, but heartbeat is reestablished by appropriate resuscitative methods. Tests reveal minimal barbiturates in the blood and the patient is respirator-dependent. Cephalic reflexes are absent. EEG is isoelectric. CT scan is consistent with brain edema (swelling). The patient is again in a clinical state compatible with brain death. However, the likely etiology of her condition—cerebral anoxia—may be completely irreversible, but there is a remote possibility that the small amount of barbiturates present could contribute to her condition. The physician elects to do four-vessel angiography, which reveals absent intracranial blood flow, thus confirming the diagnosis of brain death.

In both of these patients the clinical criteria of unresponsive coma, absolute apnea, and absent cephalic reflexes were present. These are required for the diagnosis of brain death. Reflexes below the neck may be related to a living spinal cord, and they are not significant. The absence of intoxicants is important, since they can cause reversible coma. In the first case, the EEG was confirmatory and supported the clinical picture allowing the clinician to make his diagnosis. In the second case, despite isoelectric EEG, the initial episode was reversible due to the presence of barbiturates. The etiology of the coma in the final episode—anoxia—resulted in minimal uncertainties in contrast to the first patient with the massive, demonstrable intracranial hemorrhage. Therefore, an additional test of intracranial blood flow was performed to confirm the diagnosis.

There are conditions, such as the *persistent vegetative state* (PVS), which are not brain death but which result in irreversible termination of the human being as a thinking, mentating, emotional, aware entity. Consciousness level can be anywhere from impaired to absent. While some patients in this state are arousable or even awake, there is an absence of mental content—there is no sentience. Complex stereotyped reflexes and respirations commonly occur. In this situation patients may have irreversible damage to portions of their brain rather than to their entire brain due to a variety of etiologies. They do not meet the clinical or laboratory criteria of brain death patients but have lost all that capacity that we consider fundamental to the human being.

We will illustrate this by the classic patient Karen Ann Quinlan, whom I examined in 1975 approximately six months after the onset of her condition. The patient was a twenty-one-year-old woman who was celebrating a birthday with three other friends. She drank gin-and-tonics, became ill, vomited, and aspirated vomitus into her lungs. After the aspiration she became blue, comatose, and pulseless. She was given mouth-to-mouth resuscitation. The ambulance that was called arrived in approximately 15 to 30 minutes. She was given oxygen by mask and her color improved, and spontaneous movements were noted. Her pulse and blood pressure were normal. Upon arriving at the hospital she was found to be responsive to painful stimuli, and moved all limbs and head spontaneously. Cephalic reflexes were all present with some minor abnormalities of eye movements. Breathing became impaired and she was placed on a respirator. She had some decorticate posturing, with her legs rigid and extended, but arms flexed and drawn up below her chin. She did not respond to verbal stimuli and no communication could be established. Laboratory studies immediately after admission revealed a less-than-therapeutic dose of Valium in her blood, but there were no barbiturates, opiates, or "hard" drugs found (she had two Valium pills in her purse). Quinine was present in the blood (from the tonic mixer) and no test for alcohol was performed. Within several days she had clinical and radiological evidence of an aspiration pneumonia, which was treated. Subsequently, her EEGs revealed normal to moderate diffusely abnormal activity. A CT scan was normal, as were tests for intracranial blood flow.

The patient's condition over the next six months stabilized, with decorticate posturing, four limb flexion contractures, and abnormal hyper-reflexia. Attempts to remove her from the respirator resulted in episodes of prolonged apnea. Although the patient moved spontaneously and had sleep/wake cycles, there was no evidence of ability to communicate or demonstration of awareness of her surroundings. The clinical syndrome the patient manifested was diagnosed as *persistent vegetative state* (PVS). At the time of my examination she clearly responded to painful stimuli with altered respiratory patterns while on the respirator. But all movements were stereotyped and related to complex brain-stem reflexes. There was no evidence of awareness, cognition, or goal-directed movements. She was successfully weaned from the respirator within a year of being in coma and could breathe on her own. The patient was then kept on supportive therapy, including tube feeding and turning every two hours, as well as antibiotics for infection for ten years until her death. Her mental status never reached the level of sentience. CT performed prior to her death revealed massive cerebral atrophy.

This condition—the persistent vegetative state, or irreversible non-cognitive state—may become chronic. Case reports indicate that with appropriate care patients can live as long as thirty-seven years. At a 1977 New York Academy of Sciences meeting,[8] some health-care professionals wished to include persistent vegetative state as a form of human death, especially insofar as these patients are incapable of mental function other than that described. However, it was decided that vegetative states could not be considered death, for two reasons. The first is that the certainty of diagnosis is less accurate than that of brain death. Second, and more important, if such a patient were pronounced dead, what does the physician do after the pronouncement? He has a breathing, heartbeating cadaver on his hands. In order to terminate the situation he may withdraw all treatment and feeding, but the time between the pronouncement of death and the cessation of cardiopulmonary function might still be considerable. An active measure, such as injecting the patient with an intoxicant to stop cardiopulmonary function, was considered identical to shooting the patient and, therefore, reprehensible and unethical. The specter of a Nazi medical ethics was raised. Even though one is not killing a human being—since the humanity, if the diagnosis is correct, is irreversibly gone—the act of killing is contrary to the tenets of medicine. Further, this vegetating husk is a shell of a human being and carries with it to friends, relatives, and society and culture as a whole, the aura of what that individual was. This very real, emotional problem and the requirement to terminate actively are crucial to understanding why brain death was defined as it was and excluded persistent vegetative states.

The *critical system of the brain* is irreversibly nonfunctional in these vegetative patients, in contrast to the *critical system of the human being*, which is irreversibly nonfunctional in brain death. In these clinical entities described under the umbrella of irreversible noncognitive or persistent vegetative state, several clearly defined structures or systems within the brain may be identified with sentience. Without these structures, the brain, and hence the individual, can no longer function in a manner that we may describe as human. This pathological state is devoid of sentience, mentation, emotion, and awareness, although arousal may alter with sleep/wake cycles present. Although the lighting of the stage may fluctuate according to the script of the play, no actors are onstage. Complex stereotyped reflexes related to brain-stem and spinal function persist, but this repertoire of activity has no cognitive or emotional mental content. The critical structures include the cerebral cortex, and/or thalamus, and basal ganglia, bilaterally (destruction of the basal ganglia alone may not result in PVS). Bilateral destruction or irreversible dysfunction of any set or combination of these structures will result in an irreversible noncognitive state. In addition, a single lesion destroying the midline upper brain-stem ascending reticular formation prior to its splitting into two parts in the thalamus can also cause a persistent vegetative state in and of itself. Most often patients with PVS who are autopsied show a multiplicity of lesions with severe involvement and atrophy of the above-described structures. The brain of one patient in persistent vegetative state for seventeen years was reduced to twenty percent of the normal weight of three pounds.

We will consider the cerebral hemispheres in their entirety and the ascending reticular portion of the midbrain to comprise the critical system of the human brain. This excludes the cerebellum and most of the brain stem. Thus, on clinical and pathological grounds we have defined the critical system required for the functioning of the essence of a human brain.

In anencephalic malformations we have the unusual situation in which the critical system of the brain has never developed. The more typical case history is where the mother, usually prior to term, delivers this pathological specimen (I do not believe it is accurate to use the term "infant"), which may have the appearance of a troll, with no forehead or skull, and most if not all of the cerebral hemispheres missing. Fortunately, most of these pathological entities are stillborn and those that survive and have spontaneous respirations rarely live for any significant period. However, some cases may breathe for prolonged periods—from weeks to months. The disorder usually can be diagnosed early in pregnancy by special tests, including amniocentesis and sonography, and therapeutic abortion may be undertaken. Even more rarely, the birth of what appears to be a normal infant occurs at term. The repertoire of behavior at birth and in the first week of life includes breathing, sucking, withdrawal from pain, and random eye movements, all derived from the brain stem. Only after several weeks is the behavioral lag noted, with lack of attention, absence of awareness or eye contact, and other forms of inappropriate behavior becoming obvious. If the child is held up to a light bulb the skull transilluminates, revealing the absence or marked diminution of cerebral contents. In one such case, when a flashlight was placed at the back of the head two beams of light shone, one from each pupil. The skull is essentially full of cerebral spinal fluid, and the disorder is called hydroanencephaly. These specimens may live for an unspecified period if they are carefully cared for or treated. They will never attain sentience. A colleague of mine knew of a case that was maintained to the age of seventeen years—tied to a chair, diapered, and lovingly fed by his mother in the backwoods of Kentucky. The importance of these anencephalics is twofold; first is the classification of their problem, and second is that they may be used for organ transplants.

They cannot be considered brain dead, since they may have a living brain stem that maintains them. They are essentially analogous to the persistent vegetative state, with one significant exception: They never develop even the beginnings of a person. It is our thesis that they were never alive as a human being, since they never developed an operational critical system of the brain.

From this point we may consider the definition and diagnosis of the onset of the individual—the earliest beginnings not of human life but of the human being as an entity—a "person."

Utilizing the constructs previously defined in relation to brain death and persistent vegetative state (PVS), we will attempt to define and diagnose the onset of the life of a human being. The focus will be on the critical system of the brain rather than the entire brain (the critical system of the organism). For the practical and ethical reasons discussed above, PVS cannot be used to define brain death as a diagnostic entity. However, it is clear that the termination of the life of the human being in every sense occurs in the PVS. It is for this reason that the reciprocal, inverse, or opposite of PVS (rather than brain death) will be used to approximate the emergence of the human being. In order to determine when the life of the human being begins, we will review the *ontogenesis of the human brain*—more specifically, that of the cerebral hemispheres along with the ascending reticular formation. The period when human life begins will be defined as corresponding to the construction of these systems and the development of their functional capacity. We wish to establish the earliest limits relating to the completion of major construction and the incipient onset of function.

In order to make the diagnostic statement that a human life has begun, we must have available tests and measurements to use as indicators of the state of development and functional capability of the critical system of the brain. Others have chosen to link the emergence of the life of a human being to events or processes such as fertilization or conception, embryonic segmentation, electrical activity of any neurons in the fetal brain, quickening, viability, or the moment of birth. Although each of these has proponents, and some of these events, such as the moment of birth and the time of conception, are clearly demarcated, none is consistent with definitions relating to the termination of human life. One problem is that from the time of conception through the time of birth, adolescence, and adulthood, the human organism is always alive, although it has not yet become a human being in its earliest stages. What we must include in our definition relates to a set of characteristics that are invariant and define a human being from its earliest stages until its termination. We will assume that diagnosed states are "real" states of being in transition but not potential ones. Thus, the process is considered as the set of states observed during the period of transition.

Fetal development will be analyzed to derive a period that can be considered as a transition state marking the emergence of the critical system of the brain of the human being—the construction of the cerebral reticular complex. All embryological and fetal ages will refer to age from onset of fertilization. Although structure and function are inextricably interwoven, the nature of the research and data available forces us to separate them into different aspects of fetal ontogenesis. This simplified description will be modified and revised depending on new knowledge.

The fusion of the sperm and egg results in a zygote with a new mixture of DNA. This single cell is triggered for action by fertilization. There is an impetus for rapid and massive reproduction of cells. The underlying mechanism of reproduction in each cell requires nucleic acids—DNA as the recipe and RNA as the translator of the recipe into operational components—such as proteins. The first step is replication of DNA—producing more and more copies of the required recipe for the organism. In each cell transcription of DNA to RNA follows. This step results in the creation of the components for and assembly of the necessary parts for cell function. This translation of RNA to protein using amino acids leads to the production of parts for the dynamic operation of all aspects of cell metabolism and function, even feeding back to maintain the DNA and RNA. On the multicellular level, gross parts of the organism are being created, but we do not yet have the semblance of a human being.

As cell reproduction proceeds they form a ball, which becomes hollow and invaginates—the blastula-gastrula stage. Chemical gradients and structural forces form a "morphogenetic field," which results in a sculpturing of this embryonic organism from within and without. It is impossible for the DNA to specify the development of the entire organism. Rather, the DNA sets in motion other (epigenetic) mechanisms, such as protein enzymes, which, through competition and interaction with the local environment, specify the building of the organism within restricted limits. Thus, the development of an invaginated, cylindrical, three-layered structure in three dimensions begins. The dimensional aspects are along head–tail and back–front axes with right–left symmetry. The layers from inside to out are called endoderm, mesoderm, and ectoderm, respectively.

The indentation that occurs from head to tail on the back surface of the embryo forms the beginnings of the nervous system. From the ectoderm the neural groove becomes a neural tube, finally expanding and segmenting to develop the early structures that are antecedents to the brain and spinal cord. At three weeks after fertilization the embryo is about one-eighth of an inch long. This period, called neurulation, lasts until six weeks, ending with the cleavage of the cerebral hemispheres and deep structures. Neuronal development has occurred in the spinal cord and brain stem to a significant degree but lags markedly in the cerebrum. At about eight weeks there is a transition from the embryonic to the fetal stage. Significant features of the embryo at this stage include head, eyes, limbs, fingers—all in a one-and-one-quarter-inch organism. The minuscule brain at this time is composed of a well-developed brain stem with a smooth cerebrum of the same size. While the fetus more than doubles its weight at thirteen weeks, the cerebral hemispheres become dominant, overshadowing the brain stem and cerebellar structures. The cerebral hemispheres are still smooth, undifferentiated without convolutions, and microscopically neuronal development is just beginning. There is thickening of the cortical wall with the beginning of a neuronal stratification: synaptic organization (neuronal interconnections) is nonexistent.

During the period from ten to twenty weeks the major event of *neural proliferation* occurs, and *neural migration* begins in the cerebrum.[9] The construction of the cerebral hemispheres from primitive neuroblasts, the precursors of neurons, occurs by the utilization of a process described as *interkinetic nuclear migration.* This phrase attempts to describe the reproductive ritual dance of neurons. The primitive cells lie deep within the cerebrum on the surface of the ventricle (a natural cavity within the brain). Some of these primitive cells proliferate—dividing by mitosis. The daughter cells then migrate toward the cortical plate by entwining themselves around the elongated process of a radical glial cell (nonneuronal component of the nervous system involving supportive functions) and ascends much like a snake climbing up a vine. Some neurons will climb to a predetermined level and remain there, beginning the layering of the cortex. These have been *determined* and will subsequently *differentiate* into a specific neuron. Other daughter cells will return, descending to the ventricular surface only to reproduce again and repeat the cycle. This dance of reproduction, migration, and return continues to oscillate until the cortical layers are saturated. In this manner, at an estimated rate of 250,000 neurons per minute,[10] the stratification of the cortex is virtually complete in terms of its neuronal complement at twenty weeks.

There is marked overproduction of neurons in virtually all cell assemblies of the developing nervous system. This occurs in the spinal cord and in the neuronal groups of the brain stem, thalamus, and cerebral cortex. This overproduction is a normal ubiquitous occurrence in ontogenesis of the central nervous system and is later followed by massive neuronal death. The reasons for this unusual phenomenon in ontogenesis are directly related to the interconnecting of groups of neurons with one another. After neurons have developed and differentiated, short processes called dendrites and long ones called axons begin to grow. Bundles of axons form tracts from one neuronal group (cell assembly or nucleus) to another, where they interconnect on their cell bodies and dendrites. These connections are termed *synapses*. The processes underlying the mapping of connections among different neuronal groups are elaborate, dynamic, and competitive. Part of the process involves neuronal overproduction. In order to have sufficient neurons to match one group with another, an extra reproductive cycle occurs to ensure that there will be no deficiency in the number of cells required. This results in doubling the number of neurons needed. After the competition for synaptic connections, a large mass of unmatched cells—the losers of the competition—dies. The final stages of synapse formation and cell-assembly matching involve modification and retraction of the synaptic connections. The crux of the function of the nervous system is keyed into the (synaptic) connectivity among individual neurons and neuronal cell assemblies. It is this crucial stage of development that begins the separation of anatomical structure from functioning systems. Consider the analogy of a computer system before and after its components are wired together—it is totally inoperable prior to there being connections between parts.

We are primarily interested in connections within the cerebrum and to the brain stem and spinal cord in fetal development. These represent a measure of structural completion of the critical system of the brain and its proximity to onset of function. By twenty weeks of fetal age the complement of cerebral neurons is virtually complete, but migration continues. The essential migration of cortical neurons is complete at about twenty-one weeks. The cortical-spinal tract, which descends to superimpose its control over spinal reflex mechanisms, reaches the spinal cord during the fifteenth to nineteenth week. Within the cerebrum, thalamo-cortical fiber connections—which relay sensory information—are present at about seventeen weeks, while the corpus callosum, which interconnects the two cerebral hemispheres, approaches completion at eighteen weeks. Tract development and interconnections of neurons continue for longer periods. There is a significant delay between projection of pioneer fibers to a target and the onset of function. These data represent the beginnings of the cerebral structural substrate for information input, processing, and output.

What probably occurs toward the end of this twenty-week period is the projection of the neurons of the cerebrum to and from infracerebral structures, with modification due to information input at this time. The significance of synaptic development relates to the ability of neurons to process information essential for the operation of the critical system of the brain. We are not focusing on when this process is complete; it may in fact go on for the entire life of the individual. Rather, we wish to delimit the beginnings of this process in the cerebrum. Synaptic development of the spinal cord occurs at a much earlier time, occurring in phases from six to fourteen weeks. The brain stem likewise has evidence of synaptic activity at an early stage in fetal development—the development of the trigeminal nucleus (subserving sensation from the face), for example, has been traced from its inception at about six weeks to up to twenty-two weeks, when significant maturation has occurred. The cerebrum, on the other hand, matures late, and synapto-genesis begins after nineteen to twenty-three weeks in the cortical plate, continuing through the postnatal period and probably through the preadolescent period.

Thus, the structural substrate for function exists quite early in the spinal cord but only begins to develop at about twenty weeks in the cerebrum, from which time it becomes progressively more elaborate in terms of intracerebral and extracerebral projections (to the brain stem and spinal cord). It should be clear that as the cerebral structures superimpose their effects on the brain stem and spinal cord by tract growth, changes occur in these infracerebral structures. The dynamism and competition of the changes are significant in that they represent the instability of the earlier developmental neural states in relation to their transition to the more mature operational state. This flux is the major indicator that we are dealing with only a partial system prior to the establishment of the major outlines of brain structure. We wish to ascertain the range of the lower limit—or rather the initial boundary conditions that reflect the earliest structural and incipient operational phases of the critical system of the brain.

The invariant anatomical substrate is composed of the structures and connections of the ascending reticular system and the cerebral hemispheres. These structures change with development, but the beginning of the invariance occurs when the structure is first being built and is in the process of becoming operational. This functional state is characterized by its ability to be modified by informational input. The earliest time at which the cerebrum may be significantly modified by informational input via the neuronal route on the synaptic level in a manner remotely similar to that of the adult organism occurs at about twenty weeks.

Neurotransmitters are molecules, produced at synapses, allowing them to function as a conduit for information. They transmit information through excitation or inhibition across the synapses. Quantitative studies in the human fetus have been performed on several of these neurotransmitters.[11] Although minuscule amounts of these agents may be present in the fetal nervous system prior to eighteen weeks, significant increases occur in the last half of fetal life and continue to increase exponentially after birth. This exponential rise, starting at about eighteen weeks, indicates the onset of cerebral neurotransmitter function related to synaptic activity. Detailed analysis of neurotransmitter-related enzymes indicates that the picture above is an oversimplification; but it serves as a first approximation. The findings are compatible with the timing of the impact of the developing cerebrum on the remainder of the nervous system after the twentieth week.

The nature of the electrophysiological activity of the fetal brain is of paramount importance in evaluating the presence and function of neuronal activity and synaptic transmission. Neural tissue is most appropriately studied by evaluating spontaneous electrical activity (the electroencephalogram, or EEG), changes in such spontaneous activity related to altered neural states (sleep/wake cycles). Induced electrical activity (evoked potentials) in response to a variety of sensory stimuli (somatosensory, auditory, and visual) also represents an important technique in evaluating the activity of neuronal interaction.

The first evidence of electrophysiological activity has been described variously between six and one-half and eight and one-half weeks of fetal age. EEG activity has also been described during the third and fourth month of fetal life. In reviewing these studies it becomes apparent that the size of the fetal brain is so minute and the recording techniques so gross that we are obtaining electrical activity from infracerebral structures. The most well defined of these studies were recorded from within the structures of the brain of the human fetus with needle electrodes.[12] Evidence indicated that low-voltage electrical activity could be recorded from the brain stem at eight and one-half weeks of fetal age. EEG activity arising from the cerebral hemispheres rather than brain-stem structures has been reliably described to begin at between twenty and twenty-two weeks.[13] The studies on premature neonates indicate a gradual development of EEG activity. Initially, at about twenty weeks, there is none; but as the fetus grows, there are bursts of activity, with long quiescent intervals. At twenty-nine to thirty weeks, more continuous electrical activity is observed. Sleep/wake cycles can also be more clearly distinguished at this time in contrast to the fragmentary episodes seen at twenty-four to twenty-six weeks. Sleep/wake cycles include the stage of rapid eye movements (REM) and concomitant low-voltage EEG activity and suppression of electromyographic (EMG-muscle) activity. These cycles have their source in the cerebral hemispheres, with contributions from infracerebral structures. Ascending reticular activity as demonstrated by EEG arousal and some cortical function begins at about twenty weeks. Evoked potentials have been identified between twenty-two and twenty-five weeks from the cortex but may start somewhat earlier.[14] Prior to this period, electrical activity is derived from subcortical structures in the brain stem. Some activity may arise in the limbic system (primitive cortex subserving survival of individual and species—oral-genital behavior) at about nineteen weeks.

The cerebral hemispheres and the ascending reticular formation are the critical system of the human brain—the electrical activity of these structures reflects the invariant that is the requisite of the onset of the life of the human being as an entity. This period is concurrent with the termination of a major construction phase of the cerebrum—internal components and connections as well as major input and output tracts. Thus, this transition stage occurs at about twenty weeks of fetal life based on the onset of cerebral electrical activity. The next step is to consider fetal behavior itself.

Fetal behavior will be discussed in relation to three modes of experimental observation. The first will be related to those studies in the analysis of direct fetal response outside the uterus. These include observations of spontaneous movements of the fetus and those that occur in response to stimulation of the fetus itself. The second set of studies relates to sonography and the indirect observation of the fetus within the mother's uterus. Although some of these studies attempt to stress input-output relationships, they are almost entirely related to spontaneous movements. The third and perhaps most interesting approach relates to conditioning and learning of the fetus *in utero*.

Movements in response to direct stimuli begin during the seventh week of fetal life.[15] Over the next ten weeks a progressively more complex repertoire of patterned movements is observed, including specific focal reflex patterns relating to the head and limbs. Mass reflexes of the entire body are also elicited. These are more generalized responses to localized stimuli. These stimuli are usually produced by tickling the face or extremity of the fetus with a fine hair. Both input (sensory) and output (motor) activity develop in a sequence beginning at the head and ending at the lower extremities. Immature sensory receptors in the skin and muscle develop during early periods of fetal life to form reflex arcs within the brain stem and spinal cord. By the sixteenth week the generalized patterns are more difficult to produce and focal responses are the rule. There is an increased variety in face, limb, and trunk movement.

Spontaneous movements generally occur slightly later than induced movements. These include sucking, swallowing, grasping, grimacing, and squirming, as well as spontaneous thrusting and jerking. The mother may feel these quickening at about the sixteenth week, but they can occur as early as the thirteenth week.

The neural circuitry underlying these movements is completely infracerebral, involving those components of the spinal cord and brain stem that control simple and complex reflex involuntary behavior patterns. The cerebral structures are still undergoing developmental structural changes at this time and do not contain a functioning structural apparatus.

From the seventeenth to the twenty-second week of fetal life a period of relative *behavioral quiescence* occurs. The fetus, outside the uterus, has decreased sluggish responses to stimuli. Long periods of inactivity occur and bursts of spontaneous activity are more difficult to evoke. This period terminates at about twenty-three weeks, when self-sustained respirations occur and movement patterns reappear, starting at the head and ending at the feet. We may conjecture that the quiescence is related to superimposition of cerebral on infracerebral structures. The movements occurring after this period are often described as more complex and less stereotyped; they include conjugate lateral eye movements, and indeed, these movements blend into those of the earliest viable premature infant.

In summary, responsivity to stimuli in these fetal experiments progresses from localized to generalized mass reflex response, changing gradually to more highly specific and less generalized reflex patterns as the receptive region to sensory stimuli increases. By the seventeenth week this repertoire of stereotyped movements is punctuated by quiescence and sluggish responsivity to stimuli; and the cycle is reestablished after the twenty-second week, with more complex, less stereotyped response patterns and spontaneous respirations. From here on the progression of behavior complexity increases.

Sonography allows visualization of the fetus *in utero* by means of sound waves and has been used for longitudinal studies of the development and evolution of spontaneous movements. Breathing movements are first noted at about fourteen weeks and become frequent at twenty-four weeks. Startle reactions decrease in frequency during the same period. From the twentieth to the thirtieth week responses to external stimuli are noted, such as increased heart rate to sound; habituation to this response occurs with repeated auditory stimuli. Responses to touch and light are extremely simple reactions but herald more complex ones, to be discussed under fetal learning. Additionally, at about thirty weeks sleep/wake patterns with eye movement changes are noted. These states apparently can be observed in a premature infant as well as in the fetus at the same age. Sonography has additional clinical importance in that fetal age estimates may be made with considerable accuracy by measurement of the biparietal diameter of the skull or, in early stages, crown-to-rump measurements.

In summary, what sonography has revealed is that there are apparently complex patterns that do change after twenty weeks and patterned cyclic changes evolve into sleep/wake cycles after thirty weeks. Additionally, the fetus, *in utero,* appears to be responsive to external stimuli such as sound, with capability of habituation after twenty weeks.

Recent studies on fetal learning by DeCasper and colleagues[17] will be detailed here briefly. In the first experiment a group of pregnant mothers read aloud a paragraph from Dr. Seuss's *Cat in the Hat* twice a day for the last six weeks of pregnancy. After birth the infant was tested for preferential sucking in response to two different stimuli. The first was the reading of the same *Cat in the Hat* paragraph, and the second was the reading of a matched paragraph from another story (matched for phonemes and duration). The infant clearly responded with increased preferential sucking to the Seuss story. The second experiment, similar but more elaborate, used two groups of mothers from their thirty-second to thirty-eighth week, each hearing one of two different matched stories. These were taped and played to their respective group twice a day. Fetal heart rate was measured at the end of thirty-eight weeks with both recordings played to each mother—each group acted as the other's control. In both groups the fetal heart rate slowed significantly when the story it was exposed to was played, and increased in rate in response to the story that was played for the first time. The conclusion is inescapable. The fetal nervous system at this stage has captured, stored, and retrieved complex patterned information to which it now can respond (this does not infer understanding of meaning in any manner).

The logical experiment would be to utilize this technique to find the earliest state at which the fetus could respond to an incorporated complex signal.

In view of these data on behavior, movement, and learning of the fetus, it appears clear that until the twentieth week of fetal life there is no evidence that the structure of the critical system of the brain is either complete or operational. In contrast, during the twenty-to-thirty-week period there is ample evidence that the reticular cerebral complex has some level of completeness in its structure and has begun incipient function. After thirty weeks there is no question that the cerebral-reticular complex, although immature, is structurally operational, certainly, in terms of sleep/wake patterns, eye movements, and the ability to learn and respond to complex environmental stimuli. Being conservative, we could estimate the onset of the life of a human being—as reflected by the organizational structure of the critical system of the brain and its incipient function—to be after twenty weeks; a person begins to emerge.

Evidence has been presented to support the hypothesis that the life of a human being begins with the onset of the structural organization and incipient function of the critical system of the brain—the reticulo-cerebral complex. The utility of this hypothesis is that it conforms with a large body of biological and scientific data as well as current concepts of brain death and vegetative states. The hypothesis does not depend on conception or birth; nor is it rooted in a biological function that may be altered by advancing technology. It is possible that modern technology may lead to the construction of an artificial uterus, and the entire reproductive cycle from fertilization to birth may be performed outside the woman's body. In this case a practical statement of when the life of the human being begins becomes more significant, dependent only on the invariance of the critical system of the brain.

If we accept the hypothesis, many problems may be resolved, but new and different ones will take their place. For example, the problem of organ transplants from anencephalics is resolved by considering that this partial or incomplete system is not a human being as an entity. It is not, and never was, and never will be a person. Therefore, it does not have the rights we grant to a human being and does not have to be pronounced dead. The organs may be used with the approval of the mother; if the placenta turned out to have therapeutic utility, one would require the mother's approval for its use. Current attempts at declaring anencephalics brain dead is logically incorrect and unnecessary.

Applications to the problem of abortion are also relevant. Utilizing the present concepts, abortion prior to twenty weeks does not affect a human being, since the fetus has not yet developed to this level. Sometime after twenty weeks the rights of the fetus as a human being require consideration. In obstetrical nomenclature, a fetus of less than twenty weeks is termed a spontaneous abortion, while one of more than twenty weeks is called a stillbirth. This leads to problems that relate to fetal rights. When does the fetus have rights, and what are those rights in juxtaposition to the rights of the woman carrying the fetus?

More complex problems arise in considering organ transplantation from the fetus; already, transplantation of parts of the brain have been made in the treatment of Parkinson's disease. Research indicates that portions of the fetal brain might be successfully used to treat a variety of neurological disorders—possibly the dementia of Alzheimer's disease. The primitive neurons required are to be derived from the brain of a fetus of about sixteen weeks, well within the period before which the life of the human being begins. The results of an abortion now become a product for treatment. Issues to be addressed range from the enormous benefits that may be derived for individuals who are seriously ill with brain dysfunction to the specter of harvesting fetuses for profit. How society and individuals will handle the ethical aspects of these problems will determine in part the moral shape of the world to come.

NOTES

[1] Julius Korein and T. J. Heffernan, "On the Use of Computers in Medicine: Personal Experiences and Critique," *The Jewish Memorial Hospital Bulletin*, 1972, vol. 16, pp. 1–27.

[2] J. J. Bruhier d'Albaincourt, *The Uncertainty of the Signs of Death* (London, Globe in Paterson-Row, 1746), pp. 221.

[3] Pius XII "The Prolongation of Life" (an address of Pope Pius XII to an International Congress of Anesthesiologists," in *The Pope Speaks*, November 24, 1957, pp. 393–98. 1958.

[4] Julius Korein, "The Diagnosis of Brain Death," *Seminars in Neurology*, 1984, vol. 4, pp. 52–72.

[5] "Definition of Irreversible Coma: Report of Ad Hoc Committee (Chairman, H. K. Beecher) of Harvard Medical School to Examine Definition of Brain Death," *JAMA*, 1968, vol. 205; pp. 85–88.

[6] "Guidelines for the Determination of Death: Report of the Medical Consultants on the Diagnosis of Death to the President's Commission for the Study of Ethical Problems in Medicine and Biomedical and Behavioral Research," Special Communication, *JAMA*, 1981, vol. 246, pp. 2184–85.

[7] Julius Korein, "Brain States: Death, Vegetation and Life," in J. E. Cottrell and H. Turndorf, eds. *Anesthesia and Neurosurgery*, Chapter 15, 2nd ed. (St. Louis, The C. V. Mosby Co, 1986), pp. 293–351.

[8] Julius Korein, ed., "Brain Death: Interrelated Medical and Social Issues," (*Annals of New York Academy of Sciences.*) 315:1–454, 1978.

[9] J. J. Volpe, *Neurology of the Newborn*, 2nd ed. (Philadelphia, W. B. Saunders Co., 1987), pp. 1–68.

[10] W. M. Cowan, "The Development of the Brain," *Scientific American*, 1979, vol. 241, pp. 112–133.

[11] M. V. Johnston, and J. T. Coyle, "Development of Central Neurotransmitter System," in C. Elliot and J. Whelan, eds., *The Fetus and Independent Life*, CIBA Foundation (London, Pitman Publishing Ltd., 1981), pp. 251–270.

[12] R. M. Bergstrom, "Electrical Parameters of the Brain During Ontogeny," in R. J. Robinson, ed., *Brain and Early Behav-*

ior, Development in the Fetus and Infant (London, Academic Press, Ltd., 1969), pp. 15–37.

13   J. R. Hughes, *EEG in Clinical Practice* (Woburn, MA, Butterworth Publishers, 1982), p. 235.

14   D. P. Purpura, "Morphogenesis of Visual Cortex in the Preterm Infant," in M. A. B. Brazier, ed., *Growth and Development of the Brain* (New York: Raven Press, 1975), pp. 33–49.

15   D. Hooker, "The Prenatal Origin of Behavior," Porter Lectures, Series 18, University of Kansas Press, Lawrence, Kansas, 1952, pp. 54–85 and 123–36.

16   A. Inniruberto and E. Tajani, "Ultrasonographic Study of Fetal Movements," *Seminars in Perinatology,* 1981, vol. 5, pp. 175–81.

17   A. J. DeCasper and M. J. Spence, "Prenatal Maternal Speech Influences Newborns' Perception of Speech Sounds," *Infant Behavior and Development,* 1986, vol. 9, pp. 133–50. (A. J. DeCasper, et al: "Familiar and Unfamiliar Speech Elicit Different Cardiac Responses in Human Fetuses," presented at The International Society of Developmental Psychobiology, Annapolis, MD, 1986.)

MEMES VS. GENES: NOTES FROM THE CULTURE WARS

▼

MIHALY CSIKSZENTMIHALYI

> . . . cultural forms can evolve and grow without necessarily enhancing the biological fitness of the individuals who produced them. The monks who developed European culture in the Middle Ages transmitted art and learning instead of genes. That these two ways of transmitting information across time are often in conflict was recognized long ago by the Latin saying *libri aut liberi*—books or children. It is indeed difficult to spawn biological and cultural progeny at the same time.

Humanity discovered evolution just a little more than a century ago. For the span of a few generations we thought this meant that the future belonged to mankind. During the Victorian era and up to World War I, it seemed that we were slated to be benevolent rulers of the entire planet. This brief period of optimism had barely time to blossom before it already seemed part of a nostalgic past. As we approach the end of the century it is getting more and more difficult to believe that we are making progress toward the rational control of evolutionary processes. Indeed, the very concept of evolution is coming under attack.

Despite these setbacks, evolution still seems the best way to explain what has happened in the past, what is happening now, and, to a certain extent, what will happen in the future. But in order to understand events in human history from the evolutionary perspective, which so far has taken into account changes in the biological structure and function of living organisms, must be expanded to include events of a different kind, following different laws from those that hold for the transmission of genes—changes that take place in the realm of society and culture.

Scholars have debated the relative contributions of biology and culture to human evolution, especially after Edward O. Wilson formulated the theses of sociobiological determinism. The question is whether changes in art, science, religion, economics, politics, and other cultural systems obey their own rules, or whether they are shaped by the same forces that account for the selection and transmission of genes.

It makes sense to assume that evolution consists of the interaction of two parallel but related processes, one biological and the other cultural. They have separate mechanisms for producing new information, for selecting certain variants, and for transmitting them over time.

For example, art historians trace the evolution of dome-like structures in Western Europe from the Roman Pantheon rebuilt by Hadrian in the second century, through the baptistery of Florence in the twelfth century, through Brunelleschi's dome of the Cathedral of Florence in the fifteenth century, and ending with Michelangelo's dome over St. Peter's in Rome about a hundred years later. The changing shapes of the dome were not due to genetic mutations in the architects' chromosomes, but to attempts to improve on culturally mediated instructions—plans, theories, calculations, and information passed on from masters to apprentices. Each dome may not have been "better" than the previous one, but it is clear that one "evolved" from the other in the sense that the latter included the technical and aesthetic knowledge of earlier forms, plus changes that had not been possible before.

This means that cultural forms can evolve and grow without necessarily enhancing the biological fitness of the individuals who produced them. The monks who developed European culture in the Middle Ages transmitted art and learning instead of genes. That these two ways of transmitting information across time are often in conflict was recognized long ago by the Latin saying *libri aut liberi*—books or children. It is indeed difficult to spawn biological and cultural progeny at the same time.

Occasionally people try to eliminate information they fear. The Romans systematically destroyed everything written in Etruscan so that they could impose their cultural hegemony over Italy. When the great library of Alexandria was put to the torch, much of our Greek heritage perished with it. During the Great Cultural Revolution the Chinese lost so much of their culture that very few people are left now who know how to read the ancient texts that were saved from the flames. But the opposite also happens: Ideas, beliefs, and wrong information kill people perhaps more often than the other way around. Sometimes a small difference in religious interpretation leads to the death of tens of thousands of people, as during the Albigensian wars of the thirteenth century.

Cultural forms depend on the environment of human consciousness. Ideas and artifacts reproduce and grow in the mind, responding to selective pressures that are in principle independent of those that constrain genetic evolution. Because of this independence, it is perfectly possible to start up trains of thought that in the long run will be injurious to our survival. We tend to select new cultural forms that promise to give more power, comfort, or pleasure. But like selective mechanisms that operate in biological evolution, this one, too, has potential dangers as well as obvious advantages.

Cultural evolution can be defined as the differential transmission of information contained in artifacts—in objects, concepts, beliefs, symbols, and behavior patterns that exist only because people took the trouble to make them. While artifacts are human products, they in turn shape human consciousness. A person with a gun, for instance, is different from an unarmed man. It makes no sense to say, as the National Rifle Association does, that "guns don't kill people, people do." People in the abstract don't exist. They are made by the culture in which they live, by the objects they use, the words they hear, the ideas they come across. We have biologically programmed propensities for aggression as well as for compassion and for cooperation. Which of these potentials we realize depends on the cultural environment. When everyone carries a gun, it becomes "natural" to act out the aggressive script instead of the cooperative one.

Artifacts contain implicit instructions for how to behave

because they define the reality within which we operate. Children born in a fishing village automatically adapt to a technology of boats and nets, just as spontaneously as they adopt the local language. Some artifacts also contain *explicit* directions for action; they are the norms, regulations, and laws. They parallel even more clearly the function of genetic instructions that direct behavior. But while genetic instructions are coded chemically in the chromosomes, the information contained in artifacts is coded and stored outside the body—in the action potential inherent in objects, drawings, texts, and the behavior patterns of other individuals with whom one interacts. We might use the term "meme," coined by Richard Dawkins for the replicating unit of cultural information.

We like to believe that cultural evolution serves the goal of human adaptation. According to this view, memes survive only if they enhance the inclusive fitness of the individuals who use them. Artifacts evolve because they help to make our lives better. Cultural forms become destructive and dangerous only when they are misused. For instance, the reason armaments have evolved from stone axes to space lasers is that we have not been able to resolve competition for resources without resorting to aggressiveness. If men only learned to curb their belligerence, weapons would cease to multiply. This perspective on the evolution of culture is basically reassuring because it holds that the growth of artifacts is held in check by human control.

But thinking this way might blind us to the real state of affairs. It is possible that weapons and other artifacts evolve regardless of our intentions. In effect, the multiplication and diffusion of artifacts follows its own logic to a large extent independently of the welfare of its carriers. The relationship of memes to humans is sometimes symbiotic, sometimes parasitic. Although they need consciousness as their growth environment, this dependence is not different, in principle, from our dependence on plants or on a breathable atmosphere. And just as we might kill the environment that made and supported us, the artifacts we created could well destroy us in the end.

Memes often spread in human cultures despite people's initial opposition. Some of the most important steps of civilization, such as the transition from the free life of the hunters to the more regimented life of the nomadic shepherds, and then to the even more restricted life of the farmers, were at first bitterly resisted. The diffusion of coins and currency across the globe initially caused an enormous amount of unhappiness. People just didn't take easily to a money economy, which seemed so much more impersonal and arbitrary, and so much less fun, than bartering had been.

Whenever there is a change in the culture, we assume that it was something we meant to happen, even though on reflection it seems that we are rather helpless in the matter. For instance, most people believe that new car models are introduced because manufacturers are greedy. But in reality they can't help doing what they do. As long as customers automatically prefer novelty, each new advance in technology makes it mandatory to add the latest gimmicks to existing models. In a free market this means that even if all the manufacturers declined to change, new capital would be attracted to produce a car that included the up-to-date features. We are in the habit of thinking that businessmen use technology to achieve competitive advantages. From a less anthropocentric viewpoint, the same scenario could be described as technology using producers and consumers as a medium in which to prosper. Unless actively restrained, memes continue to grow and multiply on their own.

Cultural evolution has its own propaganda apparatus, complete with ideology and slogans that people repeat over and over mechanically. One of my favorites is the phrase ''It's here to stay,'' applied to new products and processes. It serves as a handy Trojan horse to lull our sense of judgment. This innocuous-sounding phrase heralds the territorial ambitions of the meme: Ready or not, here I come.

Weapons provide a clear example of how memes change and propagate. The information in a weapon, when decoded by our mind, says that the amount of threat must be countered with a weapon that contains at least as much threat as the first, and possibly more. Thus, the threat of the knife begets the sword, the sword begets the spear, the spear begets the arrow, the arrow begets the bolt, the bolt begets the bullet . . . and so on to Star Wars. This progress may or may not benefit the biological survival of the human host. There is no evidence, for example, that the people of the Tuscan city of Pistoia, who first manufactured the pistol more than five centuries ago, have received any particular benefits in terms of inclusive fitness over their neighbors. On the other hand, the relative decline of the American Indians is due in large part to the fact that the Caucasian invaders had more and better firearms.

Like other patterns of organization, whether physical, chemical, biological, or informational in their composition, memes will propagate as long as the environment is conducive to growth. There is no reason to expect, for instance, that weapons will stop taking over more and more resources unless their growth environment in human consciousness is made less hospitable. The problem is, of course, that many people find the information contained in weaponry congenial. For some, paradoxically, weapons provide a relief from existential anxiety. Others find in the manufacture of weapons a source of profit. A few are intellectually challenged by the technology—Robert Oppenheimer used to refer to his work on the nuclear bomb as ''that sweet problem.''

Weapons are an obviously problematic species of memes, but the same argument holds for cultural forms that on the surface appear to be more benign. The control over the transformations of matter that modern physics and chemistry have brought about, when translated into uncontrolled technology, has reached a point of diminishing returns. Physical energy gets compressed in ever more explosive concentrations, without a clear idea of whether we shall be able to control its release. New substances are being created regardless of how useful they are, simply because it is possible to produce them. As a result the planetary environment, polluted by noxious substances, is getting to be increasingly unfit for human existence. And when genetic engineering becomes a going concern, it is doubtful that the new forms of life that gene splicing makes possible will be designed with the ultimate welfare of human life in mind—partly because it is impossible to know at this point what that is. Rather, the proliferation of new life forms will be dictated by whatever the technology can accomplish, regardless of consequences. Unless, of course, mankind realizes that its physical survival might be threatened by the evolution of culture, and it is willing to take this threat seriously.

Because artifacts are born and develop in the medium of the human mind, in order to understand the dynamics of cultural evolution it is necessary to consider how consciousness selects and transmits information.

While the *content* of socio-cultural evolution exists outside the body, the *process* that makes it possible takes place within consciousness. The three phases common to all evolutionary processes—variation, selection, and transmission—are mediated by the mind. Cultural variation begins when new memes arise as ideas, actions, or perceptions of outside events. Selection among variant memes, and retention of the selected ones, also involves a more or less conscious evaluation and investment of attention. And so does the transmission of the retained meme. Unless people invested time and attention—psychic energy—in the new variant, it would not survive long enough for the next generation to be aware of its existence. New products, political ideas, and path-breaking works of art will disappear without a trace unless they find a receptive medium in the minds of a large enough audience.

This difference between biological and cultural evolution

has some important consequences. Perhaps the most important is that in genetic evolution, selection is to a very large degree accomplished by impersonal environmental conditions. Whether a given mutation will be retained or not generally depends on the climate, the nature of the food supply, the mix of predators and parasites, plus a myriad of other factors that interact with the mutation and determine its contribution to the fitness of the organism. In socio-cultural evolution, selection is mediated by consciousness. Whether a new idea or practice is viable does not depend directly on external conditions, but on our choices.

This does not mean, of course, that such things as climate or predators have no effect on cultural evolution. To the contrary, external conditions often dictate which innovations are selected. Two of the most fundamentally early cultural inventions, fire and stone weapons, are obvious examples: They were selected because they helped us cope with the climate and compete for the food supply. Our current fascination with nuclear physics is basically not that different: The energy of the atom is sought both to warm our homes and to destroy our enemies. But in cultural evolution the constraints of temperature and competitive pressure do not affect the survival of information through the differential reproductive rates of the organisms that carry it. The constraints are represented in human consciousness, and it is there that the decision is made whether to replicate the meme. It is clearly not the case that atomic reactors have multiplied because those who developed them have had more children—if anything, the contrary is probably true.

Because the variation, selection, and retention of memes occur in consciousness, we must consider their dynamics in order to understand socio-cultural evolution. Perhaps the most fundamental issue is the limitation of the mind as an information-processing apparatus. There is so much we will never know, simply because our brain is not equipped to handle the information. The limitation is both qualitative, referring to the kind of things we are able to recognize, and quantitative, referring to how many things we can be aware of at a given time. Although the qualitative limitations of consciousness are probably the most interesting in the long run, in this context only the consequences of quantitative limitations will be explored.

Information matters only if we attend to it. It is impossible to learn a language or a skill unless we invest a sizable amount of attention in the task. This means that each person is an informational bottleneck; there are only so many memes that he or she can process at any given time. According to the best estimates, the human organism is limited to discriminating a maximum of about seven bits—or chunks—of information per unit of time. It is estimated that the duration of each "attentional unit" is of the order of 1/18 per second; in other words, we can become aware of about 18 times seven bits of information, or 126 bits, in the space of a second. Thus a person can process at most in the neighborhood of 7,560 bits of information each minute. In a lifetime of 70 years, and assuming a waking day of 16 hours, it amounts to about 185,000,000,000 bits of information. This number defines the upper limit of individual experience. Out of it must come every perception, thought, feeling, memory, or action that a person will ever have. It seems like a large number, but in actuality none of us finds it nearly large enough.

To get a sense for how little can be accomplished with the amount of attention at our disposal, consider how much it takes just to follow an ordinary conversation. It is claimed that extracting meaning from speech signals would take 40,000 bits of information per second if each bit had to be attended to separately, or 317 times as much as we can actually handle. Fortunately, our species-specific genetic programming allows us to chunk speech into phonemes automatically, thereby reducing the load to 40 bits per second—or approximately 1/3 of the total processing capacity of attention. This is why we cannot follow a conversation and at the same time do any other demanding mental task.

Just to decode what other people are saying, even though it is to a large extent an effortless and automated process, preempts any other task that requires a full commitment of attention.

As the above example suggests, "chunking" information greatly extends the limits for processing it. Some people conclude from this fact that consciousness is a boundless "open" system, and that the information we can attend to can be indefinitely multiplied. This optimistic reading of the situation, however, flies in the face of the facts. Despite our spectacular success in chunking phonemes, it is still impossible to listen to more than three conversations at the same time. It is unlikely that we will ever be able to pull up two socks simultaneously, and it is difficult to imagine a person being able to talk to a child and write a sonnet at the same time.

Because attention is the medium that makes events occur in consciousness, it is useful to think of it as "psychic energy." Any nonreflex action takes up a certain fraction of this energy. Just listening to an ordinary conversation closely enough to understand what is being said takes up one-third of it at any given time. Stirring a cup of coffee, reaching for a newspaper, and trying to remember a telephone number all require information-processing space out of that limited total. Of course, individuals vary widely in terms of how much of their psychic energy they use (how many bits they process), and in terms of what they invest their energy in.

The limitations on the information-processing capacities of consciousness have clear implications for the evolution of culture. Only a few new memes out of the variations constantly being produced are noticed, few are retained, and even fewer are transmitted to a new generation.

The rate at which new variations are produced depends to a large extent on how much attention free from survival demands is available. In addition, it depends on what cultural instructions there are regarding new memes. Some cultures, like the ancient Egyptian civilization, actively discouraged variants. Others, like current Western societies, are ideologically primed to encourage their overproduction. Thus, how frequently new memes appear is a function both of the basic scarcity of attention and of the social organization of attention that may either facilitate or inhibit the emergence of new artifacts.

After a new meme is produced, its retention is also constrained by the amount of attention available in the given human environment. According to the census there are at present about 200,000 Americans who classify themselves as artists. It is probably safe to assume that no more than 1 in 10,000 from among their works will be preserved even one generation from now as part of the information that constitutes the symbolic system of the visual arts. Every year about 50,000 new books are published in the United States. This number already constitutes a selection from probably 1,000,000 manuscripts submitted, most of which do not get published. But how many of these volumes will be remembered in ten years, how many in a hundred? The same argument holds for scholarly articles, inventions, popular songs, or new products. The environment of consciousness that allows artifacts to exist is restricted and provides a severe selective pressure on their survival.

The rate of selection and retention of new memes is again a function of both the scarcity of attention and the social organization thereof. Each person must have a theoretical upper limit on how many paintings he or she can admire, how many scientific formulas he can remember, or how many products of each kind he can consume. Thus, societies must also have limits on how many works of art, scientific facts, or commercial products they can recognize and assimilate. It is naïve to assume that progress can be enhanced by encouraging more people to be creative: If there is not enough psychic energy available to recognize creative changes, they will simply be wasted. At certain historical periods, some communities have disposed of unusual amounts of free attention. Greece twenty-five centuries ago, Florence five hundred years ago, and Paris in the nineteenth century were able to stimulate and to retain cultural variations at unusually high rates. Occasionally communities become specialized niches for certain kinds of memes; music flowered in eighteenth- and nineteenth-century Vienna; Göttingen in the late nineteenth century and Budapest in the early twentieth century provided fertile soil for mathematics; Goethe's Weimar was receptive to poetry, and so forth. But eventually no human community has enough attention to keep more than a few of the many new artifacts that are constantly produced. At the point of saturation, a selective process begins to operate.

Of the few innovations that eventually end up in the symbolic system of society, even fewer will be transmitted to the next generation. It is not enough for a meme to be preserved in a book or an object. To survive, it has to affect the consciousness of at least some people. A language that is no longer spoken or at least read becomes a "dead" language. When people forget the key to its meaning, as has happened with Etruscan, the language loses its informational structure and stops growing and reproducing. The transmission of cultural information through time requires expensive investments of attention. Several institutions exist primarily to carry out this function. For instance, schools specialize in the transmission of memes, although anyone familiar with them knows what a small fraction of the cultural heritage is actually passed on within their walls. Another example are the public behavioral instructions codified in political constitutions. All of the nations of the world have constitutions that specify appropriate behaviors concerning the same dozen or so units of information (such as work, property, income, education, decision-making, and so on), although the hierarchical relations between these units vary. The continuity of constitutional texts can be traced back to Roman law and the British Magna Charta. But they don't survive naturally. Great social resources must be invested for their preservation. Without courts, judges, lawyers, police, schools, and a host of other institutions, the instructions contained in constitutions would be disregarded and eventually forgotten.

Human environments favorable to cultural evolution are characterized by surplus attention, by a social organization that encourages novelty, by social arrangements that facilitate the retention and transmission of new variants, and by informational skills that are far enough developed to recognize and integrate the variation within their symbol systems. When a society has these characteristics, it becomes a favorable medium for the spread of artifacts. But whether this will benefit the people who become hosts to cultural evolution is another issue entirely.

The survival of new memes does not depend only on environmental factors, such as the amount and the social organization of attention in the human milieu. It also depends on how the information itself is patterned. In other words, some memes are fitter than others in the sense that the information contained in them is going to spread to more minds, and to be remembered longer. It is impossible to give a general description of what makes a new artifact successful, any more than it is possible to describe a successful genetic mutation, and for identical reasons. Just as the fitness of a new mutation depends on the environment to which the phenotype is adapted, so is the viability of a new cultural form dependent on the prior state of the culture and the human environment in which it appears.

Nevertheless, it is possible to point out some characteristics of memes that help their diffusion in a wide range of contexts. The first requirement of a new cultural form is that it be identifiable as such. Every symbolic domain has formal or informal criteria for establishing whether a meme is a genuine new variant. The Patent Office and the copyright laws use formal definitions, while in other fields like science and art a consensus of experts decides whether an artifact is really new. To be so identified a variant must depart from previous artifacts to a substantial extent, yet not so much as to be unrecognizable. The range of optimal variation is one characteristic that defines the viability of new memes.

In social contexts where new memes are seen to be dangerous, elaborate institutions might be established to test new ideas and other artifacts to determine whether they constitute variations from the accepted orthodoxy. In some historical periods the Christian Church spent great efforts to identify "heresy," which referred to cultural variants that had to be eliminated from the consciousness of the population. Even now the function of the Vatican's Sacred Congregation for the Doctrine of the Faith, a successor to the Inquisition and to the Holy Office, is to eliminate books and teachings that introduce unacceptable variations into the religious meme pool. Similar institutions exist in the Soviet Union, and in all societies built on the assumption that the structure of information they already have is superior to any possible new form. Such mechanisms of social control try to separate new artifacts that are beneficial to the commonwealth from those that are not. In principle this could be a useful function once it is admitted that cultural evolution need not coincide with human welfare. Historically, though, the censorship of new ideas has been informed more often by the desire to maintain a particular power structure than by the desire to maximize the well-being of the population.

Once it is established that an artifact is genuinely new, the next question becomes: Should it be preserved? A great variety of reasons determines why one meme will be selected for retention while thousands of others are eliminated and forgotten. Economy is one general criterion. Any artifact that saves scarce human resources has a better chance of surviving. And, attention being one of the most precious resources, artifacts that save time and concentration generally have an edge in fitness. Thus, the evolution of symbol systems representing language, quantities, and other forms of representation always tends toward memes that will accomplish equal or better effects with a saving of attention. The ascendancy of the metric system over competing systems of measurement or the general adoption of the North Semitic alphabet are good examples of how savings in attention will positively select a more efficient set of symbols. The same is true of the evolution of tools, appliances, and social customs. A cheaper price is just a corollary of the same principle, since the advantage of saving money is simply a special case of saving attention—money being what is exchanged for psychic energy invested into productive tasks. If a book or a car is less expensive than an equivalent brand, buying the cheaper one saves psychic energy that would have gone into earning the difference in price; the attention saved can then be invested either into making more money or into pleasurable experiences.

While economy of attention is a very important criterion for the selection of artifacts, it is certainly not the only one. Perhaps the most universal qualification of positively selected artifacts is that they improve the quality of experience. Whenever a new cultural form promises pleasure or enjoyment, it will find a receptive niche in consciousness. This reason for the adoption of a new artifact is well expressed by the Greek poet who welcomed the invention of the water mill two thousand years ago, as quoted by the historian Marc Bloch: "Spare your hands, which have been long familiar with the millstone, you maidens who used to crush the grain. Henceforth you shall sleep long, oblivious to the crowing cocks who greet the dawn." Compared to the millstone, the water mill offered women smoother hands, less physical effort, and more disposable time—presumably adding up to an overall improvement on the quality of life.

Clearly enjoyment is the main reason why we select and retain most works of art. Painting, music, drama, architecture, and writing are symbolic skills adopted because they produce positive states of consciousness. So do mystery novels and television programs, which appear to "waste" psychic energy but do so while providing pleasurable information in return for the investment of attention.

But some of the most utilitarian artifacts also survive because they provide enjoyment to those who use them. In discussing the introduction of the first metal objects at the end of the Stone ages, Colin Renfrew writes:

> In several areas of the world it has been noted, in the case of metallurgical innovations in particular, that the development of bronze and other metals as *useful* commodities was a much later phenomenon than their first utilization as new and attractive materials, employed in contexts of display. . . . In most cases early metallurgy appears to have been practiced primarily because the products had novel properties that made them attractive to use as symbols and as personal adornments and ornaments, in a manner that, by focusing attention, could attract or enhance prestige.

Products with novel properties continue to attract attention regardless of utilitarian considerations. Interest in automobiles started not because of their usefulness, but because stunts and races captured people's imagination. A recent promotional brochure from Alfa Romeo states: "In 1910, a car company was created that was destined to distinguish itself from all others. A company built on the simple philosophy that a car shouldn't be merely a means of transportation, but *a source of exhilaration* . . ." This is wrong only in claiming that such a "philosophy" was unique to this particular manufacturer; in fact, most early cars were built with that goal in mind (a point recognized six pages later in the same brochure: "The Triumph TR3. The Austin Healey 3000. The Jaguar XKE . . . They were sleek, sensual, agile . . . Designed and built for the sheer joy of driving, *they made no pretense whatsoever of practicality*"). The same trend can be recognized at the inception of many cultural innovations, from the airplane to the personal computer.

According to the great Dutch cultural historian Johan Huizinga, human institutions originally arise as games that provide enjoyment to the players and the spectators; only later do they become serious elements of social structure. At first, the thoughts and actions these institutions require are freely accepted; later they become the taken-for-granted elements of social reality. Thus, science starts as riddling contests, religion as joyful collective celebrations, military institutions start as ceremonial combat, the legal system has its origins in ritualized debates, and economic systems often begin as festive reciprocal exchanges. Those forms that provide the most enjoyment are selected and transmitted down the generations.

But once a set of memes, for whatever reason, finds a niche in consciousness, it can go on reproducing without reference to the enjoyment of its hosts. Coins were first minted to enhance the prestige and the economic power of kings and to facilitate trade. When the exchange of necessary products becomes dependent on a monetary system, however, people become helpless to resist its spread and will have to adapt to it whether they like it or not. As Max Weber noted, capitalism began as an adventurous game of entrepreneurs but eventually became an "iron cage," an economic system with peculiar shortcomings from which it is very difficult to escape.

If it is true that artifacts exploit enjoyment as their medium for survival, any account of cultural evolution must give consideration to what people enjoy doing. People enjoy experiences in which they are faced with opportunities for action—or challenges—that are high and that are matched with an equivalent level of personal skills. Worry and anxiety result when there are more challenges than skills, apathy and boredom when the situation is reversed. When challenges and skills are out of balance, people seek to restore the optimal condition in which their experience is most positive. The simple formula for enjoyment, Challenges/Skills = 1, was originally developed in the context of empirical studies with urban American adults. Since then it has been confirmed by studies in a variety of European and Asian contexts.

Because of this relationship, people tend to overreproduce memes that raise the level of existing challenges, provided that at the same time they can raise the level of their own skills. Anything we do for a long time eventually becomes boring. At that point we look for new opportunities for action, which in turn forces us to develop greater skills; this dialectic leads to a process of *complexification*. This principle accounts for both the generation of new artifacts and, to a lesser extent, for their subsequent acceptance and transmission.

The relationship between complexification and enjoyment does not mean that people are constantly motivated to seek higher challenges. In fact, the opposite is true. When free to use time at their discretion, most people most of the time prefer to relax. They engage in low-intensity activities such as sitting with a bottle of beer in front of a television set. "Pleasure" is a homeostatic principle that drives people to save energy whenever possible, and to derive rewards from genetically programmed actions that are necessary for the survival of the species, such as eating and sexuality.

Enjoyment that requires developing new skills to meet increasing levels of challenge is relatively rare. Yet this is the experience that people all around the world mention as the high point of their lives. Thus, while pleasure is generally conservative, selecting and transmitting already existing artifacts, enjoyment that leads to complexification is more often responsible for generating and selecting new cultural forms.

At the most general level, then, it can be said that the process of complexification, which is experienced as enjoyable, defines the symbiotic relationship between the evolution of human beings and the evolution of culture. Cultural forms that offer the possibility of increasing enjoyment will survive by attracting attention. Similarly, people who invest attention in such forms acquire a more complex consciousness. In each generation, individuals who develop and learn to use new artifacts form a new breed.

Up to a point, this coevolution is beneficial both to us and to the world of things. However, there is always the possibility that memes will move from a symbiotic to a parasitic relationship. To prevent this from happening, we must entertain the possibility that culture does not exist to serve our needs. As organized matter and information, artifacts compete for energy with other forms of organization, including ourselves. When this possibility is faced, it becomes easier to evaluate cultural forms more objectively, and to make decisions on a sounder basis concerning which ones to encourage and which ones to restrain.

The joint complexification of consciousness and culture, brought about by the evolved trait of finding joy in complexity, has given the human race a great advantage in its competition with other forms of organized matter. Because the mind enjoys a challenge, people have lustily explored the hidden potential in all forms of information, thereby acting as midwives to artifacts of every kind. In so doing they have learned how to survive at the expense of other animals and plants they found useless. But just because enjoying the challenge of complexity has served us in the past does not guarantee that it will do so in the future. There is increasing evidence that this Faustian restlessness is making us vulnerable to the mindless replication of artifacts. If we are to take charge of the direction of evolution, a first step might be to recognize the fact that unless we find ways of controlling the evolution of culture, our own survival might be in serious jeopardy.

EXPLORING FUTURE TECHNOLOGIES

▼

K. ERIC DREXLER

Nanotechnology will be based on molecular machines and molecular electronic devices. With computers and robotic arms smaller than a living cell, it will enable the construction of almost anything, building up structures atom by atom.

Everyone knows that technology has reshaped our world. Advances in technology have transformed a world of isolated peasants toiling for a handful of lords into a world where ever more millions of people are free to roam a globe echoing with satellite newscasts. Most of us suspect that advances are far from over. Fewer have tried to understand future breakthroughs. Many would call the effort futile.

Yet if understanding is possible, it seems worth seeking. If the gross trends in technology are any guide to the future, we will face dramatic advances in a time frame for which we pretend to make serious plans.

Bureaucrats blithely project Social Security budgets for the year 2025, as if they know what another thirty years' progress in computers, artificial intelligence, and robotics will mean for economic productivity—and as if they know what another thirty years' progress in the biotechnology revolution will mean for health care and life expectancy. To assume no change in these fields would be ridiculous, and to assume that the future will *merely* bring longer lives and better factories seems an exercise in fantasy.

Parents plan college for newborn infants, implicitly planning career preparations for a stranger in a strange world. They save for their own retirements, and a personal journey into that world. If we make long-term plans for saving and spending, then surely it makes sense to consider developments that will determine what our money can buy—if, that is, there is anything of importance we can puzzle out. My purpose here is to show how one can puzzle out something of importance about future technologies, and to sketch a few of the larger results.

These results, if correct, should affect public policy decisions. It seems that certain lines of work will lead to technologies of great power. If so, then—given standard policy assumptions, in a competitive world—it makes sense to pursue those technologies, to try to gain their benefits while forestalling their abuse. Research-and-development budgets in the U.S. alone total tens of billions of dollars annually, and long-term prospects affect short-term research goals. With a better understanding of the future, we could invest more wisely today.

To think productively about future technologies is largely a matter of *exploratory engineering*. To do a better job of understanding the future, we need to do a better job of understanding, practicing, and judging efforts in exploratory engineering. The following sections of this essay examine this field, comparing it to science and standard engineering.

Exploratory engineering involves designing things that we can't yet build. This may seem a dubious proposition. "If we can't build something, who will pay for its design? Surely, the designs will be sketchy and inadequate. And, if we can't build it, how will we test it? Surely, any conclusions about its workability will be tentative and inadequate." These are natural questions, and the answers to them revolve around the counter-question, "Inadequate for what?"

One shouldn't expect the exploratory engineer to concoct specific designs and propose them as the definitive machines for the 2006 model year. Not only are present engineers too ignorant to do so (a basic problem), but we lack the resources. Modern industrial designs are often complex and sophisticated; future designs will likely be more so. On a small budget, one could not possibly design today's machines, much less the future's.

So why bother with exploratory engineering? Because, just as one can have a general knowledge of today's machines and what they can do—without knowing their detailed designs—so one can, perhaps, gain a general knowledge of some of tomorrow's machines. A general knowledge can include important facts, and detailed, sophisticated designs are not essential to a general understanding. It is one thing to know about cars, roads, petroleum, and suburbs; it is another thing to know about the complexities of internal combustion engines and how these affect car weights and gas mileage.

Likewise, consider nuclear bombs. The key points in a general understanding of them are simple: They work by nuclear reactions, initiated by fission, releasing nuclear levels of energy and producing active nuclear debris. This general understanding (and more) was possible before the Manhattan Project, and hence before the first bomb. Sophistication was secondary. The first, crude bombs were grossly inefficient by today's standards, yet they beat conventional explosives by orders of magnitude. Even the still-cruder, exploratory designs for these bombs must have shown the possibility of this, because the basic potential lay not in the sophistication of the designs but in the fundamental principles of the technology.

The lesson in this is simple: In new technologies of fundamental power, even clumsy, conservative designs can sometimes give awesome performances. Exploratory engineering works best in these new domains, where crude designs can beat the most sophisticated systems possible with present technology. The chief example explored here is a domain called *nanotechnology*, a technology based on molecular machines able to build molecular machines—and anything else. Here again, crude, exploratory designs are enough to reveal great power.

By its very nature, however, exploratory engineering has nothing to say about the timing of events. There is nothing in the design of a machine that tells how long a community of human beings will take to develop all the technologies needed to build it, or whether they will try. Dates do not fall out of design calculations.

These uncertainties limit the value of exploratory engineering, if one seeks predictions of future events rather than the directions of future progress. One might guess at matters of timing, but it is wise to be cautious in these guesses. What "cautious" means, of course, depends on the issue at hand: A technophile's optimism is a technophobe's pessimism, and vice versa. If one considers the unprecedented economic and health care benefits promised by nanotechnology, the cautious assumption is that it will take a long, long time to arrive. If one considers the unprecedented potential for abuse of nanotechnology, however, the cautious assumption is that it will arrive with startling speed. For those chiefly concerned with the direction of progress—with choosing productive lines of research, for example—uncertainties about the timing of long-term goals are less important.

Exploratory engineering, more than most engineering, builds on science—yet this does not make it a branch of science, any more than bridge design is a branch of science. And this is important to recognize, because the confusion between science and engineering is fatal to understanding the future of technology. To judge by newspaper and television coverage, space flight is a great achievement of science, and scientists spend a lot of time trying to make rocket engines work. Any scientist or engineer, of course, will tell you that space flight—though it has benefited from science and in turn yielded scientific knowledge—is itself an achievement not of science but of engineering. Understanding the difference between these fields is vital: If engineering were a science, then exploratory engineering would be impossible.

Science and engineering build on each other and use similar tools, but they have different goals. Science aims to understand how things work; engineering aims to make things work. Science takes the thing as given and studies its behavior; engineering takes a behavior as given and studies how to make something that will act that way.

This difference makes foresight impossible regarding scientific knowledge, but not regarding engineering ability. The limit on foresight regarding knowledge is simple and logical: If one were to *know* today what one will "discover" tomorrow, it wouldn't be a discovery. Since engineering is about doing rather than discovering, no such logical problem arises. There is no contradiction in saying, "We know that we will be able to land a man on the moon," as Kennedy's advisers did in the early 1960s. When scientists do make predictions about their future knowledge, they predict what they will learn *about* rather than what they will learn. And this is often a matter of engineering: "We will learn about the composition of the lunar surface—because engineering will take us there."

Because of this situation, confusion about science and engineering hinders understanding of future technologies. If we confuse engineering with science, then we will think that little can be said about its future—that engineering *projections* are as poorly founded as scientific *speculations*. And we will tend to think that scientists (with their proper and ingrained distrust of speculation) are the right experts to ask about the future of technology. Scientists have little reason to ponder the nature of engineering and often misunderstand how it differs.

"Thus, we conclude that engineers can, through the discipline of exploratory engineering, tell us solid facts about future technological prospects. We need only ask them, and listen to their answers." This is, of course, nonsense.

Standard engineering has a short-term perspective for a simple reason: Employers will not pay engineers to think about what can be built in another fifty years, because there is no money in it. In the U.S., companies seldom pay engineers to think about what can be built in ten years. Medium- and long-term exploratory engineering are little practiced today. What is more, the discipline of exploratory engineering differs so greatly from that of standard engineering that standard engineers may be excused for doubting whether it even makes sense.

Engineering is about designing things—ordinarily, things that one can build, test, and redesign in the short term. Exploratory engineering is about designing things that can be built, but only with tools that we don't yet have; this makes it a different sort of endeavor.

The differences begin with motive. Standard engineering receives massive funding to help achieve a competitive advantage in the world—to build a more attractive CD player or a more aggressive jet fighter, and to do it soon. Exploratory engineering, to the extent that it is practiced at all, seeks to construct not a physical artifact but a rough understanding of future technological capabilities.

The exploratory engineer must still do design work of some sort, or there would be nothing to discuss, no real ideas to criticize. But those designs may omit many details and still make a solid case for a future capability. In standard engineering, the job isn't done until every detail is specified, since every detail must be built. This makes the exploratory engineer's job simpler.

Since exploratory engineering aims to build a solid case rather than to outperform the best similar system, it need not try to push the limits of the possible. This has profound consequences for the nature of the intellectual enterprise. Again, it makes work simpler.

In standard engineering one seeks a net advantage in any way that works, regardless of whether we understand *why* it works. Engineers must seek lower-cost manufacturing, which forces them to work with all the complexity of factory operations. They must seek better materials, which drives them to confront all the complexity of metallurgy and polymer chemistry, as in manufacturing turbine blades for jet engines and composite materials for wings. They may have to push the limits of precision, cleanliness, purity, and complexity, as in state-of-the-art microprocessor production. And almost any production process is likely to use a big bag of tested, reproducible black-magic tricks: Add a pinch of this, a dash of that, and clean the glass with Alconox™ detergent before step five.

Though engineers eagerly use (and produce) scientific knowledge, they no more *need* to understand how a process works than a bird needs to understand aerodynamics. Cut-and-try works in engineering as it works in other evolutionary systems. Once discovered, a process may work, prove its reliability in testing, and provide a real competitive advantage—yet it may remain utterly beyond analysis and simulation based on current knowledge. Competitive pressures encourage engineers to increase their understanding, but those same pressures do not allow them the intellectual luxury of staying on well-understood ground.

Competition pushes engineering beyond the limits of what can be analyzed or simulated. In practice, the tools of analysis and simulation alone never yield competitive systems and hence can never support the full burden of standard engineering. This requires testing, not only to get the details right, but to discover valuable yet mysterious processes. But exploratory engineering must rely almost exclusively on these limited tools: One can't test and learn from what one can't build. The standard engineer, looking at this situation, has the strong gut feeling that analysis and simulation will prove inadequate—as indeed they would, if the goals and designs were those of standard engineering. But when a design need not be competitive, then—at least in some instances—it need not go beyond what can be analyzed in terms of well-understood laws of nature.

In these instances, analysis and simulation can give strong reason to think that a rough, exploratory design could in fact be made to work. To make such a case, the designer must pay attention (explicitly or implicitly) to a host of questions. What are the relationships among materials properties, component shapes, strengths, forces, speeds, energies, temperatures, voltages, currents, chemical reactions, and so forth? The list is long, but (for any particular class of physical system) it is still finite.

Uncertainties in analysis and simulation pose problems. Different fields suffer different problems from uncertainty; once again, confusion about the differences separating science, standard engineering, and exploratory engineering can confuse our efforts to understand the future of technology.

In exploratory engineering, one can't test and measure, so uncertainties may remain large. Some can be dealt with by leaving large margins for error in a design. If you don't know how strong the material will be, assume the worst and beef up the thickness of the part to match. Where a standard engineer would be forced by competitive pressures to leave only an adequate margin for safety (after testing to probe the limits of workability), the exploratory engineer can design in a huge margin for ignorance, just to make a more solid case.

In an unknown environment, uncertainties may also be unknown. Accordingly, exploratory engineering is easier when the designer can assume a simple or well-defined environment. For parts inside a machine, the machine is the environment and is itself a known part of the design.

A more subtle problem arises when a precise result must follow from a combination of uncertain quantities. For example, a spinning part may require perfect balance yet be made of two parts of unknown density bolted together. Here one must ask if there are enough "degrees of freedom" to satisfy the constraint. In this case, the unknown density-ratio between the parts is no problem, so long as we are free to adjust the size of at least one part to bring the assembly into balance. This gives us the degree of freedom we need to compensate for the uncertainty.

This line of reasoning shows how the exploratory engineer can make a solid case for a device despite uncertainties about many of its properties and design details. It also shows how uncertain properties can create *compensating* uncertainties in design details (as in the example given, where an uncertain density leads to a corresponding uncertain size). This shows that "uncertainties" can come in planned sets that cancel out rather than adding up. The notion of uncertainty in exploratory engineering plays other tricks. Ignorance of these can lead one to confuse confidence-building factors with confidence-eroding factors. We need to avoid confusions about uncertainty, especially in large systems of ideas.

Uncertainties play different roles in science, standard engineering, and exploratory engineering. The usual intuitive rule about uncertainty in large sets of ideas or proposals is simple: If a conclusion or design rests on layer upon layer of shaky premises, it will surely fall. But this intuition sometimes misleads. To see where it works and where it doesn't, consider an imaginary proposal—a theory—in science, and another—a design—in engineering. Each proposal will have five essential parts and ten equally plausible possibilities for each part.

The theory might have to explain: 1. what something is; 2. where it came from; 3. how it survived the last million years; 4. why it hasn't been detected with X rays; and 5. what it does when baked. Only one possibility can be right for each part of the theory, so with our assumed ten equally plausible possibilities for each part, a choice will have only a one-in-ten chance of being right. For a specific version of the theory, the chances of getting all five parts right (assuming no additional data) are no better than 1/10 to the fifth power. For a theory to be true, all its parts must be true, and so for any specific version the odds against it are at least 100,000 to one.

This artificial example shows how uncertainties combine in building real scientific theories: They combine adversely indeed. A scientific theory is a single-stranded chain that can break at any link. A chain with many dubious links is almost certainly worthless. This shapes the scientist's attitude toward uncertainty.

Uncertainties in exploratory engineering work in a different way. Consider a superficially similar design problem: a mechanism requiring five essential parts, with (again) ten equally plausible possibilities for each part. The design might require: 1. a power supply; 2. a motor; 3. a speed controller; 4. a locking device; and 5. an output shaft. But here, more than one possibility may work: Unlike theoretical proposals, engineering possibilities are not mutually exclusive. What is more, in exploratory engineering the typical problem is to build a case for the workability of the mechanism, not to specify a detailed, workable design—it is enough for there to be *one* working possibility.

In accord with these points, imagine that each of the ten possibilities for a part has a fifty–fifty chance of working. The chance of all ten possibilities failing, leaving no workable design for the part, is 0.5 to the tenth power—less than 1 in 1,000. With five parts facing this risk of unworkability, the overall chance that some essential part won't be possible is less than 5 in 1,000, making the overall probability of a workable design better than 99.5 percent. Real examples can give even better results: There may be a hundred ways to build each part, and several may be essentially sure bets.

In exploratory engineering, the "uncertainty" resulting from many possibilities may lead to a virtual certainty that at least one will work. An exploratory design concept can be like a massive, braided cable, in which many strands must fail before the link is severed. Uncertainties do not combine adversely, as do the superficially similar uncertainties of science (in science, a closer parallel would be a claim that *some* correct theory can be found, but even this suffers from the problem that only one choice can be right, and that choice may not be known). Standard engineering, however, is a bit closer to science in this regard.

In an idealized competitive world, only the best design would do. And choosing the *best* design, like choosing the true theory, means choosing the uniquely right possibility for each part. In the real world, the best isn't necessary, but competitive pressures still narrow the acceptable choices.

Further, in standard engineering it isn't enough to establish that there is a workable design somewhere in a forest of alternatives—one must propose a specific design, build it, and live with the consequences. Time and budgets are limited, and the failure of a large system may leave no resources for another try. In our model above, this would mean making five choices with a fifty–fifty chance of success with each part, making the overall chance of success about 3 percent. (This motivates careful testing of parts before building systems!)

All these factors combine to make exploratory engineering more feasible than it might seem. Designs need not be competitive with other, similar designs; they need only be workable. To make them workable, they can be grossly overdesigned to compensate for uncertainties. Since their purpose is to provide a case for a possibility, not a blueprint to guide manufacture, they can omit details and include room for adjustment. All this aids in building a solid case for specific kinds of mechanisms, and concepts for whole systems of mechanisms can be solid even if they are built on layer upon layer of shaky cases for specific parts.

In the first half of the twentieth century, work in exploratory engineering persuaded knowledgeable individuals that space flight would be possible. Today, the most important field for exploratory engineering is perhaps nanotechnology: It is clearly foreseeable and will be of immense practical importance. It can serve as a prime specimen of the process.

Nanotechnology is (or, rather, *will be*) a technology based on a general ability to build objects to complex, atomic specifications. We live in a world made out of atoms, and how those atoms are arranged makes a tremendous difference. This is why nanotechnology will make a tremendous difference.

Today's technology is a *bulk technology*: It handles atoms, not as individuals, but as crowds. We make things by heating, stirring, molding, whittling, spraying—all processes that move trillions of atoms at a time, with only crude control over the patterns they form. Chemistry and genetic engineering use clever bulk-technology techniques to achieve specific molecular results, but only within narrow limits. No technology today gives us a general ability to build objects atom by atom.

Nanotechnology will be based on molecular machines and molecular electronic devices. With computers and robotic arms smaller than a living cell, it will enable the construction of almost anything, building up structures atom by atom. Among the products will be:

- Pocket computers with more memory and computational capacity than all the computers in the world today put together;
- Large objects, such as spacecraft, made from light, super-strong materials and as cheap (pound for pound) as wood or hay;
- Machines able to enter and repair living cells, giving medicine surgical control at the molecular level.

How can one draw such conclusions? A more detailed exposition is spread over several papers and a book (*Engines of Creation;* Anchor/Doubleday, 1986), but the outlines are straightforward.

The idea of nanotechnology resulted from applying an engineering perspective to the discoveries of molecular biology, and one path to nanotechnology lies through further advances in biotechnology. Regardless of how nanotechnology emerges, however, the facts of molecular biology provide a direct demonstration of principles that can be used by future molecular machines. (A rule of exploratory engineering: If one knows that it happens, one can assume it is possible.)

Cells contain enzymes, some of which function as molecular jigs and machine tools, assembling small molecules to build larger molecules. Enzymes themselves are made by ribosomes (which are in turn made by enzymes and earlier ribosomes). Ribosomes are complex molecular machines, programmed by the genetic system. Together, enzymes and ribosomes demonstrate that molecular reactions can be guided by molecular machines under programmed control, building up complex structures—including more molecular machines.

One path to nanotechnology, then, would use these biochemical machines to build new machines of our own design. This, however, means learning how to design protein molecules (the products of ribosomes), and this is a tough job. The biotechnology industry is hard at work on this problem, and making slow but real progress. Another path to nanotechnology would use chemical techniques to build non-protein molecular machines—using nature's principles, but not nature's materials. The 1987 Nobel Prize in chemistry was presented to Jean-Marie Lehn, Donald Cram, and Charles Pedersen for work that leads in this direction. Yet another path would use the technology of the scanning tunneling microscope—which can position a needle to atomic precision near a surface—to manipulate molecules and so build molecular machines. No one has yet built a specific molecular structure this way, but the technology is still young, having been announced in 1982.

Thus, multiple paths lead from present technology toward a technology able to build complex molecular structures, including molecular machines able to build better molecular machines. The conclusion that we can build such machines gains strength from what may be termed our "uncertainty regarding how to proceed"—that is, from the presence of many apparently workable options. This uncertainty does not spill over into nanotechnology itself, however, because all these developmental paths lead to the same destination.

Full-fledged nanotechnology will rely on molecular machines able to position reactive molecules to atomic precision, building up complex structures a few atoms at a time. These molecular construction machines are called "assemblers"; some advanced versions will resemble submicroscopic industrial robots. Nanotechnology is virtually synonymous with assembler-based technology, since only assemblers seem likely to give us the control needed to build complex structures to atomic specifications.

Nanotechnology is not defined by its size, even though the prefix "nano" means "billionth," just as "micro" means "millionth." Not everything that produces micrometer-scale objects qualifies as microtechnology: Exhaling particles of cigarette smoke fails the test. Likewise, not everything that produces nanometer-scale objects qualifies as nanotechnology: Burning hydrogen to make water molecules and etching ultra-fine lines on a silicon chip fail the test. Nanotechnology, like microtechnology, is characterized not by the scale of its products but by the sorts of techniques used and the sorts of things those techniques can build. Microtechnology makes intricate micron-scale patterns using etching, vapor deposition, photolithography, and the like; nanotechnology will make intricate nanometer-scale patterns by building objects atom by atom.

Multiple paths lead to the land of nanotechnology. What lies within?

To explore the domain of nanotechnology means exploring the world of things—especially molecular machines—that can be built using atoms as individually arranged building blocks. Knowledge of the forces within and between molecules tells us of the forces within and between the parts of molecular machines. The field of "molecular mechanics," developed by chemists, describes these forces and the resulting molecular motions, often quite well. The exploratory engineer can compensate for inaccuracies in modern molecular mechanics descriptions by overdesigning parts, by allowing large margins of safety, and by paying attention to the number of degrees of freedom in a design.

The most fundamental fact about molecular mechanics is that molecules can be thought of as objects. They have size, shape, mass, strength, stiffness, and smooth, soft, slippery surfaces. Large objects are made of many atoms; molecules are objects made of only a few atoms.

Molecular mechanics describes what happens when the atomic bumps of one surface slide over the atomic bumps of another—and shows, surprisingly, that the resulting motion can be so smooth as to be almost frictionless, at low speeds. This makes possible good bearings. Molecular mechanics can also describe how friction builds up with speed, but the analysis is complex and has not yet been done. Until it is, the exploratory engineer can design using low sliding speeds, and only then assume low sliding friction.

The story continues through other molecular devices. Meshing atomic bumps can serve as gear teeth. Helical rows of bumps can slide smoothly over other helical rows, serving as threads on nuts and screws. Tightly bonded sets of atoms—like tiny bits of ceramic, diamond, or engineering plastics—can form strong, rigid parts. Rotors, bearings, and electrodes can form electrostatic motors a few tens of billionths of a meter in diameter, and producing an incredible amount of power for their size (many trillions of watts per cubic meter).

Motors, shafts, gears, bearings, and miscellaneous moving parts built in this way can combine to form robot arms less than one-tenth of a millionth of a meter long. Owing to a fundamental law relating size to rate of motion in mechanical systems, a robot arm this size can perform operations in one ten-millionth of the time required for an analogous device a meter long. Equipped with suitable tools, these arms can work as assemblers, building other machines at a rate of millions of molecular operations per second.

This sketches some of what seems clear from the exploration of nanotechnology. Many uncertainties remain, particularly in molecular electronics. Molecular *mechanical* devices can be analyzed using molecular mechanics and the familiar, Newtonian laws of motion (augmented by statistical mechanics, to describe thermal vibrations). Molecular *electronic* devices, in contrast, demand a quantum mechanical analysis, which is far more complex. Until a useful set of devices is designed and subjected to a clear, sound analysis, the exploratory engineer cannot design systems that assume the use of molecular electronics.

This might seem a grave limitation, since computer control has become so important in conventional engineering. Nonetheless, molecular *mechanical* computers (with properties supporting the above projection of "pocket computers with more memory and computational capacity than all the computers in the world today put together") can readily be designed. Although molecular electronic devices should be orders of magnitude faster, and may even outcompete molecular mechanical computers in all respects, the analyzability of molecular machines gives the mechanical approach a decisive advantage—not to the standard engineer of the future, but to the exploratory engineer of today. Analysis shows that molecular mechanical computers can be made to tolerate the jostling of thermal vibrations, and that these computers can run at about a billion cycles per second (somewhat faster than today's electronic machines), while consuming (roughly) tens of billionths of a watt of power. This technology will pack the memory and computational ability of a mainframe computer into the volume of a bacterial cell.

These mechanical nanocomputers can control assembler arms, directing their work. If a computer contains instructions (on molecular tape, say) for constructing a copy of an assembler and its raw-materials feed system, a copy of the computer, and a copy of a tape-duplicating machine, then the whole system can build a copy of itself. In short, it could replicate like a bacterium. Calculations indicate that a replicating assembler system of this sort could copy itself in less than an hour (remember the speed of assembler arms), using cheap industrial chemicals as raw materials. It is left as an exercise for the reader to calculate how long it would take one replicator, with a mass of (say) one-trillionth of a gram, to convert a million tons of raw materials into a million tons of replicators. (Hint: A ton is a million grams, and the answer is measured in days.) Slower-working replicators could run on air, water, sunlight, and a pinch of minerals. For safety they would need reliable, built-in limits to growth, but that is an issue addressed elsewhere.

These results, plus the observation that molecular machines can build large things, such as redwood trees, lead to the conclusion that teams of replicating assemblers can build large objects. By building atom by atom, they can build these objects from materials that are today impractical for structural engineering—materials such as diamond. This supports the above projection that nanotechnology will enable the construction of "large objects, such as spacecraft, made from light, super-strong materials and as cheap (pound for pound) as wood or hay." This, in turn, will make possible inexpensive housing, consumer goods, spacecraft, and so forth. These can be as inexpensive as other, more complex products of self-reproducing, solar-powered molecular machines: Crabgrass is harder to synthesize than diamond, unless one has crabgrass seeds to help. With seeds, making crabgrass is no trouble at all; with suitably programmed replicators, making simple things like spacecraft will be equally convenient.

The last projection listed above, "machines able to enter and repair living cells, giving medicine surgical control at the molecular level," is in a special category of difficulty and importance. The essential argument is simple. We observe molecular machines working within cells and able to build anything found in a cell—this is, after all, how cells replicate themselves. We observe that molecular machines can enter tissues (as white blood cells show), enter cells (as viruses show), and move around within cells (as molecular machines inside cells show). Molecular machines can also recognize other molecules (as antibodies do) and take them apart (as digestive enzymes do). Now combine these abilities—to enter tissues and cells and recognize, tear down, and build molecular structures—with control by nanocomputers, and the result is a package able to enter and repair living cells—almost.

The only substantial reservations about this conclusion involve knowledge and software. Knowledge about cells, and the difference between diseased and healthy cells, is not the problem. Though this will be new scientific knowledge, and hence not predictable in its particulars, acquiring that knowledge is a problem amenable to an engineering solution. In the early 1960s one could project that we would learn the composition of the lunar surface through rocketry; today, one can project that we will learn the particulars of cell structure through nanotechnology (if not sooner, by other means). Knowledge of how to build software able to perform complex cell diagnosis and repair processes, however, is harder to project. This will involve building software systems of greater complexity than those managed in the past, requiring new techniques. Progress in these aspects of computer science has been swift but is hard to project.

Simple cell repair systems are within the range of confident projection today. Repair systems able to tackle more complex problems (such as repairing severe, long-term, whole-body frostbite) seem likely, and can be analyzed in many details today, but discussing them appears to involve an element of speculation regarding future progress in software engineering.

As the last example shows, on the frontier of the domain of exploratory engineering lie problems characterized more by their complexity than by their physical novelty. These are problems whose solutions will demand new design techniques.

Attempts to project new design techniques can run afoul of a problem like that of trying to project future scientific knowledge: New design techniques will often stem from new insights, and if we could say what the insights will be, we would have already had them.

Other attempts pose fewer problems. For example, if faster, cheaper computers are the key to a new design technique, then the possibility of that technique becomes fair game for exploratory engineering. Curiously, the idea of building devices that can think like engineers, but far faster, can be examined in this way. While this capability seems most likely to be achieved in some novel way based on new insights, it *could* be achieved through the use of nanotechnology to study and model, component by component, the functions of the brain. Then, without necessarily *understanding* how the brain works, one could build a fast, brainlike device. This would not really be artificial intelligence, however; it would merely provide a new physical embodiment for the intricate patterns of naturally evolved intelligence.

Issues of complexity are not central to nanotechnology itself. Assemblers need be no more complex than industrial robots. Nanocomputers need be no more complex than conventional computers. Even replicating assembler systems seem no more complex than modern automated factories. The fundamental capabilities of nanotechnology thus entail no more complexity than we have already mastered. Though nanotechnology will permit engineers to build systems of unprecedented complexity in a tiny volume, it does not *demand* that they do so.

Exploratory engineering has limits, but there is much to be achieved within those limits. Successful exploratory engineering can be of great value from a variety of perspectives. For the technophile, it can reveal directions for research that promise great benefit, increasing the returns on society's investment. For the technophobe, it can reveal some of the dangers for which we must prepare, helping us handle new abilities with greater safety. Success in exploratory engineering, and in heeding its results, may be a matter of life and death. If so, then it seems we should make some effort to get good at it.

The first step is to recognize and criticize it. No field can flourish unless it is recognized as having intellectual standards to uphold; to have a discipline, one must have discipline. Exploratory engineering has too often been seen as not-science and not-(standard) engineering, and hence lumped together with scientific speculation and science fiction. Since speculation and fiction make no pretense of solidity, they are not subject to rigorous criticism to separate the solid from the erroneous. Exploratory engineering is different, and should be criticized on the basis of its aims. Those aims, again, are not to prophesy new scientific knowledge, not to prognosticate the details of the competitive designs of the future, but to make a solid case for the feasibility of certain classes of future technology.

In the absence of criticism, nonsense flourishes. Where nonsense flourishes, sense is obscured. We need to recognize and criticize work in exploratory engineering, in order to make a bit more sense of our future.

COUNTING THE WAYS: THE SCIENTIFIC MEASUREMENT OF LOVE

ROBERT STERNBERG

Each aspect of love can be viewed as generating a different side of a triangle. Each individual in a given loving relationship has his or her own triangle, and these triangles may or may not correspond closely. Moreover, each partner has an ideal triangle, which represents that partner they would like to have, and an action triangle, which represents the extent to which their actions speak for their feelings in each of the three domains of intimacy, passion, and commitment.

SHE: "Do you love me?"
HE: "Of course I do."
SHE: "How much do you love me?"
HE: "Oh, lots and lots."
SHE: "But really, how much?"
HE: "Eight, on a one-to-nine scale."

In a romantic conversation, his last remark might seem somewhat incongruous, but in the scientific study of love, it would not be incongruous at all: The claim of this article is that love, like other psychological constructs, can be studied scientifically, and that, like other psychological constructs, it can also be quantified and measured.

There are good reasons to study love scientifically, despite the resistance psychologists studying love scientifically often encounter from laypersons and scientists alike. A first and not inconsequential reason is simply to show it can be done: Senator Proxmire, in bestowing a Golden Fleece Award upon an internationally famous love researcher, was not alone in his belief that the study of love should be left to poets. Even many psychologists have been skeptical as to whether love can be studied scientifically, and as a result, the field languished for many years. Love is a key aspect of many interpersonal relationships, and it is in some ways rather odd that, for so many years, the study of interpersonal relationships flourished in psychology at the same time that the study of love languished.

A second reason is that with the divorce rate in the United States approaching fifty percent, there is a societal as well as a scientific need to understand what love is, and what leads it either to grow or to die. If we could measure love, then we might be able to ascertain what kinds of feelings and actions lead to its growth or decline. We might also be able to use these measurements to predict which relationships are likely to succeed and which to fail.

Third, if we could measure love in close relationships, we ultimately might even be able to use these measurements to intervene therapeutically and suggest to individuals and couples ways in which they could improve their relationships. Rather than making guesses about which aspects of relationships need improvement, we might be able to identify these aspects scientifically, and then set about correcting them, wherever possible.

We might worry that measuring love would simply tell us what Grandmother already knows—in quantified form with impressive statistics that Grandmother never needed. But the measurement of love has led to a number of scientific observations that are anything but routine. For example, Susan Grajek, a former graduate student at Yale, and I found that, on the average, whereas men love their lovers more than their best friend of the same sex, women love their lover and best friend of the same sex about equally, and actually like their best friend of the same sex somewhat more than their lover.[1] Michael Barnes, a graduate student at Yale, and I found that the best predicter of satisfaction in an intimate heterosexual relationship for a given partner is not how much one loves one's partner, or even how much one's partner loves oneself, but, rather, the difference between how much one perceives one's partner to love oneself and how much one ideally wants to be loved by one's partner.[2] We can feel "starved" by too little love from our partner, but we can also feel "suffocated," in some relationships, by too much of it. In predicting satisfaction, Michael Barnes and I found that there is not a particularly high correspondence between how much one thinks one's partner loves one and how much one's partner actually loves one. Moreover, in predicting satisfaction, once one has entered into the prediction equation how much one thinks one's partner loves one, how much one's partner *actually* loves one makes no difference to one's satisfaction. In short, the findings that emerge from scientific studies of love are by no means routine or obvious and do, indeed, take us beyond Grandmother's knowledge of love and its consequences.

The study of love has by no means been the exclusive province of psychologists. Plato, in the *Symposium*, suggested that people were originally of three kinds—male, female, and androgynous. Androgynous individuals were round, with their backs and sides forming a circle. They had one head with two faces looking in opposite directions, and had four hands and feet, as well as two sexual organs. But the gods came into conflict with humanity, and in their determination to cripple humanity, the gods cut all humanity into two parts. The males became homosexual, the women, lesbian, and the androgynous, heterosexual: Each of the three kinds, to this day, is seeking his or her lost part, seeking to complete himself or herself.

Many philosophers and writers since Plato have had a great deal to say about love, but in psychology, the origins of theorizing about love, as about so many other things, date most clearly to Sigmund Freud. Freud, like many others, believed that the origins of love are sexual: The infant is narcissistic, loving only himself or herself.[3] Soon, the love of the infant is directed toward the parents, and especially the parent of the opposite sex; but later, because of incest taboos, this love is ultimately directed toward an opposite-sex partner outside the immediate family. For Freud, love is essentially sublimated sexuality—that is, sexuality redirected in a socially appropriate way.[4] Harry Harlow, formerly a psychologist at the University of Wisconsin, viewed love in terms of attachment toward another, and Erich Fromm identified love with feelings of care, responsibility, respect, and knowledge of another.[5] Abraham

Maslow, formerly a psychologist at Brandeis University, distinguished between two kinds of love: deficiency love, which arises out of a person's insecurities and lower-level emotional needs; and being love, which arises out of a person's higher-level emotional needs, and especially the desire for self-actualization and the actualization of another.[6] Maslow's deficiency love is similar to Theodor Reik's conception of love as the search for salvation—finding in another what one cannot find in oneself.[7] Ultimately, this conception probably harks back to Plato's ideas about the search for completion.

The scientific study of love was placed on an entirely new footing through the research of a graduate student in psychology at the University of Michigan, Zick Rubin (now at Brandeis). Rubin believed that love could be quantified and, hence, measured.[8] In a landmark article on "the measurement of romantic love," he proposed two scales, one of which was purported to measure love, and the other of which was purported to measure liking.[9] Subjects were asked to indicate their level of agreement with each of a series of statements, and their levels of agreement were quantified on a 1-to-9 scale. The love scale had items measuring what Rubin believed were three main aspects of love: attachment, caring, and intimacy. Examples of scale items measuring each of these characteristics of love were: "It would be hard for me to get along without ———" (attachment); "I would do almost anything for ———" (caring); and "I feel that I can confide in ——— about virtually everything" (intimacy). Three characteristics of liking were measured by the liking scale—admiration, respect, and perceived similarity. Examples of liking-scale items were "I feel that ——— is unusually well adjusted" (admiration); "I have great confidence in ———'s good judgment" (respect); and "I feel that ——— and I are quite similar to one another" (perceived similarity). The full love and liking scales, containing thirteen items each, can be found in Rubin's *Liking and Loving: An Invitation to Social Psychology*.[10]

Of course, anyone can claim that a proposed scale measures love or liking. For any scale to win acceptance, it has to be shown to be reasonably internally consistent, or reliable, and to have some kind of empirical validity. Rubin, aware of this problem, showed both the reliability and validity of his scales. Not only were the scales internally consistent, but they proved to have a number of interesting correlates in studies of college students. For example, love-scale scores were fairly highly correlated ($r = .59$ for both men and women, on a $0 = $ low to $1 = $ high scale) with partners' estimates of the probability that they would marry, whereas liking scores were only moderately correlated with these estimates ($r = .35$ for men and $.32$ for women). Love scores were also correlated with measured levels of intimate disclosure to one's partner ($r = .46$ for men and $.51$ for women), with liking scores also showing positive but lower correlations ($r = .21$ for men and $.37$ for women). Love scores were also correlated with the amount of gazing into each other's eyes partners did while waiting to participate in the experiment; and for those who believed love to be an important aspect of deciding upon a marital partner, love scores were correlated with the longevity of the intimate relationship. Loving and liking are themselves correlated, although in Rubin's studies, the correlations are only in the middle ranges ($r = .56$ for men and $.36$ for women).

In sum, Rubin's work essentially started a new field—the measurement of love. Investigators took off from Rubin's seminal work in a number of directions, most of which attempted to put the study of love on a more theoretical footing. Rubin's theory, although based to some extent on factor-analytic data, was largely intuitive. Some of the subsequent work has attempted to elaborate on and modify our theoretical understanding of love.

Some investigators have explored ways of measuring particular aspects of love. For example, Elaine Hatfield, a psychologist at the University of Hawaii, has concentrated on the measurement of passionate love, whereas Ellen Berscheid, a psychologist at the University of Minnesota, has concentrated on emotion and intimacy in close relationships.[11] Other investigators have attempted to measure both liking and loving, conceptualizing them in ways somewhat different from Rubin. Keith Davis, a psychologist at the University of South Carolina, for example, has proposed that love is liking plus physical attraction and caring beyond that found in liking.[12] But still other investigators have tried to generate measurements of love based on global theories of the nature of love.

One attempt to place the study of love on a more theoretical footing was made by an investigator whose earlier research had been in a field seemingly as distant from the field of love as could be possible. The distant field was intelligence; the investigator was myself. In an initial article, Susan Grajek and I made what might seem like a strange proposal—that three alternative structural models of intelligence might be carried over to the study of love.[13] These three models are shown in Figure 1.

The first model was based upon the thinking of Charles Spearman, a British psychologist at the turn of the century who had proposed a "two-factor" theory of intelligence, according to which there is a general factor pervading all intellectual performances, as well as a set of less-interesting specific factors, with each of the latter limited to performance on a single task.[14] Similarly, one might conceptualize love in terms of a single general factor, which would be an undifferentiated "glob" of highly positive and emotion-charged affect that is essentially nondecomposable. To experience love would be to experience this glob of highly positive affect.

The second model was based upon the work of Godfrey Thomson, a British psychologist, who had proposed that the mind possesses an enormous number of bonds, including reflexes, habits, and learned associations.[15] Intellectual performance on any one task would activate a large number of these bonds. Related tasks, such as those used in intelligence tests, would sample overlapping subsets of bonds.

Three Alternative Models of Love

"Spearmanian" Model

"Thomsonian" Model

"Thurstonian" Model

Figure 1

A factor analysis of a set of tests might therefore give the appearance of a general factor, when, in fact, what is common to the tests is a multitude of bonds. In terms of a structural model of love, one might conceptualize love in terms of a set of affects, cognitions, and motivations that, when sampled together, yield the composite emotion that we label love. In this view, though, the composite is not an undifferentiated unity; rather, it can be decomposed into a large number of underlying bonds that tend to co-occur in certain close relationships and that in combination result in the global feeling that we view as love.

The third model was based upon the work of Louis Thurstone, a psychologist of the early 1900s at the University of Chicago who had proposed a theory of intelligence comprising seven primary and equally important factors, such as verbal comprehension, memory, and inductive reasoning.[16] The underlying idea was that intelligence is composed of a relatively small set of correlated primary mental abilities. Applying this notion to love, one would emerge with a theory viewing love in terms of a small, consistent set of emotions, cognitions, and motivations that are of approximately equal importance and salience in the overall feeling we describe as love. Love is not one main thing, whether decomposable (Thomsonian model) or not (Spearmanian model). Rather, it is a set of primary structures that are best understood separately rather than as an integrated whole.

Susan Grajek and I administered the Rubin Love and Liking Scales as well as using an instrument based on the Levinger, Rands, and Talaber Interpersonal Involvement Scale. Our subjects were eighty-five adults from the greater New Haven area who had answered a newspaper advertisement.[17] All were primarily heterosexual, eighteen years of age or older, and had been involved in at least one intimate relationship. They filled in the Rubin and Levinger *et al.* scales not only for their lover, but for their mother, father, sibling closest in age, closest same-sex friend, and oldest child. (Data about children were discarded because the number of subjects having children was not large enough for adequate statistical analysis.) Two main statistical techniques were then applied to the data: factor analysis, which seeks to discover the latent structure underlying a data set in terms of continuous dimensions; and cluster analysis, which seeks to discover latent structure in terms of discrete groupings, or clusters.

The factor-analytic results for all of the interpersonal relationships indicated a strong general factor. The general factor was labeled "interpersonal communication, sharing, and support," based upon items from the Rubin and Levinger *et al.* scales that showed particularly high correlations with the factor. The emergence of this general factor supported the models of Spearman and Thomson, but not of

Thurstone. In order to distinguish between the former two models, it was necessary to discover whether the general factor could be broken down. Analysis revealed ten distinct and identifiable clusters, thereby supporting the model of Thomson over that of Spearman. The ten clusters were a desire to promote the welfare of the loved one, experienced happiness with the loved one, a high regard for the loved one, being able to count on the loved one in times of need, a mutual understanding with the loved one, sharing of oneself and one's possessions with the loved one, receipt of emotional support from the loved one, giving of emotional support to the loved one, intimate communication with the loved one, and valuing the loved one in one's life.

As sometimes happens after findings on love are reported in a scholarly scientific journal, the general media picked up on some of our results. The reporters who talked to me all seemed to make the same point: Isn't the view of love that emerged from this study a rather tame one, one that does not seem to take into account the hotter, or more passionate, aspects of love? At first, I argued that these hotter aspects of love are concomitants of love rather than part of the love itself. This line wore rather thin after a while, though, and I began to think about how the Sternberg–Grajek "Thomsonian" model might be elaborated to view love in a broader way. In particular, I became concerned that the Rubin and Levinger *et al.* scales might have sampled only a narrow subset of love as a complete entity, and that the results that had emerged from our study were all thereby conditionalized upon the possibly narrow sampling of aspects of love in the questionnaires.

According to my triangular theory of love, love comprises three components: intimacy, passion, and decision/commitment. Each component manifests a different aspect of love.[18]

Intimacy refers to feelings of closeness, connectedness, and bondedness in loving relationships. It thus includes within its purview those feelings that give rise, essentially, to the experience of warmth in a loving relationship. The ten clusters obtained in my study with Susan Grajek mentioned earlier represent some of the elements of intimacy: desire to promote the welfare of the loved one, being able to count on the loved one in times of need, and mutual understanding with the loved one.

Passion refers to the drives that lead to romance, physical attraction, sexual consummation, and related phenomena in loving relationships. The passion component includes within its purview those sources of motivational and other forms of arousal that lead to the experience of passion in a loving relationship. It includes what Elaine Hatfield and William Walster refer to as "a state of intense longing *for union* with the other."[19] In a loving relationship, sexual needs may well predominate in this experience. However, other needs—such as those for self-esteem, nurturance, affiliation, dominance, and submission—may also contribute to the experiencing of passion.

Decision/commitment refers, in the short term, to the decision that one loves a certain other, and in the long term, to one's commitment to that love. These two aspects of the decision/commitment component do not necessarily go together, in that one can decide to love someone without being committed to the love in the long term, or one can be committed to a relationship without acknowledging that one loves the other person in that relationship.

Each aspect of love can be viewed as generating a different side of a triangle. Each individual in a given loving relationship has his or her own triangle, and these triangles may or may not correspond closely. Moreover, each partner also has an ideal triangle, which represents the partner they would like to have, and an action triangle, which represents the extent to which their actions speak for their feelings in each of the three domains of intimacy, passion, and commitment. Geometrically, the size of a triangle represents the amount of love one partner experiences toward the other, and the shape of a triangle represents the balance of the three components of love in the relationship, as shown in Figure 2.

Different Amounts and Balances of Love According to the Triangular Theory of Love

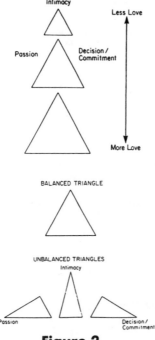

Figure 2

The three components of love generate eight possible subsets when considered in combination. Each of these subsets gives rise to a different kind of love: nonlove, liking, infatuated love, empty love, romantic love, companionate love, fatuous love, and consummate love. The particular combinations of components generating each of these subsets are shown in the following table.

Nonlove refers simply to the absence of all three components of love. Liking results when one feels closeness, bondedness, and warmth toward another without feeling intense passion or the desire for long-term commitment. Infatuated love is essentially passionate "love at first sight"

Taxonomy of Kinds of Love

	Component		
	Intimacy	Passion	Decision/ Commitment
1. Nonlove	−	−	−
2. Liking	+	−	−
3. Infatuated Love	−	+	−
4. Empty Love	−	−	+
5. Romantic Love	+	+	−
6. Companionate Love	+	−	+
7. Fatuous Love	−	+	+
8. Consummate Love	+	+	+

NOTES: These kinds of love represent limiting cases based upon the triangular theory. Most loving relationships will fit between categories, because the various components of love are expressed along continua, not discretely. "+" = component present; "−" = component absent.

and results from high psychophysiological arousal in the absence of intimacy or commitment. Empty love results when one feels committed to a "loving" relationship in the absence of feeling either intimacy or passion. Romantic love results from a combination of intimacy and passion, such that one feels romantic toward another but friendly as well. Companionate love emanates from a combination of intimacy and commitment and tends to characterize long-term relationships in which the passion that was once there has died. Fatuous love, deriving from passion and commitment in the absence of intimacy, results when a couple commit themselves on the basis of attraction without enabling or possibly allowing the development of intimacy. Consummate love results from the combination of intimacy, passion, and commitment and is the love toward which many of us strive in close, heterosexual relationships.

Each of the proposed components of love shows a different time course, with both intimacy and passion exhibiting some susceptibility to habituation over time. In other words, over time, the components of love may decrease unless efforts are made to maintain variety and challenge in a relationship. Much of the success of a relationship can depend upon the couple's success in counteracting habituation.

I performed a validation of my theory of love in which I sought simultaneously to test the theory and a measure of it. The subjects in my study were eighty-four New Haven area adults, equally divided among men and women and ranging in age from nineteen to sixty-two, with a mean age of twenty-eight. All were involved in intimate heterosexual relationships whose duration ranged from about a month to twenty-two years with a mean of four and a half years.

All subjects received a series of questionnaires, including the Sternberg Triangular Love Scale,[20] as well as the Rubin scales, as described earlier. Included among the questionnaires was also a satisfaction measure that contained nine items querying the subjects regarding their satisfaction with their current intimate relationship. On my scale, subjects rated on a 1 (low)-to-9 (high) scale their responses to seventy-two statements, half of which reflected feelings and half of which reflected actions. The action questions were the same as the feelings questions, except that they were preceded by the phrase "My actions reflect . . ."

Twelve of the feelings questions were written to measure intimacy, twelve to measure passion, and twelve to measure decision/commitment. The different kinds of statements were intermixed in the questionnaire, so that subjects could not readily perceive which statements measured what. Of course, subjects were not informed in advance of the nature of the triangular theory or any other theory. Examples of intimacy, passion, and decision/commitment questions, respectively, are: "I strongly desire to promote the well-being of ———"; "Just seeing ——— is exciting for me"; and "I am committed to maintaining my relationship with ———." Half the subjects were instructed to rate all of the statements for six different love relationships (mother, father, sibling closest in age, lover/spouse, best friend of the same sex, and ideal lover/spouse) in terms of how *important* each statement was, in the subjects' minds, to each of the six relationships. The other half of the subjects were instructed to rate the statements on how *characteristic* each was in their own lives for each of the six relationships. Importance is a value judgment, characteristicness a judgment of the actual state of an existing relationship.

The three subscales proved to be internally consistent. The overall scale reliability was in the high .90s (where 0 indicates no reliability and 1 indicates perfect reliability). Feelings and action ratings were very highly correlated (generally in the .90s), indicating that people generally believed that their patterns of actions reflected their feelings. However, the reflection was imperfect, because the means of the action ratings were lower than those of the feelings ratings. In other words, people's actions reflect their feelings, but not the full extent of them. The three subscales were fairly highly intercorrelated with one another, although the extent of the correlations differed across relationships. Overall, the highest correlation for characteristicness ratings was between intimacy and commitment (.81), and the lowest between passion and commitment (.68—where 0 indicates no relationship and 1 indicates a perfect relationship).

Factor analyses were performed on both the characteristicness and importance ratings in order to determine whether the patterns of inter-item correlations accurately reflected the theory underlying the scale. Factor analysis is a statistical technique that identifies underlying sources of variations in a set of data. Three factors emerged from the overall characteristicness ratings. These factors reflected the constructs of decision/commitment, intimacy, and passion. A comparable factor analysis of the overall importance ratings resulted in four factors, which were the same as the factors for the characteristicness ratings except that the decision and commitment subcomponents of the decision/commitment component split off from each other.

Scores from both mine and Rubin's scales were used to predict scores on the satisfaction questionnaire the subjects had received. For my subscales, correlations with the satisfaction questionnaire were .86, .77, and .75 for intimacy, passion, and decision/commitment, respectively, on the 0-to-1 scale. Comparable correlations for the Rubin scales were .36 and .59 for the liking and loving scales, respectively. These correlations indicate that the scale based upon my triangular theory was quite successful in predicting satisfaction with a current intimate relationship, and thus that the scale might be useful for practical as well as research purposes.

Although the results for my scale were quite good, they were by no means perfect. A couple of items just did not work. "I view my commitment to ――― as a matter of principle" proved to be a poor item, showing only trivial correlations with scores on the decision/commitment scale of which it was a part (after total subscale scores were corrected for contribution of that item). Another item, "My relationship with ――― is very 'alive,' " was supposed to measure passion, but proved to correlate more highly with intimacy than with passion scores (again corrected for the contribution of the item to the subscale score).

An alternative approach to a theory of love has been taken by investigators studying styles of loving. John Lee, a sociologist at the University of Toronto, has proposed a set of different "styles" of loving.[21] According to Lee, there are three primary styles of love: eros, the love style characterized by the search for a beloved whose physical presentation of self embodies an image already held in the mind of the lover; ludus, which is Ovid's term for playful or gamelike love; and storage, a style based on slowly developing affection and companionship. There are also three secondary styles: mania, a love style characterized by obsession, jealousy, a great emotional intensity; agape, which is altruistic love in which the lover views it as his or her duty to love without expectation of reciprocation; and pragma, a practical style involving conscious consideration of such characteristics of the loved one as social class, religion, and ethnic group.

These styles are not unrelated to those in my triangular theory. For example, eros might be regarded as fairly close to romantic love, and storage as fairly close to companionate love. But there are also some clear noncorrespondences. Ludus, for example, would not be regarded as a kind of love in my triangular theory, but rather as a style of interrelating that people can use in various kinds of loving relationships.

The first attempt to measure Lee's six love styles was made by Thomas Lasswell and Terry Hatkoff, clinical psychologists, who devised a fifty-item true-false scale to measure the six styles of loving.[22] A more extensive attempt to measure the constructs of the theory and then to test the theory has been made by Clyde Hendrick and Susan Hendrick of Texas Tech University.[23] In the series of two studies, the Hendricks used a forty-two-item questionnaire with seven items measuring each of the styles of love on two large samples. Styles of loving were shown to be related to various demographic and gender-related variables. For example, males were significantly more ludic than females, and Orientals were less erotic in orientation than were blacks or Hispanics.

A quite different approach to styles of loving has been taken by Philip Shaver, currently at the State University of New York at Buffalo, and his colleagues.[24] These investigators have followed John Bowlby, a British scholar, in suggesting that styles of romantic love seem to correspond to styles of infants' attachment to their mothers.[25] Shaver and his colleagues have used Mary Ainsworth's attachment theory to elaborate upon this notion.[26]

According to these investigators, romantic lovers tend to have one of three different styles in their relationships. Their style is a stable characteristic and derives in part from the kind of attachment they had to their mother when they were young. Secure lovers find it relatively easy to get close to others. They also find they can be comfortable in depending on others, and in having others depend on them. They do not worry about being abandoned or about someone getting too close to them. Avoidant lovers are uncomfortable being close to others. They find it difficult to trust others completely and difficult to allow themselves to depend on others. They get nervous when anyone gets too close, and often they find that their partners in love want to become more intimate than they find comfortable. Anxious-ambivalent lovers find that others are reluctant to get as close as they would like. They often worry that their partners do not really love them or won't want to stay with them. They want to merge completely with another person, and this desire sometimes scares others away.

In their research, Shaver and his colleagues found that about 53 percent of their subjects were secure, 26 percent avoidant, and 20 percent anxious-ambivalent, percentages that correspond roughly to percentages of the three kinds of attachment relations in infants. Shaver and Cindy Hazan, of the University of Denver, have developed a scale for measuring tendencies toward each of the three kinds of love, and their results are consistent with the notion that people tend toward one or another of the attachment styles. Shaver's work is complementary to that of theorists such as myself and Lee: Different styles of attachment could lead to different preferred shapes of triangles for people or, in Lee's theory, to different styles of loving.

Since the 1970s, rapid progress has been made in the conceptualization and operationalization of love. Rubin's seminal work showed that it is possible to theorize about love in a way that is empirically testable, and subsequent developments have refined and expanded our notions both about love and how it can be measured. Although thinking about love goes back a long, long way, the scientific study of love is, by almost any standard, still in its infancy. Perhaps the greatest revelation of this work is not that any single theory or measure is clearly preferable—the field is too young for this kind of conclusion—but that love can be studied scientifically in the first place.[27] What had seemed to be as elusive and as ineffable as any psychological construct has proven itself tractable in terms of the same kinds of scientific methods used in other domains of psychology. Love may or may not conquer all, but it now appears that the study of love can be conquered by the theories and methods of science.

Currently, my graduate student Michael Barnes and I are pursuing an approach to the study of love that is quite different from the approaches described earlier. This approach concentrates on people's conceptions of love—what they think it is. We believe this direction to be a promising one, because what a person believes love to be will determine, in large part, how he or she relates to another in a loving relationship. We have found, for example, that people distinguish among three levels of intimacy—what is good for relationships in general, what is good for them individually, and what is good for them in a particular relationship with another. By studying both scientific and popular conceptions of love, it is possible to achieve a kind of balance in one's thinking about love that I believe could not be achieved by considering one kind of information alone.

NOTES

1 Robert J. Sternberg and Susan Grajek, "The Nature of Love," *Journal of Personality and Social Psychology*, 1984, vol. 47, pp. 312–29.

2 Robert J. Sternberg and Michael Barnes, "Real and Ideal Others in Romantic Relationships: Is Four a Crowd?" *Journal of Personality and Social Psychology*, 1985, vol. 49, pp. 1589–96.

3 Sigmund Freud, *Three Contributions to the Theory of Sex* (New York: Dutton, 1905/1962).

4 Sigmund Freud, "Certain Neurotic Mechanisms in Jealousy, Paranoia, and Homosexuality." In *Collected Papers* (London: Hogarth, 1922/1955), vol. 2, pp. 235, 240, 323.

5 H. H. Harlow, "The Nature of Love," *American Psychologist*, 1958, vol. 13, pp. 673–85.

E. Fromm, *The Art of Loving* (New York: Harper, 1956).

6 A. H. Maslow, *Toward a Psychology of Being* (Princeton, NJ: Van Nostrand, 1962).

7 T. Reik, *A Psychologist Looks at Love* (New York: Farrar & Rinehart, 1944).

8 Zick Rubin, "Lovers and Other Strangers: The Development of Intimacy in Encounters and Relationships," *American Scientist*, 1974, vol. 62, pp. 182–90.

9 Zick Rubin, "Measurement of Romantic Love," *Journal of Personality and Social Psychology*, 1970, vol. 16, pp. 265–73.

10 Zick Rubin, *Liking and Loving: An Invitation to Social Psychology* (New York: Holt, Rinehart & Winston, 1973).

11 Ellen Berscheid, "Emotion," in H. H. Kelley, E. Berscheid, A. Christensen, J. H. Harvey, T. L. Huston, G. Levinger, E. McClintock, L. A. Peplau, and D. R. Peterson, eds., *Close Relationships* (New York: Freeman, 1983), pp. 110–68.

Elaine Hatfield, "Passionate and Companionate Love," in R. J. Sternberg and M. Barnes, eds., *Psychology of Love* (New Haven: Yale University Press, 1988), pp. 191–217.

Elaine Hatfield and G. W. Walster, *A New Look at Love* (Reading, MA: Addison-Weasley, 1981).

[12] Keith Davis, "Near and Dear: Friendship and Love Compared," *Psychology Today*, February 1985, vol. 19, pp. 22–30.

[13] Robert J. Sternberg and Susan Grajek, "The Nature of Love," *Journal of Personality and Social Psychology*, 1984, vol. 47, pp. 312–29.

[14] C. Spearman, *The Abilities of Man* (New York: Macmillan, 1927).

[15] G. H. Thomson, *The Factorial Analysis of Human Ability* (London: University of London Press, 1939).

[16] L. L. Thurstone, *Primary Mental Abilities* (Chicago: University of Chicago Press, 1938).

[17] Robert J. Sternberg and Susan Grajek, "The Nature of Love," *Journal of Personality and Social Psychology*, 1984, vol. 47, pp. 312–29.

Zick Rubin, *Liking and Loving: An Invitation to Social Psychology* (New York: Holt, Rinehart & Winston, 1973).

George Levinger, M. Rands, and R. Talaber, *The Assessment of Involvement and Rewardingness in Close and Casual Pair Relationships*, National Science Foundation Technical Report DK (Amherst, MA: University of Massachusetts, 1977).

[18] Robert J. Sternberg, "A Triangular Theory of Love," *Psychological Review*, 1986, vol. 93, pp. 119–35.

[19] Elaine Hatfield and G. W. Walster, *A New Look at Love* (Reading, MA: Addison-Wesley, 1981).

[20] Robert J. Sternberg, *Construct Validation of a Triangular Theory of Love* (Manuscript submitted for publication, 1987).

[21] John A. Lee, *The Colors of Love: An Exploration of the Ways of Loving* (Don Mills, Ontario: New Press, 1973).

[22] T. E. Lasswell and M. E. Lasswell, "I Love You but I'm Not in Love with You," *Journal of Marriage and Family Counseling*, 1976, vol. 38, pp. 211–24.

[23] Clyde Hendrick and Susan Hendrick, "A Theory and Method of Love," *Journal of Personality and Social Psychology*, 1986, vol. 50, pp. 392–402.

[24] Philip Shaver and Cindy Hazen, "Romantic Love Conceptualized as an Attachment Process" (paper presented at the International Academy of Sex Researchers, Seattle, September, 1985).

Philip Shaver, Cindy Hazan, and Donna Bradshaw, "Love as Attachment: The Integration of Three Behavioral Systems," in R. J. Sternberg and M. Barnes, eds., *Psychology of Love*. pp. 68–99. (New Haven: Yale University Press, 1988)

[25] J. Bowlby, *Attachment and Loss—vol. 1, Attachment* (New York: Basic Books, 1969).

[26] M. D. S. Ainsworth, "The Development of Infant–Mother Attachment," in B. M. Caldwell and H. N. Ricciuti, eds., *Review of Child Development Research* (Chicago: University of Chicago Press, 1973), vol. 3, pp. 1–94.

[27] R. J. Sternberg, *The Triangle of Love: Intimacy, Passion, Commitment* (New York: Basic Books, 1988).

PSYCHOTHERAPY SYSTEMS AND SCIENCE

ROBERT LANGS, M.D.

I mean something different by the term unconscious. I don't understand the word to designate a repository for emotional blueprints that make of every new situation the same old defensive fortress. I understand the term to designate a process, whereby emotionally charged information is systematically screened out of awareness, essentially for the purpose of survival.

The status of psychotherapy, whatever forms it may take, should be of concern to virtually everyone within its sphere of influence. And few of us today in Western culture operate outside that influence. Psychotherapy encompasses multitudes of practitioners with myriad aims and tactics; it also encompasses research into the means by which we store and process emotionally charged information. In a culture avidly interested in formulae that will ensure both personal and professional fulfillment, every line of research is a potential pop-psych article on achieving self-worth and a satisfying relationship. At stake here are basic insights into the nature of human functioning. Yet psychotherapy often seems to function less as a science of human emotional processing than as a kind of parascience, inferring "laws" from commonsense observations and assumptions, and expressing them by way of metaphors that have no measurable analogues.

It would be nearly impossible to imagine a hydroelectric plant being built and operating before the existence of physics and engineering; yet Freudian psychoanalysis has spawned a vast and complex network of therapeutic systems that stand suspended, as it were, in midair, having no substantial scientific foundation. Even the nineteenth-century ideas that informed Freud's theory functioned as analogies rather than hypotheses proper. One is reminded

I am particularly grateful to Lenore Thomson for her work on this essay.

of the Chinese proverb, "Theory without observation is like a bird without feet." The fundamentals of psychotherapy stand as theoretical postulates, figments of the imagination of formulating psychotherapists rather than outgrowths of solid scientific observation.

Why, then, have we—lay public and mental-health professionals alike—so easily tolerated this anachronism in our midst? Are there ways of conceptualizing the transactions of psychotherapy and the processing of emotionally charged information that can both help us to understand this state of affairs and to move ahead? As physicists and biologists become more concerned with the role of consciousness in their own domain of research and theorizing, what might psychoanalysis contribute that would be useful to them in their work with the complex issues raised by mental phenomena?

These are but a few of the pressing questions that need our attention. I intend here, without extensive attempts at documentation, to develop perspectives that will help to answer these questions as they bear on the state of psychotherapy both as a science and as a treatment technique, and on our understanding of ourselves as interactive human beings.

Rather than begin from the vantage point of the field or process of psychotherapy as such, I would like to focus for the moment on the inner domain that we have called, for the most part, "unconscious." Most forms of psychotherapy are based on the idea that an individual's behavior may be influenced by feelings and reactions that are not immediately accessible to awareness. Those forms of psychotherapy that are closely allied to the basic concepts of classic psychoanalysis understand this to mean that the individual will strive to gratify unconscious instinctual desires, or that the individual will accommodate his or her immediate perceptions to archaic patterns of defensive behavior learned in childhood. I mean something different by the term *unconscious*. I don't understand the word to designate a repository for emotional blueprints that make of every new situation the same old defensive fortress. I understand the term to designate a process, whereby emotionally charged information is systematically screened out of awareness, essentially for the purpose of survival. This screened-out information is subsequently "worked over" outside of awareness, freeing the conscious mind for situations that require immediate and direct action.

All of us have different thresholds for the direct realization of emotional pain. And, of course, beyond our own inclinations, certain traumas cannot be avoided, at least in terms of perceiving the fact of their existence—the so-called acts of God, fire, flood, and social disaster, the death of a loved one. Nonetheless, we are inclined to detach ourselves from even these irrepressible emotional assaults, and to screen out many of the implications and ramifications of this type of terrible experience. We know that these implications and ramifications have registered because of the way in which we also tend to minimize direct communications in response to such incidents, resorting instead to communications that are indirect; that is, instead of talking about the charged event that has set us off, we talk about something else, using that secondary topic as a vehicle for the feelings we haven't yet recognized in response to the incident proper.

Thus, for example, a young man who lost his father in an airplane crash spoke for some fifteen minutes in a psychotherapy session of his grief, of the suddenness of the loss, of his anger at his father for needing to travel, and of other additional, direct, undisguised, manifest, and conscious responses to the event. The therapist, himself inclined toward probing experiences of this kind, responded with intense questions that did indeed elicit reactions in the young man not previously disclosed—for example, a small sense of relief over the death of his father, who had been unsympathetic and at times even brutal toward his son. This was a feeling that had occasioned a sense of guilt, which the patient had not previously brought into focus.

The young man was grateful to the therapist for this illumination of his feelings, then went on to speak of an uncle who had been at his father's funeral and barraged his nephew with a series of infuriating questions. It was the young man's opinion that the uncle was enraged by his brother's death because he had relied on him for important business connections, and that he had chosen to take out his fury on the nephew. Besides, the patient said, this uncle was a dishonest businessman; in fact, he wished that his uncle had died instead of his father.

In this instance, we see an individual processing a series of conscious reactions to a sudden and terrible loss. With probing, additional conscious responses are elicited, and they manifest as direct reactions to the trauma. Granted, this kind of direct processing of emotionally charged information is difficult and painful; however, I would contend that its manifestation as direct information is an *a priori* confirmation of its nature as consciously perceived information.

When emotionally charged information cannot be tolerated and processed in awareness, it is screened out and processed unconsciously. When something is processed unconsciously, we are simply unaware of what has been perceived. If these emotionally charged perceptions reach consciousness at all, they do so only indirectly. In the example I just gave, the young man was talking about a painful situation directly, and then he shifted away from the immediate trauma and talked about something else that was related, but less disturbing. Consciously, the patient was no longer thinking about the initial hurt; he was thinking over and working over something else. *Yet, all the while, he was still processing the first trauma, albeit without awareness.* Because unconscious working over is displaced and often disguised or symbolized, we say that the mental processing is silent, and that the communication is indirect or encoded.

The young man in question was actually working over two traumas that were represented by one set of images. This is a process that Freud first recognized as a property of dream imagery; he called it *condensation*. Although the young man consciously shifted topics and began to talk about his uncle, unconsciously he was still talking about his reactions to the sudden death of his father. As the father's brother, the uncle handily lent himself to this displacement of themes, but it is important to understand that the uncle's assaultive behavior was a factor as well. The uncle's behavior provided the young man with a ready vehicle to express the extent to which he had experienced his father's death as a personal attack. The young man also knew that his father had been involved in a number of dishonest business dealings that had jeopardized the entire family. Thus, the patient's painful feelings and thoughts—his sense of rage and indignation and his feeling that his father deserved to die—which could not be expressed or directly experienced after his father's death, found a ready means of displaced or encoded expression in his comments and feelings about his father's brother.

My hypothesis, then, is that emotionally charged situations in everyday life will set off both conscious and unconscious processes and communications. Broadly speaking, one might say that these traumatic experiences are first cousins to Freud's "day residues" in dreams, given the fact that dreams were Freud's particular model of inner mental processing and communication. I say "first cousins" simply because Freud's idea was that day residues were commandeered by instinctual desires for disguised gratification in dreams. My idea is that emotionally charged situations are stimuli that "trigger" unconscious processing of the perceptions involved. Triggers, then, are traumatic stimuli that contain information that sets off parallel processing and two-level communicative responses.

I should explain here that the conscious mind screens out a surprising amount of information, simply because the situations perceived will not admit of a direct or immediate course of action. Most of the reactions that we express indirectly, once recognized consciously, are ordinary enough; but they are guilt-evoking or reveal emotional ambivalence that is difficult to resolve. As human beings, we are exquisitely sensitive to ambiguity and feelings of guilt and rejection; a particular thought or feeling that seems not especially terrible to an outside observer can be unconsciously experienced as shattering and intolerable by the person involved. It would be difficult to overestimate the enormous vulnerability we feel at times of emotional stress. And once we have unconsciously elected to divert a particular set of perceptions and reactions to unconscious processing, we will do virtually anything we can to keep the information unconscious. In fact, as already noted, direct access to this information is possible only by recognizing that some other direct expression has been serving indirectly as its vehicle. That is, we need to decode unconscious messages before we can understand them consciously.

Again, Freud discussed this type of decoding procedure as early as 1900 in *The Interpretation of Dreams*; but I would maintain that encoded communication exists in every human context, not just in dreams. We are constantly using displaced images to work over painful trigger situations indirectly. What we can tolerate knowing, we allow immediately out into the open; but what we feel we cannot tolerate knowing, we keep buried at all costs. This becomes particularly relevant in the psychotherapeutic process, where the intimacy of relationship and the yearning expectations of the patient for acceptance and a sense of well-being make for a highly charged atmosphere. But without a sense of how unconscious processing works, this particular level of experience goes unrecognized. The psychotherapeutic process, ironically, can function as a defense against the unconscious material it claims to unearth and interpret.

This point can be brought home clearly by returning to the example of the young man who lost his father. I said this patient was working over two unconscious traumas by way of one set of conscious images. We saw how the first trigger for his associations to his uncle was his perception of his father's death as a personal attack and his sense that his father actually deserved to die. The second trigger for his associations to the uncle was more immediate—his experience of the therapist's interventions. As described, the therapist had decided to ask the patient a series of probing questions. The patient accepted these questions, responded to them directly, and was grateful for the insight they afforded him. This was the young man's conscious perception of and response to the situation. But the patient also had an unconscious view of the therapist's probing style of operation. The young man's feelings about his uncle's behavior at the funeral served as a vehicle for that unconscious view as well as for his unconscious view of his father's death.

Note, again, that the unconscious view of the therapist, which was displaced onto the story about the uncle, is not an old tape loop out of childhood that has encouraged the patient to distort the therapist's behavior. Neither animals nor human beings distort at the level of initial perception; indeed, perception, conscious and unconscious, is essential to survival. The story of the uncle reflects a valid displaced perception of the ramifications of the information contained in the therapist's effort. And clearly, these displaced images are rather different from the young man's conscious view of and response to that effort. The story of the uncle indicates that the therapist's questions were unconsciously perceived as an assaultive barrage. And if we extend the connection of the story about the uncle to the young man's unconscious perceptions of the therapist, we get a view of the therapist as a dishonest person, a destructive person, someone venting his rage on a substitute party, someone who deserves to die. Small wonder, sitting there in the presence of the psychotherapist, that the patient found such emotionally charged perceptions intolerable and unutterable directly—though amply stated in encoded expressions.

We can see, too, that the truths of unconscious perception are intolerable for both patient and therapist. Rare, indeed, is the psychotherapist who can bear the reflection of himself in his or her patient's associations as inadvertently assaultive, dishonest, and even criminal in his or her manner of analytic conduct. And equally rare, though we might expect otherwise, is the patient who can tolerate knowing that he or she has validly perceived the implications of a hurtful or dishonest intervention. In the long run, an exploitative or dishonest therapist can reassure a patient that his or her own defenses and denial will not be subjected to therapeutic scrutiny.

The small vignette that we have been examining has many ramifications. Perhaps most fundamental is the postulate that we process information in two different ways. I think of these as separate systems, and I realize that I am resorting to metaphor in order to describe the processing involved. One system is conscious, and it processes information directly—particularly practical information that issues in direct action. Of course, we are not aware at all times of every piece of information that we process directly. The conscious system encompasses a kind of storage house, a subsystem, for information that was perceived directly but is not currently the focus of our awareness—memories, recent and old impressions, thoughts, feelings, all of which are directly accessible to awareness again. If we want to retrieve a memory—say, the name of that restaurant someone recommended, or the date of someone's birthday—we perform an act of recollection, or we may let our mind wander until the relevant information comes into focus. This sort of direct processing is the hallmark of the conscious system and its component subsystem.

The second system is the deep unconscious system. This system is not equivalent to Freud's original definition of an unconscious domain. Freud believed this domain to be rather like a large garbage bin that functioned as a repository for anything the conscious mind disowned; he assumed that the conscious mind had perceived phenomena that triggered shameful fears and desires and had repressed awareness of those perceptions or disguised them before the perceptions could register. He believed that under the right conditions one could be led to admit those perceptions back into consciousness and deal with their ramifications consciously. My idea is that the deep unconscious system is a parallel system; whatever its storage capacity, it has been designed specifically to process emotionally charged information outside of awareness. This information entirely bypasses the conscious system. The conscious system has no way to retrieve it. And the conscious system has no access to the information unless it is expressed indirectly, by way of something that is already conscious and does not carry the same degree of emotional trauma.

I do not wish to imply that the deep unconscious system is making some kind of decision about which perceptions to divert from conscious awareness. When I say parallel systems, I mean that the two systems work simultaneously, and they are essentially perceiving different things about the same phenomena. The conscious system is perceiving directly accessible and observational phenomena; it is noticing that the traffic light has changed, that a man two cars back is honking his horn. One becomes directly aware of the need to move. The deep unconscious system is perceiving the same set of elements, but it is registering another set of meanings; some of them are only indirectly evident or implied. For example, this second system may register the feeling of humiliation attending one's lack of attention to that traffic situation. It may register the peripheral impression that the man honking the horn resembled a colleague at work. The deep unconscious system also perceives encoded messages from others. For example, the therapist in the vignette is unconsciously perceiving his patient's unconscious criticism of him via the story about the assaultive uncle.

We enter here, to some extent, the familiar world of subliminal perceptions, though with a more elaborate conceptualization. That is, the deep unconscious system is capable of processing information that is unconscious to the sender as well as to the receiver. Indeed, this deep unconscious system receives the very information that the conscious mind prefers to do without, and it works over this information with intelligence, sensitivity, and perceptivity well beyond the capacity of conscious processing. (One of my students calls this capacity the mind's UQ, as opposed to the mind's IQ.) It is actually a distinct disadvantage to be consciously aware of emotionally charged information; the unconscious system is better equipped to deal with it. On the other hand, it is our misfortune that the work of the deep unconscious system is not directly available to the conscious system, where its conclusions could be used as a tool for coping.

As I once explained to a business friend, the situation is something like having a computer that can store and process every conceivable fact known about IBM, but being unable to use that information to predict the company's future because the printout is encoded. It follows from this analogy that we can make use of our unconscious intelligence only by decoding the indirect messages that convey its perceptions and reactions.

I started this discussion with the idea that psychotherapy operates without the support of a scientific foundation. One of the reasons for this state of affairs is the fact that psychotherapy has not been based on verifiable phenomena. Of course, there are many levels of truth in life, but in the realm of emotionally charged information processing, there are only two: conscious and unconscious. And, as our little example suggests, the truth of one system is often diametrically opposed to the truth of the other. Most of our psychotherapies today are based on the truth of the conscious system and its subsystem of directly perceived information.

In general, the conscious system is designed for utility, immediate reactions, matters of survival, self-protection, and, where possible, companionship and perpetuation of the species. The language of desire, which Freud invented in terms of his ideas about instinctual striving for gratification, is well suited to the designs and stratagems of the conscious system, which measures out success in terms of the distance between wanting and having. But there is little room here for the kinds of emotional issues processed by the unconscious system, which do not admit of quick solutions, and whose realizations initially make for anxiety rather than relief.

The problem, of course, is the fact that the information perceived by the deep unconscious system is legitimately unconscious. Thus, we are in the paradoxical position of facing the truth of our emotional lives when we don't know that we are doing so, and avoiding the truth when we give the subject our undivided, conscious attention. Unconscious perceptions are revealed only indirectly; so we must know what has triggered them before we can recognize them in disguise.

Much of psychotherapy is conducted in a way that avoids the indirect language of the deep unconscious system. Take another look at our vignette: A conventional therapist might have recognized the young man's displacement of anger toward his father onto his father's brother; but the recognition of his own contribution to the unconsciously displaced perceptions is unlikely. This is because much of psychotherapy is still operating on the assumption that the therapist can essentially observe the patient empathically and infer from his or her own feelings and associations what the patient must be feeling. This is to ignore one of the most important elements of a modern scientific worldview—the fact that the patient and therapist together create a system that functions *as a system*. The patient/therapist system is surrounded by a psycho-physical boundary created mainly by the physical space and the ground rules of the treatment situation. Both parties are perceiving the situation consciously and unconsciously. Unless both levels of truth are taken into account, the therapy is based on a lie, however empathic the therapist, however well-intentioned the patient, however lasting the relief a lie may admittedly bring.

This is an important issue—the fact that we offer a service to our patients. A patient comes into therapy because he or she is unhappy and wants to feel better. By accepting this patient as a client, we are implying a contract whose ultimate aim is in concert with the patient's. But this service is not the foundation for a scientific pursuit of the truth about emotional functioning in human beings. It can't be.

And, ultimately, a lie cannot be the foundation for psychological growth, even if it does stop the pain of an ill-lived life. Nor can a lie foster an expanding conception of the therapeutic interaction.

There is much to be said on the interplay between psychotherapy, psychoanalysis, and science. Elsewhere, I have written extensively on the proposition that psychoanalysis, defined as the investigation of the processing of emotionally charged information, has not yet become a science because it is mired in an Aristotelian paradigm of "what things are." A Galilean science would ask, "How do things work?" A post-Galilean science would ask, "How do the systems that contain and define things work?"

In order to move—at the very least—from an Aristotelian framework into a Galilean mode of thinking, psychoanalysis requires a systemic and quantitative foundation. As I said earlier in this discussion, psychoanalysis is based instead on common-sense impressions that are enormously vulnerable to self-deception. One of those impressions is the concept of "transference," which holds that distorted archaic needs and the defenses against them that were acquired during childhood will emerge in the therapeutic interaction in relationship with the therapist. In the vignette that we've been discussing, a classically oriented therapist might suggest that the young man had experienced his therapist as assaultive and dishonest because he had reestablished in the analytic situation a pattern of relationship whose source was the archaic parental imago. This suggestion seems to contain both insight and validity, but it is hardly a fact that can be proved; nor can the establishment of transference be measured or predicted, because it is assumed to emanate from the patient's expectations for the relationship.

Transference is actually a proposition masquerading as a fact, and it largely serves to protect a therapist from being charged with ill-considered behaviors and interventions.

Attention to unconscious communication suggests, rather, that patients tend to perceive quite accurately the implications of their therapists' behaviors; they do not distort what they have perceived. They very naturally respond to those perceptions in keeping with their early-life experiences. That is what we all do when we perceive emotionally charged situations. We may cast about in life, looking for hooks on which to hang our unresolved emotional issues, but that's the point: The hook is a real component of the situation. The therapist described in the vignette did barrage his patient with intrusive and assaultive questions, and the patient responded quite validly, albeit unconsciously. And he naturally associated the therapist's methods with the already admitted and recognized brutality of his father.

Unfortunately, psychoanalysis has grown in upon itself and become an esoteric enterprise, isolated from interaction with the scientific community. For this reason, the field has failed to benefit from the remarkable developments in most other sciences, and in many important respects has remained unchanged in its first hundred years of existence.

As is true of all Aristotelian sciences, psychoanalysis does have its scientific researchers. But much of this work is statistical, assuming that the average situation is paradigmatic, whereas a Galilean science does not traffic in situations at all but in the laws that govern situations. Many years ago, a well-known Gestalt psychologist, Kurt Lewin, contrasted the methods of Aristotelian and Galilean thinkers. For an Aristotelian thinker, he said, a ball rolling down an inclined path has an ultimate goal: The approach to that goal can either be facilitated or impeded by some external force. This is how a conventional psychotherapist understands a patient: as a self whose life's plan may be encouraged to unfold or robbed of its impetus. For a Galilean thinker, the rolling ball is not understood to have a "goal" independent of its surroundings or context. Galileo was interested in the course of the ball, given the angle of the inclined plane. In other words, the ball and its surface constitute a single system, a unity.

On the basis of the idea of parallel processing of information, I have developed a research instrument that treats the psychoanalytic dyad as a system. (It is here that certain aspects of Aristotelian teleology reenter the picture.) I am looking at this system as a structural entity that has specific operational laws. In the service of this research project, carried out in collaboration with Lenore Thomson, I am working with a scoring system of sixty items (a sixty-dimensional space). Videotaped psychotherapy sessions are transcribed and then scored for every two lines of recorded dialogue on such items as: Who is talking? For how long? What is the sphere of reference? Is there continuity of theme? Is the material narrative or intellectualization? These items are scored for patient and therapist alike. In this work we are quantifying, among other dimensions, the intensity of the themes, along with their positive and negative valences, and we have just begun to track the interplay of these dimensions from moment to moment, using dynamical, mathematical models as our guide. There are suggestions of characteristic trajectories for each patient-therapist system, a finding all the more striking since it has proven possible to obtain consultation sessions in which a single patient is seen by three different psychotherapists.

The fundamental conception of this work is that the patient and therapist constitute the basic therapeutic system, as influenced by the boundary conditions—for example, in this particular instance, the conditions of the videotaping of the consultation.

In one initial study, using special, educational consultation sessions, the gender material—family interactions, sexuality, concern with sexual identity, and the like—was rated for one particular unmarried female patient who was seen in consultation by each of three male psychotherapists. The first therapist evoked little in the way of gender material from this young woman, and the second responded only to allusions to family interactions. In marked contrast, the third therapist pressured the patient intensely about her sexual feelings and even suggested that there was sexual involvement between the patient and her present treating psychotherapist. When the patient tried to move away from themes of sexuality, the therapist repeatedly brought her back to this particular line of exploration.

An analysis of the complexity of the information being exchanged between this patient and her three consultant therapists also proved feasible. Working closely with a mathematician-physicist, Dr. Paul Rapp, of the Medical College of Pennsylvania, and using a program designed by mathematician Dr. Miguel A. Jimenez-Montano, of the Universidad Veracruzana, Mexico, it proved possible to show that the first therapist in general created an interaction with the patient that was rather simple and uncomplicated, with repetitive rather than distinctive patterns of exchange—a finding that also suggests a low level of meaning in the information the two exchanged. The second interviewer, the one interested in the patient's family, shifted about in these areas of gender and identity and created a pattern of information exchange that was especially rich and complex. This high level of complexity suggests either a relatively chaotic or disordered system or one that is richly and elaborately structured with multiple layers of organized meaning. (Inspection of the consultation hour seemed to favor the latter formulation.) Finally, with the third therapist, the one interested in the patient's sexuality, the exchanges between patient and analyst were intermediately complex, falling between the other two. This level of complexity was largely the result of the patient's attempting for much of the session to change the subject and remain on safer ground.

Although this research is too new to anticipate specific conclusions, it has raised fresh issues with respect to our view of the psychotherapeutic experience. This particular data, and other data on the richness of imagery and themes, suggests that there are two broad ways in which therapists bring relief to their patients. In the first, virtually all levels of information and meaning, conscious and unconscious, are reduced to a minimum. The resulting system is highly predictable, well organized, ordered, and constrained, relatively low in complexity and information content, and relatively low in entropy (*i.e.*, in the degree of disorder or randomness that characterizes this system)—if the concept can be applied there. To the extent that patients obtain relief within such systems, they do so through the avoidance and destruction of emotionally relevant meanings.

In contrast, other therapists produce with their patients systems of great complexity, great richness of information, a sense of disorder and uncertainty, and perhaps a high degree of entropy. Such systems are either enormously chaotic or extremely and richly complex, suggesting two possible avenues of emotional change. In the first instance, order might emerge out of chaos, a possibility that has of late gained much attention. On the other hand, systems rich in conscious and especially unconscious meaning lend themselves readily to interpretations that take unconscious perception and response into account, and they may well produce a cure in this particular way.

I personally believe that psychotherapy is on the brink of a renaissance; but we are still in the dark ages. I hear myself use such words with some discomfort, but I do understand this research as a kind of "quest"—as a search for enlightenment, together with other seriously concerned researchers who worry about the field and its practices and are working to give psychotherapeutic techniques the kind of foundation and basis for growth and evolution that supports every worthy scientific discipline today.

WHAT NARCISSUS SAW: THE OCEANIC "I"/"EYE"

▼

DORION SAGAN

As a virus reproduces itself by infiltrating the cell, so some notions would appear to latch on to the human imagination by being suggestive, self-contradictory, or symbolic. The great ideas leave an "empty space" in which the believer recognizes himself or herself. Fascinated with their own reflection, intrigued with the way a notion speaks directly to their own experience, the converted then proselytize to others on behalf of the idea and its amazing truth. Yet in reality they may be just passing a mirror and saying: "Look."

Sense-knowledge is the way the palm knows the elephant in the total pitch-dark. A palm can't know the whole animal at once. The Ocean has an eye. The foam-bubbles of phenomena see differently. We bump against each other, asleep in the bottom of our bodies' boats. We should try to wake up and look with the clear Eye of the water we float upon.[1]

—Rumi (1207–1273)

Certain ideas take root in the psyches of their believers, coloring all their perceptions. Kierkegaard noticed that the less support an idea has, the more fervently it must be believed in, so that a totally preposterous idea requires absolute unflinching faith. This perverse balance helps account for the wide variety of beliefs—some "self-evident," others dogmatic—to which people attribute certainty. Abstract and profound ideas, like drawings with an unfinished quality, may contain a certain open-endedness that makes them appeal to many different people. As a virus reproduces itself by infiltrating the cell, so some notions would appear to latch on to the human imagination by being suggestive, self-contradictory, or symbolic. The great ideas leave an "empty space" in which the believer recognizes himself or herself. Fascinated with their own reflection, intrigued by the way a notion speaks directly to their own experience, the converted then proselytize to others on behalf of the idea and its amazing truth. Yet in reality they may be just passing a mirror and saying: "Look."

Whether true or not, subscription to certain philosophical notions puts hinges in the mind with which we can swing open the doors of perception. You may believe (with the Buddhist) that time, space, and individuality are illusions (perpetrated by samsara, the merry-go-round of regeneration). You may believe, as Nietzsche did, that everything you do will recur in the future an infinite number of times—or, conversely, like novelist Milan Kundera, that each act in the play of reality comes only once (floating away into "the unbearable lightness of being"). For the Nietzschean, each thought can have an immense significance: It will be repeated throughout eternity. For Nietzsche the thought of the eternal recurrence of the same raises the stakes of being, since any crisis or pain must be dealt with not just here and now, but forever. For the Kunderan, however, events and thoughts may have no special significance, and may appear meaningless, arbitrary, and random, slipping into the future never to return. Since Nietzsche's idea of the eternal recurrence and Kundera's notion of the lightness of being are diametrically opposed, they cannot both be continually entertained. Yet each dramatically colors the perception of the true believer.

Again, if you hold that your life has been preordained by God, or that interacting waves and particles whose antecedents were present at the origin of the universe determine your every thought and action, you may be inclined to act less responsibly—and more nihilistically—than if you believe you have perfect freedom of choice. Nietzsche sought to prove his doctrine of cosmic rerun with reference to thermodynamics. Using the example of a Christian belief in eternal damnation, he indicated that an idea need not be true to exert a tremendous effect. The truth or falsity is not a prerequisite for ideational power, the ability of an idea to transform a consciousness. Whether there is heaven and hell or starry void, free will or predestination, reality recurring forever or never, there will be believers. The human mind abhors uncertainty; in the absence of tutelage, whatever philosophy is current will rush in to fill its vacuum. (The disturbances generated by French philosopher Jacques Derrida's torturous prose result precisely from his "deconstructive" ploy of making scintillating suggestions but anticipating and defusing all would-be conclusions.[2])

People ascribe certainty to their beliefs, reality to their perceptions. From an evolutionary epistemological approach, existence is hindered, discourse impeded by the playful suspension of disbelief. So belief returns. Sheer survival requires that we arrive at and act upon conclusions, no matter how shoddily they are based. Doubt is a stranger to the human heart: To love or live we must believe—in *something*.

Let us explore now the perceptual implications of one powerfully riveting idea—that the Earth is alive. This is one of those doors which, swung open, reveals a changed world. Many in the past have believed that the whole universe is alive. A corollary of this is that the Earth's surface—our planet with its atmosphere, oceans, and lands—forms a giant global organism. We can say that the Earth is alive. But what does that *mean*?

Imagine a child of a present or future culture inculcated from childhood to believe that the planetary surface formed a real extension of his or her person, a child whose language implicitly reinforced this connection to such a point that to him or her it would not even seem to be a connection but rather an *equation*. Such a person would make sense differently. Were nature not a dead mechanism but an immense "exoskeleton" (as the more limited exoskeleton or protective shell of a lobster is not only its house but part of its body), he would be less concerned by what we could not explain. And his perception of the organic would be altered. The arrangement of objects in his home, offhand comments by strangers, walks in the woods, cinema, and vivid dreams would all be linked to the organization of a living organism whose fullness of activity would be beyond his powers of comprehension. His ego no longer encapsulated by skin, he would experience the seas, sands, wind, and soil as numb parts of a body—just as feet and fingers, which, while open to tactile sensation, were yet incapable of speech and sight. The mountains between earth and air would seem to him anatomically placed, as "our" skeleton is between "our" bone marrow and flesh. Putting ourself in his shoes, landscapes from jungles and glaciers to deserts and glens become body parts in a new anatomy, even if, from the limited perspective of that body's minute and only partially sentient parts, the global or geoanatomy remains largely unintelligible. The incomplete sensations of the planetary surface as a live body is no more a metaphor for ignorance than the idea of a skin-encapsulated anatomy. Take an ant crossing a bare human foot. Does it perceive it is touching a life form? With this scale of differences, would it be able to distinguish a toe-nail from a rock or shell? Or, what can a bacterium living in the human gut conclude about the life form that feeds it? Likewise, if we in our daily activities were meandering about upon the surfaces of a giant being, it need not be immediately apparent. Indeed, if one (not a positivist) believes in the necessity of metaphor as a system of explanation to "make known" our ignorance, then the image of a live planetary surface may itself—like Democritus's theory of atoms—be enough to launch an entire new epoch of scientific research and individual action. Though inevitably we would reach the borders upon which such a program would be based, it is possible to imagine language itself embedding the structure of such an altered state of affairs and "making it real." The blue Earth itself would color all our perceptions.

Imagine someone from this culture picnicking. She believes her environment—and not just individual plants, animals, fungi, and microbes—to be part of her self. The grass on which she sits is a patch of tissue lining the inside of the superorganism of which she forms a part. The bark at her back, the dragonflies, birds, clouds, the moist air and ants tickling her foot—all these sensations represent from her point of view not "her," but that which from our point of view we pedantically term "the self-perception at one site of a modulated environment." Like the ants, "she" senses what is beyond "her." When "she" pulls her T-shirt over "her" knees, this is no longer human, but one locus of sensation within the kaleidoscopic entrails of a planet-sized photosynthesizing being.

The physiology is vast. The prostaglandins in people's bodies have many functions, ranging from ensuring the secretion of a protective stomach coating that prevents digestive acids from acting on the walls of the stomach to causing uterine contractions when ejaculated along with sperm in the male semen. So, too—looking at it now from an artificial position outside the physiology—the whole woman, by what she says, makes, and does, performs multiple functions within the global anatomy. A hormone is a biochemical produced in one part of the body that is transported through the circulatory system and causes biological reactions. The pituitary gland, at the base of the human brain, for example, stimulates sex hormones in the ovary and testes, causing pubic hair to grow. As an animal in the Earth breathes, it affects the entire system. Water and atmosphere act as veins conveying matter and information within the geoanatomy. Indeed, the environment is so "metabolic" that minor actions may be amplified until they have major effects, while seemingly major effects may be diminished or negated. The ground is a live repository for metabolisms like the rings of tissue left in the wake of a growing tree. Treelike, the Earth grows, leaving behind it archaeological and paleobiological rings. The "woman" herself is part of a currently active geological stratum; and, far from dead, the air around the body that we, from habit, distinguish as human is fluid and thriving, part of an external circulatory system exploited by life as a whole. To one raised to believe in the textbook notion of a static geology to which biology adapts, the young woman seems to be eating alone, surrounded only by plant life. Yet from "her" perspective the environment around "her" pulses with communicative life; "she" is at a busy intersection in the heart of nature. A part of nature, "she" is not simply "human" but an action within the self-sensing system of a transhuman being. (Indeed, language's personal pronouns falsify; they do not do justice to "her" but make "us" see "her" as a "thing" in a way that is in fact alien to "her." The self-extension to the environment has altered everything.)

Bearing in mind the idiosyncrasies of "her" perception, let us return to more ordinary language on the condition that without quotations "she" and "her" are still recollected as being imprisoned in such jail bar-like quotes by our more fractured word-biased views. With that said, there are things that to her would seem bona fide but remain quite mysterious from our worldview. Being called by a long-lost friend during the very moment she was thinking of him would not necessarily strike her as being what Carl Jung termed "synchronicity"—coincidences with such deep significance that one concludes they are more than mere coincidences. For her, strange coincidences come from her ignorance of the huge physiological system of which she forms a small part. Rain forests and seaside sludge she *sees* as vital organs, as inextricable to the biosphere as a brain or heart is to an animal; humans, however, she may construe as lucky beneficiaries of the establishment of superorganism, fluff like fur or skin that can be sloughed off without incurring major harm to the planetary entity as a whole. Her uncle, a "geophysician," tells her that humanity has caused in the biosphere a physiological disturbance. "The Earth," he says (in so many words), "is oscillating between ice ages and interglacials; it has the global equivalent of malarial chills and fevers. . . . Oil in the ground has become a gas in the atmosphere . . . tall tropical forests are being flattened into cattle . . . our vital organs are plugged with asphalt." Deserts, he tells her, are appearing like blotches on the fair face of nature. "But," he tells his niece, "we don't even know if these 'symptoms' are indicative of transformative growth—in which case we are experiencing normal 'growing pains'—or debilitating disease. Perhaps it is both, as in pregnancy, which, if encountered by a being as minute in relation to a pregnant woman as we are in relation to the Earth, might be misdiagnosed as the most bloated and dangerous of tumors.''

Let us adopt the mask of metaphysical realism for a moment, and peer through the empty spaces, the (w)holes, which are all it has in the way of eyes. The example of the physical appearance of the Earth's altering due to the popularity of an idea—whether true or not—is an indication of what can happen when philosophy meets technology. But all this speaking of the Earth as if it had a "face" and a "fever"—as if it were some sort of comprehensible living entity—begs the question: Is the Earth really alive? And, if it is an "organism," what kind of organism is it? Can it think? Certainly the biosphere cannot be an animal, but only animallike. And if the Earth does not resemble any other organism we know, have we *reason* to call it an organism at all?[3]

Scientific evidence for the idea that the Earth is alive abounds. The scientific formulation of the ancient idea goes by the name of the Gaia hypothesis. The brainchild of British atmospheric scientist James Lovelock, the Gaia hypothesis proposes that the properties of the atmosphere, sediments, and oceans are controlled "by and for" the biota, the sum of living beings. In its most elegant and attackable form, the hypothesis lends credence to the idea that the Earth—the global biota in its terrestrial environment—is a giant organism. Lovelock's Wiltshire neighbor, the novelist William Golding, suggested the name Gaia after the ancient Greek goddess of the Earth. In part because Gaia resonates with a pre-scientific animism and can bring about a radically different way of perceiving reality, it has been the object of academic dismissal, suspicion, and, now, close scientific scrutiny. The British evolutionary biologist Richard Dawkins (a metaphysical realist if ever there was one) rejects Gaia, arguing that since there is no evidence for other planets with which the Earth has competed, natural selection could never have produced a superorganism. Without planetary competition, how could homeostatic or self-regulating properties on a global scale arise? Nevertheless, evidence for organismlike monitoring of the planetary environment does exist. Reactive gases coexist in the atmosphere at levels totally unpredictable from physics and chemistry alone. Marine salinity and alkalinity levels seem actively maintained. Fossil evidence of liquid water and astronomic theory combine to reveal a picture in which the global mean temperature has remained at about 22 degrees Centigrade (room temperature) for the last three billion years: And this constancy has occurred despite an increase in solar luminosity estimated to be about 40 percent. Under the Gaia hypothesis such anomalies are explained because the planetary environment has long ago been brought under control, modulated automatically or autonomically by the global aggregate of life forms chemically altering one another and their habitats. All these anomalies suggest that life keeps planetary house, that the ''inanimate'' parts of the biosphere are in fact detachable parts of the biota's wide and protean body.

It was during the NASA Viking mission to Mars with its quest to find life there that Lovelock first thought to use his telescope ''like a microscope,'' pointing it toward the laboratory of the skies. As a thought experiment he examined the red planet from Earth for signs of life. His discovery of an unremarkable absence of reactive gases produced under the control of life led him to conclude before the spacecraft landed that Mars was uninhabited (which, however, it became as soon as the outer human or Earthly limb of the sensing spacecraft landed).

To answer Dawkins and others who required a mechanism of how a self-regulating biosphere could arise in the absence of other competing biospheres, Lovelock and his associate, Andrew Watson, developed computer models that simulated the ecology of a planet containing only light and dark daisies. These models show that neither populations of planets nor foreknowledge on the part of organisms is necessary to stabilize environmental factors on a global scale. Individual organisms grow selfishly when they can bring their environment under control merely by their activities, their continuous metabolic existence. In the model, Daisy World cools itself off despite the increasing brightness of a nearby sun. The cooling comes naturally as clumps of black and white daisies absorb and reflect heat as they grow within certain temperature levels that would be normal for them in any field.

On Earth, temperature modulation may be accomplished, at least in part, by coccolithophores, a form of marine plankton invisible to the naked eye but shockingly apparent in satellite images of the northeastern Atlantic Ocean. These tiny beings produce carbonate skeletons as well as a gas called dimethyl sulfide. The gas, pungently redolent of the sea itself, reacts with the air to produce sulfate particles that serve as nuclei for the formation of raindrops within marine stratus clouds. The plankton, then, by growing more vigorously in warmer weather, may enhance cloud cover over major sections of the Atlantic Ocean. But the enhanced density of the clouds leads to more reflection of solar radiation back into space so that the same plankton growing in warm weather cool the planet. In these sorts of ways the subvisible but remotely sensible beings may be part of a global system of temperature control similar to the thermoregulation of a mammalian body. Without attributing consciousness or personifying them as minute members of some global board of climate control, the organisms may be seen to act together as part of a system of thermoregulation like the one that in us stabilizes our body temperature at approximately 98.6 degrees Fahrenheit. Locally acting organisms apparently can affect the entire planetary environment in a way that builds up organismlike organization.

In a way it is not so surprising that individual action leads to the appearance or, indeed, the actuality of global controls. Academically, the disinclination to accept the possibility that the Earth regulates itself in the manner of a giant living being seems to have less to do with physical and chemical evidence—which lends itself to such interpretation—than it does with the status of modern evolutionary theory. Darwin considered the individual animal to be the unit of selection, but in the modern synthesis of neo-Darwinian theory, natural selection is seen as operating on genes as much as individuals, and evolution is mathematicized as the change in frequency of genes in populations consisting of individual animals. So, too, altruism in sociobiology is often seen as the tendency of genes to preserve themselves in their own and other gene-made organisms; biologists tend to dismiss the idea that groups above the level of the individual can be selected for, since they are not cohesive enough as units to die out or differentially reproduce. Evolutionary biologists lump arguments for selection of populations of organisms with the archaic oversimplification ''for the good of the species''; they then perfunctorily dismiss such arguments as misguided, if not altogether disproved. Yet, as elegant as the mathematics combining Mendelian genetics and Darwinian theory sometimes may be, sociobiologists have a deep conceptual problem on their hands with their insistence that natural selection never works at a level above genes and/or the individual.

First of all, it is not clear what sociobiologists think an ''individual'' is; they fail to analyze or define this term, assuming that it is self-evident because of a parochial focus on the animal kingdom. The problem is that certain microscopic entities, cells called protists, which in the form of colonies must have given rise to the ancestors of all modern plants, animals, fungi (as well as ''protoctists''—algae, slime molds, protozoans, and the like), did, and still do, assume the form of individuals. How, then, can evolution not work at a level above that of the individual, if the very first animals were themselves multicellular collections—populations—of once-independent heterogeneous cells?

The animal body itself has evolved as a unit from a morass of individuals working simultaneously at different levels of integration. Sociobiologists and neo-Darwinian theorists disdain "group selection" because they don't have strong enough cases for its existence in populations of *animals*. But it may well be that, due to their large size and late appearance on the evolutionary stage, animals have not yet achieved the high level of group consolidation found in microbes. No matter how elegant the mathematics, dismissing "group selection" as an evolutionary mechanism requires dismissal of individual animals also: For the body of the academic itself provides a counterexample to the thesis that natural selection (if it "works" at all) never works on "groups." A person is a composite of cells. Part of the problem here is the restrictive focus on *animal* evolution when animals themselves are the result of multigenome colonial evolution and represent only a special intermediary level of individuality midway between microbes and multianimal communities. But cells, animal species, and the biosphere all evolve concurrently. The first plants and animals began as amorphous groups of cells, later evolving into discretely organized and individuated communities of interacting cells. The evolution of individual cells led to the group of cells we recognize as the animal body. Groups of animals such as insect societies and planetary human culture begin to reach superorganismlike levels of identity and organization. The human body is itself a group that has differentially reproduced compared to other, more loosely connected collections of cells. That cells of human lung tissue can be grown in the laboratory long after the victim from which they were taken has died of cancer shows that the cells in our body are tightly regimented into tissue groups but still retain the tendency for independent propagation.

To be consistent, mainstream biology should explain how something called "natural selection" cannot be "acting" on groups of organisms if the animal "individual" is in a very deep sense also a "group" of organisms, namely cells with their proposed histories and origins. Here we can accept for the sake of argument that several hundred million years ago multicellular assemblages began to evolve into the animal lineage. These groups left more offspring than their free-living unicellular relatives. Their very bodies contained the principle of social altruism, in which some cells specialized and curtailed their "selfish" tendency toward indefinite propagation for the "benefit" of the group to which they belong. Working within the framework of evolutionary theory, we must accept the argument that "group selection" exists in the *origin* of *animals*—therefore, we must (again, within this framework) concede that evolution favors populations of individuals *that act together to re-create individuality at ever higher levels*. This somewhat freaky assertion calls into question the very usefulness of trying to isolate the units of natural selection: *Because of the articulation or community relations of living things, the differential reproduction of units at one level translates into the differential reproduction of units at a higher, more inclusive level.* I anticipate that the mathematical theory of fractals, in which the same features are present in interlocking geometrical figures at various scales of analysis, may be useful in illustrating the principle of emergent identity in the series cell, multicellular organism, superorganismic society. In principle, the "animallike" nature of the Earth can be considered fractally as resulting from the Malthusian dynamics of cells reproducing within a limited space.

If this essay's evolutionary understanding (qualified by placement under the rubric "metaphysical realism") is "right," it may be that the Earth itself represents the most dramatic example of emergent identity. As in Lovelock's Daisy World, the properties of global regulation on Earth result from the metabolic activities of the organisms that comprise our biosphere; on a less inclusive scale, "global" human consciousness and unconscious physiological control mechanisms can be traced to the synergistic effects of billions of former microbes acting locally to comprise the human body and its central nervous system. As an individual, the human body has evolved in isolation from other organisms, whereas the biosphere as a whole does not even have as clear a physical boundary separating it from the abiological cosmic environment, let alone from other organisms. In this sense the biosphere is much less an individual than an animal. But the lack of biospheric individuality may be as artifactual as it is temporary. A superorganism as large as the Earth has not had the chance to evolve distinctive characters in isolation. Moreover, even if it were far more complex (anatomically, physiologically, and "psychologically") than a mammal, we may have difficulty understanding it precisely because of that complexity. In short, because the Earth is so huge, the Gaian organism may not be as apparent—or as consolidated—as a single animal. Over time, however, the Gaian superorganism can be expected to consolidate and become increasingly apparent; it may in the next centuries even become "obvious" to the majority of human beings.

Russel L. Schweickart, a NASA astronaut from 1963 to 1979, is an adviser on "Biosphere II"—a private-capital project to build a multimillion-cubic-foot-biosphere near Tucson, Arizona, for about the price of a modern skyscraper. "The grand concept," he said recently at a meeting of those working on the project, "of birth from planet Earth into the cosmos—when, 1993, 1994, 2010, 2050, whenever—is a calling of the highest order. I want to pay a lot of respect to everyone associated with that grand vision for their courage to move ahead with this in the face of the unknowns which make the lunar landing look like a child's play toy. There were a lot of complexities there, but we were dealing with resistors, transistors, and optical systems which were very well understood. Now we're wrestling with the real question: that natural process of reproduction of this grand organism called Gaia. And that's what all the practice has been about." Many astronauts space-walking or gazing at the Earth report on the tremendous transformative power of the experience. That looking at the Earth from space could so totally change a person's consciousness suggests that the experience has not yet fully registered upon the body politic. People such as Schweickart who have seen the Earth from "outside" in space may be more prepared to accept the unorthodox idea that the biosphere is not only a living entity, but about to reproduce—as many individuals—and, indeed, many cellular groups arranged into individuals—have done "before."[4]

However, at the Cathedral of St. John the Divine in New York City in 1987, the thoughtful plant geneticist Wes Jackson protested the idea of Gaia on the basis of Gaia's "infertility." Jackson claimed there is no way the Earth could be an organism, since all known organisms, from microscopic amoebae to whales, reproduce. Since the Earth has no "kids," it cannot be a real organism. It is only a metaphor, he said—and it may even be a bad one. According to Jackson, we do not even know what the Earth is. ("What is God?" he asked provocatively, suggesting the questions were similar.) In a way I do agree with Jackson. The Earth seems indefatigable in its capacity to make us wonder about its true nature. Yet I had become convinced that the Earth is, in a sense, reproducing before ever hearing Jackson raise this counter-Gaian argument. The reason for my conviction that the biosphere is on the verge of reproduction has to do with two things: 1. the growing number of scientists and engineers involved in designing, for a variety of reasons, closed or self-sufficient ecosystems in which people or aggregates of life can live; and 2. my assumption that humanity is not special but part of nature. For, if we are part of the Earth, so is our technology, and it is through technology that controlled environments bearing plants, human beings, animals, and microbes will soon be built in preparation for space travel and colonization. In space these dwellings will have to be sealed in glass and metal or other materials so that life will be protected inside them. Such material isolation gives the recycling systems discrete physical boundaries—one of the best indications of true biological "individuality." Thus, the bordered living assemblages necessary for long-term space travel and planetary settlement by their very nature bear a resemblance to biological individuals at a new, higher scale of analysis. They look startlingly like tiny immature "earths"—the biospheric offspring Jackson claims must exist for the Earth to be a true organism.

We can trace a progression in size in these man-made containers of recycling life. Claire Folsome of the University of Hawaii has kept communities of bacteria enclosed in glass and they have remained healthy and productive since 1967. There is no reason to think they may not be immortal despite being materially isolated from the global ecosystem. Similarly, Joseph Hansen of NASA has developed a series of experimental desktop biospheres consisting of several shrimp, algae, and other organisms in sealed orbs half filled with marine water. These last for years, and in some crystal balls the hardy animals have even reproduced. On a still larger scale, private and governmental space administrations in the Soviet Union, the United States, Japan, and other countries are developing the art of creating materially closed perpetually recycling ecosystems. Crucial not only to space travel and colonization, these miniaturized ecosystems could also protect endangered species, maintaining air, water, and food supplies, and allow, in the long term, the possibility of social, cultural, and biological quasi-independence on the ever more crowded and homogenized Earth. If successful, controlled ecosystems will carry a powerful educational message about the need for cooperation of people with one another as well as with the other species that support the global habitat. And, if perpetually recycling ecosystems can be erected and maintained, a whole new scientific discipline may arise from the possibility, for the first time ever, of comparing "parent" and "offspring" biospheres. Former astronaut and physicist Joseph Allen points out that the quantum mechanical revolution that so marks modern physics derives from the comparison by Niels Bohr of helium and hydrogen nuclei: Having more than a single biosphere to observe may likewise revolutionize biology. Communication established between two semiautonomous biospheres may resemble in emotional impact the relationship of a mother or father to a daughter or son. Yet the "children" will teach: The safe modeling of potential ecological disasters within a new biosphere may provide dramatic warnings and even perhaps usable information on how to ward off the environmental catastrophes—from acid rain to pesticide contamination of foods—that potentially await us. New biospheres thus may serve as living whole-Earth laboratories or "control worlds," inaugurating differential reproduction on the largest scale yet.

The importance of the development within the biosphere of such enclosed ecosystems cannot be overestimated. Whether or not individual, national, or private venture-capital models succeed or fail is irrelevant. What we see, rather, is the *tendency* of the Earth (or Gaia, or the biosphere) to re-create herself in miniature. Since we, from an evolutionary perspective, are natural and not supernatural creatures, the Earth is, through the high-tech expedient of modern world civilization, re-creating versions of the global ecosystem on a smaller scale. To some the view of an Earth biospherically splintered into semiautonomous ecosystems would be a technocratic blunder equivalent to the formation of a planetary Disneyland. But even if the Earth is saved as a single biosphere, such materially closed ecosystem technology will be necessary for extended human voyages into space or the settlement of off-world sites for emigration or long-term exploration. Thus, we do seem to be caught in precisely that historical moment when the Earth is begetting its first, tentative batch of offspring. That humankind is currently the only tenable midwife for Gaian reproductive expansion is a gauge of our possible evolutionary longevity and importance—provided that the violently phallic technology that promises to carry life starward does not destroy its makers first.

The "Gaia hypothesis" is at once revolutionary science and an ancient worldview, with the power to spur not only scientific research but religious debate. If we take it to its logical extremes, it says not only that the Earth is alive but that it is on the verge of producing offspring. From a strict neo-Darwinian perspective this may be a mystery, for how can a giant organism suddenly appear *ex nihilo* and then just start reproducing? Yet, from a broader philosophical perspective, the reproduction of the biosphere makes perfect sense. We are animals whose reproduction is an elaboration of the reproductive efforts of cells: The organismic and reproductive antics of the Earth *have not* appeared in an evolutionary vacuum. Gaia's weak, immature attempts at "seed" formation and reproduction result from the sheer numbers of organisms reproducing at the Earth's surface. What before occurred in the living microcosm of cells is now transpiring in the larger world of animal communities. The Malthusian tendency to increase exponentially in a limited space beyond the resource base apparently may account for more than just the evolution of new species: It leads also to the appearance of individuality at ever greater levels and scales of analysis.

This essay broaches what might be termed a "Nietzschean ecology." That is, it attempts to hint at an art of biology whose unveiling may be as important as biology itself, at least as regards biological understanding as it applies to the "individual" in his/her/its restless search for meaning. (Academicians, guard your territory!) The appearance of closed "offspring" biospheres from the original open biosphere repeats or continues the process by which "individual" plants, fungi, and animals appeared from communities of microbes. As the folk saying goes, *plus ça change, plus c'est la même chose:* The more things change, the more they stay the same. As Nietzsche scrawled in one of his notebooks: "Everything becomes and recurs—forever!"

As we have seen, even a false idea may color our views of the world, and where there is a chance of changing the world, there is the chance of bettering it. Gaia is such an idea, yet one with the added punch that it may be proved true. (Oscar Wilde observed that "Even true things may be proved.") It was interesting to watch the debate develop in March 1988 as the Geophysical Union met in San Diego to "test" for the first time among polite scientific society the general validity of Lovelock's hypothesis. In fact, as everyone saw in the epistemology session (and *any* sort of philosophical discussions is rare at scientific meetings these days), it was fairly easy to show that Gaia is not, strictly speaking, testable. Whether one took him to be a very naïve epistemologist or an extremely sophisticated sophist, James W. Kirchner was correct when he compared the postulate that the Earth is alive to Hamlet's theory that "all the world is a stage." There is no way of proving or disproving such general notions. Kirchner pointed out that Gaia is not a valid hypothesis because it does not say something we can verify or falsify, something such as (Kirchner's example): "There are footlights at the edge of the world." In fact, Gaia is not a hypothesis. It is, like evolution, a metaphysical research program. The idea that the Earth is alive is extremely fruitful, able to suggest many scientific models and lines of inquiry. Yet ultimately it is unprovable, a matter, at bottom, of faith. It is, after all, a worldview. What positivists miss in their attack on Gaia is that they are also up to their necks in metaphor and metaphysics. There is no avoiding metaphor and metaphysics. When worldviews collide, weak ones are obliterated in the encounter. In my view, what happened at this conference was an encounter of worldviews. But it was no head-on collision. Rather, the old panbiotic or animistic worldview (at the center of the "Gaia hypothesis") sneaked its way into mainstream discussion. In a direct confrontation, the Gaian worldview would have been eaten alive by the prevailing worldview (atomistic science and its Platonic "laws" as absolute reality). But by disguising itself as a testable *hypothesis,* Gaia was smuggled into a prestigious scientific discussion. We would never expect the discussants at a serious scientific conference to bring up as the main question their own view of reality. But this is, in effect, what happened. Like the Trojan horse, the Gaian *worldview* sneaked past the well-armed guards of metaphysical realism (''science'') by disguising itself as a *hypothesis*. And now the worldview Gaia, having lodged itself inside the worldview metaphysical realism, is impossible to extract without damage to both. Our entire conception of life and its environment is being called into question. What is life? Technology? The environment?

Perhaps another Greek myth, because it has not strayed onto the dangerous battlefield of truth, better sums up the present philosophical situation: *Once Narcissus stood and eyed the still waves that reflected his own image. He had never seen himself before. He became infatuated. And now we gaze in the looking glass of satellite imaging technology. Again we see the water. Again . . . but what is ''ourselves''? And who—or what—is this body?*

NOTES

¹ The quotation is from *We Are Three, New Rumi Translations,* by Coleman Barks, Maypop Books, Athens, Georgia. Jalal ad-Din ar-Rumi Rumi (1207–1273) was a Sufi love mystic who wildly spun around as he delivered his musical verses, which were transcribed by assistants. He was the first ''Whirling Dervish,'' and it is claimed that his poetry read aloud in the Persian original is so musical it sends listeners into a trance by its aural quality alone.

² The technique of leading people in certain directions and then ''pulling the rug out from under them'' resembles the method of the sleight-of-hand artist. Both the deconstructionist and the magician present signs that are typically organized or mentally ordered into a narrative of events. A difference is that, whereas the exponent of legerdemain presents approximately the minimal number of sensory stimuli to arrive prematurely and mistakenly at a certain impression of reality, and this impression is then revealed to be ''wrong'' (that is, clearly only an image), after the performance of the ''trick,'' the deconstructionist uses language as the medium for the presentation of mirages that are more or less continuous; the deconstructionist does not entertain like the magician with a series of

discrete and contained surprises, but reveals rather that the attribution of "finished" images and mirages from unfinished signs and stimuli proceeds unceasingly. The difficulty with deconstructionism is that it shows offstage, whereas traditional magic shows onstage. But this difficulty has to do with the "broadening" of the stage, the spilling over of theater into the realms of everyday life: it cannot be gotten rid of by dismissing as unreadable all deconstructive prose. Clearly the conclusions arrived at through the use of language—and especially of "language with ordinary words"—may be as bogus as the conclusions arrived at through the motions of a sleight-of-hand artist—and especially one manipulating not apparatus onstage (where the theatrical element is expected), but small ordinary objects such as cards and coins in the home space so normally above suspicion.

3 We say all this keeping in mind that our language—and our science—bears within it its own deeply embedded and usually unexamined set of metaphysical assumptions. Derrida has unequivocally shown this. Just as Nietzsche did not need thermodynamics to be affected by the idea of eternal recurrence, one need not justify the culturally marginal notion of a living Earth by reference to or with the sanction of a cultural mainstream, a tradition of knowledge not at home with such ideas. Nonetheless, the possibility of scientific sanction indicates the reality of the approach of this notion into the mainstream.

4 Part of the problem with the whole concept of evolution—and all narrative "explanations"—may be the unexamined reliance upon the unprovable assumption of linear time, a logocentric assumption. The verb tenses of languages perpetuate the assumption of temporality. The relation of language to the bias of linear time is here dubbed "chronic." In fact, the relationship of life forms may be better seen as four- or multidimensional, in which case the evolutionary unfolding in linear time is better seen as only a "slice" through true space-time.

JOHNNY CAN'T READ (AND NEITHER CAN HIS OLD MAN)

ROGER SCHANK

The goal is not to teach reading at all. It is to teach children to be able to gather information and be critical in their understanding of that information. Naturally, books are excellent sources of new information. But in the computer age they are by no means the only source. The goal is thinking, questioning, analysis, and synthesis, not reading.

Should children learn how to read? No, just kidding. Even in the age of the computer, reading is still a valuable skill. Surely reading will be with us forever. Well, that may not be so certain, not because the medium will become unworkable, but because there may not be so many interesting books to read. Best-seller lists full of self-help books, how-to books, sex and diet books, and books of advice from famous comedians make it clear that real reading has been passé for some time. Books that challenge their readers to think about something don't sell a million copies, or even a few thousand. Why this state of affairs? The answer may be complex, striking at the roots of our society in a technological age, but one thing seems possible: People may not know how to read.

Why can't Johnny read? For one thing, no one really ever taught him to. For another, what he was taught as reading so distorted his view of the subject and the possible pleasure he might derive from it that he gave it up as soon as possible.

Part of the problem comes from the fact that understanding is not taught, while reading is. What's the difference? It is kind of difficult to imagine what it would mean to teach reading without teaching understanding. It doesn't even seem possible. And, in fact, it isn't. But this hasn't stopped the schools from trying. Reading instruction in school tends to revolve around the *mechanics* of reading—syllables, prefixes, and so on—while understanding could be taught as well by discussing movies or having conversations. In a movie of moderate depth, following what is going on entails figuring out who is doing what and why. Such details are not always spelled out in a movie since doing so would make the movie tedious. The viewer is assumed to be intelligent enough to fill in the details about motivations himself. He also is expected to make some assumptions about what is going to happen next. A good movie often violates those assumptions.

Part of understanding a movie, then, involves a process of thinking. The more complex the movie, the more thinking is involved. The same is true of reading. Books in which everything is spelled out and all future actions in the book are obvious from the start don't make great literature. Reading, or at least intelligent reading, the kind that involves thinking on behalf of the reader, requires understanding of the most complex sort.

It seems obvious that if the basis of reading is understanding, and understanding and learning to understand is the fun part of what the process of learning to read is about, then teaching reading should mean teaching understanding. And one could teach reading, to children who don't already know the mechanics of reading, by introducing movies into reading classes.

What does it mean for someone to understand? Is it really necessary to teach this? Why isn't decoding the letter combinations into words what reading is all about? To see that it isn't, read the following story:

John went to Lutèce last night. He had the lobster.

Now I am going to give you a reading-comprehension test. Your question is: *What did John eat last night?*

Can you answer it? How do you know that what you answered was correct? The story never says a word about eating. It doesn't mention restaurants, it doesn't mention that John was hungry. Somehow, we just know that the answer to the question I asked is obvious. And we know that, had the story said *He had the car* instead of *He had the lobster,* we would not even for a minute think that he ate his car. How do we do all this?

When we teach Johnny to read, we do not, nor need we, teach him that people eat lobsters but not cars. Nevertheless, this information, and a lot more like it, is an important part of what reading or understanding is about.

We can specify two distinct aspects of the reading process that have consequences for the teaching of reading. The first is the association of a sound with a given set of letters. The teaching of word recognition takes place in the early grades. By the second grade, most children can read simple words in isolation. From that point on, many school systems invest most of their effort in the second aspect of the reading process. It is hard to put a name to this second part; many schools call it ''language'' or ''language arts.'' Lumped together under this rubric are such diverse items as spelling, syllabification, and alphabetization. It is at this point that children, no matter how well (or how poorly) they have done in learning to decode the symbols that represent words on the printed page, begin to get bored with reading. Instead of teaching children to understand better, we teach them to play with language.

What does one do during the reading process? Since reading is, after all, primarily comprehension, the key question to ask is: What is a person doing when he is attempting to ''understand''? A large part of the understanding process is the attempt to make explicit what is implicit in a sentence, or in a situation in general. Language is a means of conveying information. But frequently what is expressed in an actual sentence is only a small part of what the speaker wishes to convey. Often, much of the intended information is implicit. It is the job of our memories to fill in what has been left out.

When we hear someone say that he or she likes a book, it is our memory processes that are responsible for determining that this probably means he or she liked reading the book, as opposed to holding it, for example. When we hear that John likes Mary, we can speculate that he might ask Mary for a date, if other aspects of the situation fit the rest of a pattern that we know about such things. Such additional information comes from our memories and is incorporated into our understanding of what we hear. We learn to make guesses or predictions about what we hear. We learn to make details of what we have been told. In reading, these same *guesses* apply.

This predicted information also tells us what *not* to think, in regard to what we have been told. Notice that the expectation that John will want to read Mary does not come to mind. But what is the actual surface difference between *John likes books* and *John likes Mary*? The difference between them relates to what we know about the world. It is not explained solely by saying that there are two different senses of *like*.

But talking about the different senses of *like* is what teachers like to teach in school. The concepts of synonym, antonym, and such can be taught, and students can be easily tested to see if they learned the material. But what is the relevant material? In this case, it is whatever enhances reading. Here, the fact is, a child already knows about the two senses of *like*. He needn't be taught any of it. Instead of teaching him to read, we are teaching him to take tests that force him to make explicit what he already knows implicitly about his language.

Each word's meaning affects the meaning of the words surrounding it. To decide on the correct choice of a meaning for a word, it is necessary to understand it in terms of the partially composed meaning of the entire sentence. For example, the meaning of *straw* is different in each of the next two sentences, as is the meaning of *plane* in the following two:

Sip your soda with a straw.

Lie down on that straw.

I took the plane to New York.

I used the plane in the garage.

Words have multiple possible meanings. Because of this we can never simply say: "The meaning of this word is such and such." The context that surrounds a word determines its meaning. This is true to such an extent that even in the preceding examples, we can reverse the meanings of the word *plane* simply by supplying a new sentence that provides a different context:

John needs to do some woodworking.
I took the plane to New York.

How did you get to New York?
I used the plane in the garage.

Do we need to teach people how to do this? How did you do it? People don't even see the ambiguities inherent in what they read. Of course, to be an educated person it is nice to know something about how the language one uses every day actually works. But, in order to read, one need know none of it.

To figure out correctly what these sentences mean, one has to have had the experience associated with them. So what if Johnny can make the right sounds when he sees *plane*? The question is: Does he have enough experience to guide him through these situations? If he had had no experience with either *plane,* no sounding out of the words is going to help, except to make him *sound* as if he knows what's going on.

In a sense, then, the reading process relies more heavily on one's memory of what has gone on in the past than it does on the words on the printed page. Consider the sentence: *John needs some aspirin for his cold.* We can read the words easily enough, but not to be found anywhere on the page is the fact that John intends to swallow this aspirin and that he believes aspirin cures colds. To know both of those things one has to know that the action and the belief implicit in that sentence are normal enough and follow from the concept of need in the context of medicine.

Contrast this sentence with *John needs some money for his son.* It is the same sentence, at least grammatically, but John isn't going to swallow anything, and we know nothing about his beliefs about sickness, although we may be able to guess something of his philosophy of child-raising. And what do we teach in school about such things? We teach how to parse the sentence to discover that these sentences have the same structure. A lot of use that will be later on in life. We don't attempt to teach the process of how to draw conclusions about what people believe from observing their actions. That process is what is necessary here in order to understand what the sentence means.

What matters in understanding is *inference-making.* Inference-making is the process of making best guesses about what a speaker must have meant apart from what he said explicitly. So, although the sentence does not say that John intends to put the aspirin in his mouth and swallow it, that is a very good guess (though it may turn out to be wrong). When actions aren't stated, we need to figure them out for ourselves.

When the goals of a character aren't stated, we need to figure them out as well. When we are told that someone wants to do something, we must ask ourselves why if we want to understand what is going on. To convince yourself of this, consider a story like: *John loved Mary. Somebody mugged Mary in the park. When John heard about this he was satisfied.* It is difficult here to explain John's reaction. The only way we can do so is by imagining some of John's and Mary's goals and seeking some explanation of how mugging may have been in concert with some goal of John's. The story is peculiar because the proposition that the mugging could have a good effect is peculiar. Of course, there would have been no problem had *was satisfied* been replaced by *cried.* But in the latter case we would have no conscious remembrance of searching our memories for the coherence of the goals and actions of the characters in the story, because crying is not an unusual response to the situation. But, conscious or not, an important part of the understanding process is the identification of goals, and the recognition that goals are connected to the actions intended to achieve them.

So, what does all this tell us about how to teach children to read? First, we must get rid of the idea that children enter the first grade as empty-headed beings. Of course, no teacher would actually say that he or she believed that, but this does not stop the school system from teaching children to make explicit what they already know quite well. By the age of six, most children speak their language very well. And, although they may be illiterate, they are not ignorant. They possess large vocabularies, know a great deal about the syntactic structures of their language, and have a tremendous amount of information about the world.

One of the very important tasks of the reading instructor is to assess what a child knows so that he can build upon it. Note that here I am referring to a child's knowledge of the outside world rather than his knowledge of either reading or language. Actually, the problem I am referring to can be understood by considering many other tasks that require understanding but have nothing to do with reading. For example, a six-year-old will only understand the barest parts of a movie that is not intended specifically for him because he does not have the requisite knowledge of the world.

Compounding this problem of knowledge assessment for the teacher of reading is the problem of assessing what a child knows of his language. A child who speaks well, for example, will have implicitly learned a great deal about the rules of his language. For example, it may seem quite reasonable to teachers of reading to teach children about words ending in "ly" or "er," but most children in the early grades already use such endings in their speech. Furthermore, they understand words that have such endings. They do not have *explicit* knowledge of the meanings of those endings, they don't know the word *suffix*, and probably never should, but that does not mean they lack that knowledge *implicitly*. That is, the kind of knowledge the child needs to help him read words with those endings is already present. There is no reason to teach a child to have explicit knowledge of what he knows implicitly.

What does an adult know that a child of six does not? On the face of it, this seems like a silly question. An adult has a sophisticated knowledge of the whole world; a child understands only a small part of what is present in his immediate environment. What does an adult know, then, that enables him to read that a six-year-old does not know? Or, to put this a bit differently, what is it that an adult who reads literature knows that one who can only read how-to books doesn't?

Reading means understanding, and understanding involves at least the following processes:

1. making simple inferences
2. establishing causal connections
3. recognizing stereotyped situations
4. predicting and generating plans
5. tracking people's goals
6. recognizing thematic relationships between individuals and society
7. employing beliefs about the world in understanding
8. accessing and utilizing raw facts

These eight kinds of knowledge roughly categorize what an adult knows about the world. A child in the first grade has this knowledge, too, but in a simplified form. Teaching understanding means enhancing this ability to rely upon knowledge of the world to help interpret what is going on.

The eight types of knowledge just listed help a reader to interpret what he or she hears, sees, and reads, which in turn helps him or her determine the import of what has been read. Let's consider the knowledge involved, according to these eight categories, in reading a simple story:

> John hated his boss. He went to the bank and got twenty dollars. He bought a gun. The next day at work he decided to ask his boss for a raise. But John was so upset by his own plan that he told his boss he was sick and went home and cried.

This is a simple story, on the surface. The words are easy and most third-graders would have very little difficulty reading the story out loud. Yet very few of them would feel they had understood it. Beneath the surface of some simple words are some complicated ideas that require an adult's understanding of the world to interpret. Let me illustrate just some of the ways in which each of these eight categories comes into play:

1. Inferences. In order to understand a sentence fully, it is necessary to draw conclusions from that sentence about the things that were not explicitly stated but that nevertheless are true. We must *read between the lines*. People are rarely aware that they are making an inference at any given time. They are much more aware that they have made one when that inference is violated or in error for some reason.

Some inferences necessary for understanding the above story are:

a. After buying the gun, John has the gun—*i.e.*, buying implies having.

b. The gun cost twenty dollars—*i.e.*, buying requires money.

c. John intends to use the gun—*i.e.*, one buys something for its eventual use.

d. John will threaten or possibly shoot someone—*i.e.*, functional objects (e.g., guns) are used for specific purposes.

2. Causal Connections. Adults have an understanding of how one event relates to another. There are many different kinds of causal relations. Adults attempt to determine the causal relationships inherent in what they are trying to understand. (This category and the others described below can all be seen as different varieties of inference.)

One causal relationship in the above story is:

Going to the bank enabled John to get money—i.e., "going" can suggest actions that ordinarily take place at the destination.

3. Stereotyped Situation. People have a great deal of information about stereotyped situations. In this story those that are referred to are banks, stores (the place where John bought the gun), and offices. Understanding this story requires a working knowledge of how the real world functions.

4. Plan Prediction and Generation. To understand this story fully, it is necessary to postulate a set of possible plans under which John is likely to be operating. In order to postulate such plans, however, one has to be able to generate them oneself. The more that John's actions seem to the reader to fit into a coherent plan of action, the more "understandable" the story seems. This plan-creation and understanding ability are at the heart of following a story of this kind. This is precisely where a third-grader will find himself severely handicapped when trying to understand the story. Even the simplest of plans is hard to follow if one has not learned how to follow another person's plan.

5. Goal Tracking. What is John going to do, and why is he doing it? These are the questions that occur as we read this story. However, answering such questions requires knowing about goals such as being well treated, respected, well paid, or whatever complex set of goals are reasonable to postulate in understanding this story.

6. Thematic Relationships. Understanding this story requires a good assessment of how an employee might feel toward a boss, and an interpretation of hatred in this context. A third-grader may know what "hate" means to him, but his definition is likely to be only partially relevant. Another important thematic relationship is the fear of being an outcast, an immoral person, or a criminal, all of which one can imagine to be going through John's mind.

7. Beliefs. We, as readers, believe certain things about what is right and wrong. If John is going to threaten his boss for a raise, or possibly kill him, we view it at least as misguided, and probably terribly wrong. These beliefs about what is a correct course of action in the world are very much a part of how we understand, and thus of how we read.

8. Raw Facts. Banks have money. Bosses give raises. Crying releases tension. Stores sell guns. All these are simple facts about the world, without which it would be hard to understand this story.

We are now ready to return to our three-year-old. What does he know of the world? What, within the range of these eight kinds of knowledge, is available to him to help him understand?

1. Inferences. By age three a child can make some very simple inferences. He knows that if you put something someplace, it will be there; that if you eat, you won't be hungry anymore, and so on. Recall that the ability to make inferences is dependent upon world knowledge in the first place. So, while the basic apparatus is there by age three, the only things that a child of this age can infer are those things about which he already has a good understanding, things within the child's small world.

Teaching a child to read, therefore, means teaching him to figure out what else is true besides what he was told. But whatever one teaches in this regard is likely to be fallacious, at least some of the time. Teaching what is true of the world is a subjective matter at best. Inference of the sort we are talking about is not logical in any sense. These same inference problems exist in watching movies; a story is a story, and understanding a complicated one requires that we infer.

2. Causal Connections. A three-year-old child has a very confused view of what causes what. At age three a child is willing to believe just about anything with respect to causality. Because of this, the child often cannot make the correct causal connections in what he reads.

Can you teach causality? I think so. Further, teaching how to assess a chain of reasoning or a physical chain of events is a very important part of teaching thinking. It is also a part of reading. Authors leave the chains of reasoning to the reader to fill in. The sequence *John hit Mary. She died.* means that she died because of the hit. On the other hand, *John hit Mary. She laughed.* doesn't mean that the hit caused the laugh in the same sense that hitting can cause death. Do children know this? Not so well. And they cannot read without knowing it.

3. Stereotyped Situations. Children do, on the other hand, have very sophisticated ideas about stereotypical action sequences, or *scripts*. There is evidence to suggest that children are forming scripts almost from birth. An example of a script is the restaurant script or the airplane-ride script. These scripts tell us who does what when and what we must do to play our part. Children learn all kinds of scripts, from ones about diaper-changing to their own version of the restaurant script, which misses a great deal of what is really going on in a restaurant but does get them fed. The scripts that they form are discarded or improved as the case warrants, a process that serves as one basis for learning. Thus, by age four a child has very good and detailed knowledge, albeit from his or her own point of view and experiences, of such stereotyped situations as banks, grocery stores, mealtimes, and restaurants.

Consider a conversation between a Parent (P) and a four-year-old (C):

P: Now, I want you to tell me what happens when you go to a restaurant.

C: Okay.

P: What happens in a restaurant? Start at the beginning.

C: You come in and you sit down at the table. And then the waitress comes. And she gives you a menu. And then she takes it back and writes down your order. And then you eat what she gave you. And then you get up from the table. And you pay the money and then you walk out of the store.

4. Plans. A child of three does very little planning that is not extremely simple. Consequently, he cannot track someone else's plans very well. By the age of six, a child's ability to plan for himself is greatly improved, but understanding someone else's plan can still be quite difficult. Consider the following story that was read to the same four-year-old. She was asked questions about the story. Notice her answers indicate a strong reliance on script-based knowledge and a failure to comprehend fully the plans of the characters in the story:

John loved Mary, but she didn't want to marry him. One day, a dragon stole Mary from the castle. John got on top of his horse and killed the dragon. Mary agreed to marry him. They lived happily ever after.

P: Why did John kill the dragon?

C: 'Cause it was mean.

P: What was mean about it?

C: It was hurting him.

P: How did it hurt him?

C: It was probably throwing fire at him.

P: Why did Mary agree to marry John?

C: 'Cause she loved him very much and he wanted very much to marry her.

P: What was going to happen to Mary?

C: If what?

P: When the dragon got her?

C: She would get dead.

P: Why would the dragon do that?

C: 'Cause it wanted to eat her.

P: How come Mary decided to marry John, when she wouldn't in the beginning?

C: That's a hard question.

P: Well, what do you think the answer is?

C: 'Cause then she just didn't want him and then he argued very much and talked to her a lot about marrying her and then she got interested in marrying her . . . I mean him.

The problem of planning is, for children, the single biggest obstacle in reading. It is also a big obstacle in watching a movie and in observing what their parents are doing. Adults follow complex plans and they also learn cues by which to identify one another's plans. Without information about the kinds of plans there are, how can a child understand that when a character in a movie goes to the perfume store and he is in love, it means one thing, but if he is very angry and goes to the liquor store, it means another?

5. Goals. As with plans, a child's goals are so simple that he has almost no ability to understand that someone else might have more complex goals, much less be able to track someone else's goals. This is a very important point in considering what stories are appropriate for children at any given age. If a child cannot understand the goals of the characters, in the deepest sense of understanding, he will not be able to follow the story being read, no matter how simple the vocabulary and syntax of that story.

6. Thematic Relationships. A child understands certain thematic relationships in which he himself is involved. He knows about what mothers and fathers do, for example. But his knowledge of the role of the grocer or the bus driver

is much more limited. He has only the vaguest notions about the aspects of their roles that do not relate directly to him. He may not realize that a doctor gets money for what he does, for example. Other thematic relationships, such as those involving dishonesty or malevolence, will be totally unclear to a three-year-old. Stories that use such relationships will be difficult for a young child to comprehend fully.

7. Beliefs. A child's beliefs are constantly changing. Here again, story understanding must relate to beliefs the child actually holds, if he is to understand a story. Or, he must be taught about the beliefs of others. Understanding how different cultures view the world must be an important part of education. Sometimes such things are taught in school, but usually in a social-studies class. Reading depends upon being able to figure out the beliefs of others. Consider the following story:

> The preparations were made for the tribal puberty rite. Little Nkomo was frightened and he grabbed his mother's hand. The crowd drew back in horror.

A reader doesn't know what rule Nkomo violated, but he can guess. Such guessing is an important part of reading.

8. Raw Facts. The child has quite a few of these. One reason to read is to gather new facts. Without a healthy assortment of facts at one's disposal, it is difficult to understand what is going on.

Of course, in learning to read, the child must first learn to recognize words on the printed page. After that, the fundamentals of comprehending what people are doing and why they are doing it are of more use in learning to read than any of the more traditional things taught in reading instruction. Why aren't such things taught? Why isn't there a course in understanding people? Here again, this is a suggestion that flies in the face of how the school system operates. Schools need facts to teach so that exams can be given. Children need to learn to figure out what is going on in situations they haven't encountered previously. They need to learn to reason in order to read (and in order to do quite a bit else as well).

And what is actually taught when children learn *language arts*? Here is a partial list of the units covered in the third and fourth grades in language arts:

1. the use of dictionaries
2. punctuation
3. prefixes and suffixes
4. compound words
5. reading with expression
6. using an index
7. reading a diagram
8. synonyms and antonyms
9. making an outline
10. spelling
11. syllabification
12. capitalization
13. rules of grammar

Although I make no argument that some of these things should not be taught in the schools, there is a vast difference between teaching them and teaching reading. Units on each of these subjects are interrupted by endless reading-comprehension tests. So, if learning to read isn't one long S.A.T. test for a child, it is an examination on exciting things like the catalog system in the library.

There are two questions worth addressing here:

1. Do these thirteen items have anything to do with reading?
2. Is learning to read adversely affected by coupling ''language arts'' with reading?

None of the thirteen items has anything directly to do with reading. Some of them are clearly new skills (using an index, using a dictionary, making an outline). But these new skills should be dissociated from the teaching of reading. Many people read very well but have little or no familiarity with indexes or outlines. Coupling these skills with the teaching of reading can make reading itself seem dull or, even worse, difficult. Advancing in reading is often tied to advancing through workbooks that drill children in these skills, and the child who reads well can get bored and irritated with "learning to read."

In order to see why the teaching of reading and "language arts" must be separated, we must consider the distinction between recognition memory and recall memory. This distinction is crucial for understanding what we are doing when we teach reading.

People exhibit two distinct memory capabilities. They can recognize an object, and they can recall information when they need it. Some examples of the differences between recognition and recall are:

1. We can recognize somebody we know when we see that individual, but often it is difficult to conjure up the person's image (recall the image) when the person is not present.
2. We can recognize the capital of Norway, say, when we see it in a list of three on a multiple-choice test, but we cannot recall it without those choices before us.
3. We can find our way to a place we have been only once or twice, by recognizing various clues on the way (following our noses). After we turn right at a certain corner, we are sure that that was the right thing to do, but we could never have recalled the name of that street or the identifying landmarks well enough to tell someone else how to get there.
4. We can recognize somebody we know, yet forget his or her name or occupation.

These experiences are common to everyone, because of the "division" in our memories. This division is not a literal one. There are not two different memory boxes that contain the information we need. Rather, we are relying upon two different processes for retrieving information from memory.

To see this, imagine that you are the director of a large museum with five thousand rooms, each containing one hundred art objects. As director, you might have some difficulty specifying exactly where in the museum the "blue-and-white Ming vase with butterflies on it" is located. You might have a good idea about where it would most likely be found, and where to start looking. But 500,000 items are just too many for any person to know offhand the exact location of each. On the other hand, if you were put in the correct room, you would have no trouble identifying it as such without actually having to see the vase.

Searching the human memory in a thorough manner is actually much more difficult than searching a museum. At least in a museum there is a known organization of material. Some people are better organized than others, and they would be better at recall than others. Recognition, on the other hand, is more directly correlated with knowledge. The more one knows, the more one can recognize.

Now let us return to the teaching of reading. How are these two types of memory-retrieval processes related to reading? Spelling is an example of recall memory. When my daughter was five, she hung a sign on her door that read: NOBODE ALOUD. She could read extremely well at five. However, as noted, recognition and recall are very different processes. Reading is a recognition process; spelling, a recall process. To read we must recognize each word. To do this we must rely on our prior knowledge to help us. Having seen a word before, it is easier to recognize it. We do not need to use recall in the process of word recognition. To spell, we must find the correct spelling in memory. Thus, my daughter could write "NOBODE" by sounding out in her mind "nobody" and writing letters for sounds. Naturally she wrote E for the sound that that letter makes. But if she had been asked to read what she wrote, she might have said "no bode," since she well knew the rules for word recognition in the sounding out of new words.

Despite the fact that spelling and reading rely on totally different memory processes, they are often coupled in reading workbooks and school curricula. But the ability to read really does not depend upon the ability to spell. (There are many eminent professors who can hardly spell, but no one doubts their ability to read! In some school systems, such professors would have a difficult time being promoted from the third grade.)

Capitalization and punctuation are two skills, certainly quite valuable ones, that relate to the distinction between recognition and recall. Capitalization and punctuation are taught to children as recall phenomena, even though they by now know how to treat them as recognition phenomena. That is, a child can read a punctuated text—*i.e.*, recognize it—without necessarily being able to punctuate a text. Learning to punctuate correctly is very difficult, even for adults. It should be taught as a subject in school, but, as the inability to punctuate properly does not affect one's reading ability, it should be taught separately from reading. Learning to punctuate is a recall phenomenon. In fact, all writing is a recall phenomenon, so this same argument applies to capitalization. Here again, recall phenomena must be differentiated from reading. Reading is a recognition process.

To deal with the remaining subjects on the preceding list, it will be necessary to discuss the distinction between knowledge of how to do something and knowledge about what one is doing. Perhaps the best way to proceed is by analogy. There are important differences between knowing how to drive a car, knowing how to fix a car, and knowing how to design a car, or, similarly, with understanding what goes on in a football game, being able to play football, and being able to describe the aerodynamics involved when a football is thrown or kicked. These differences carry over directly into language. We can understand and speak a language, we can edit and correct the language of others, and we can help to create a theory of language.

People are taught to understand much the way they are taught to drive a car. They see someone else do it, they themselves practice, and after they get the feel of it, off they go. You never have to know a thing about how your car runs, either in theory or in practice, to drive it competently (even magnificently). The knowledge that a performer has of his performance ability is usually limited to being able to describe crudely what he is doing. He is rarely aware of exactly what he knows; he just knows how. He may even be able to teach the "how" that he knows, because this can be done by imitation and correction. The theory need never be understood, and, indeed, if it is understood, it will usually in no way help the performance. Great musicians do not usually understand air flow, nor do they have well-developed theories of the physics of sound.

With reading it is much the same. Children learn to talk by imitation and correction. To teach reading and writing to a child capable of understanding and talking, it is necessary to give the information pertaining to reading and writing that the child does not as yet have. It follows that to teach writing, one must teach about the formation of letters, capitalization, punctuation, and other writing-specific phenomena.

Children's difficulty in reading often comes from a lack of confidence about guessing what is implicit in what they are reading. Teaching children to rely upon their prior knowledge is the crux of what needs to be taught. On the other hand, we do not want to teach children theories about the formal nature of that knowledge. An excellent example of a problem in this regard involves the teaching of grammar. These days instruction in grammar is usually part of a "language arts" curriculum. In our distinction between "knowing how" and "knowing that," it is clear that every child knows how to form a sentence. The most common definition of grammar states that grammar defines what is in a language. Since every child who speaks English is speaking English sentences, by this definition he can only be speaking grammatical sentences. To put this another way, the child has rules for putting a sentence together that he uses all the time. These rules constitute the "grammar" that he uses. It is obvious that, prior to entering school, most children who speak English have no idea what a noun is. But they do know all the rules that they will ever need for knowing how to manipulate nouns. "Noun" is part of the vocabulary of the language theorist, not the language user.

If grammatical rules in no way affect reading ability, what do they relate to? From a stylistic point of view, they relate to writing, but they do so only at a very advanced stage. Consider the rule "Do not use a preposition to end a sentence." In the first sentence of this paragraph, I violated that rule. English speakers regularly violate it, which could be seen to call into question its validity as a grammatical rule of English. Nevertheless, it is considered poor style to place prepositions at the end of sentences.

Making children aware of such rules is important, if they might need to know them. It is important to learn to write well. But writing well is something that must be learned considerably after one learns to read. Teaching grammatical notions to elementary-school children is simply premature. Furthermore, that kind of teaching may turn children off to school entirely.

With respect to grammar, then, a child who has never heard of nouns and verbs will be in no way handicapped. He will be able to read, and speak, with the best. We do not want to confuse a child who already knows how to use language by teaching him theories of language, which are at this point in a muddle. No theory has been shown to be correct as of this writing. Why teach children aspects of a theory of syntax that have never been proven and are in no way relevant to the development of skills that they will need?

The important point is that we must teach children those things that will help them in reading. Not everything that is currently part of the reading curriculum has relevance in aiding reading. A great many things that are taught are holdovers from outdated conceptions of the three R's. We most certainly do wish to make our children facile with language. But to do this requires that we first ensure that they are good readers. A child need not know the theoretical constructs of language in order to be able to use language effectively. What do we want to teach, then? The major issue is teaching reading comprehension.

Children can sound out or recognize words, many of which they may not really understand at all. They may appear to be reading, if what one counts as reading is the pronunciation of the words on the page. But comprehension is hardly indicated by whether a child can utter a string of words aloud. Try reading a foreign language that uses our alphabet—Italian or Spanish, for example. Can you "read" these languages? Since their pronunciations conform well to the way the languages are written, it is rather easy for an English speaker to become fairly competent in reading aloud. But what does this demonstrate? Certainly the ability bears no relationship at all to comprehension. A beginning reader is not unlike the English speaker who at first sight can read Italian aloud. Since an adult will want to comprehend what he is reading, teaching him to read Italian requires teaching him the meaning of the words, and that is also what the reading-comprehension process requires.

To assess the problem of what to teach in teaching comprehension, we must attempt to determine what is likely to prevent a child from comprehending a given text. Or, to put it more positively, what must a child know, beyond the issue of word recognition, in order to read a story? Let us consider an example and use it as a guide to the problem. The story I have chosen is from an edition of *Treasure Island* that is described as appropriate for children from eight to fourteen years of age. I will take seven passages and attempt to indicate the kind of trouble a child might have in reading those passages, and the source of trouble.

1. Awkward Expressions

I remember . . . when the brown old seaman took up his lodgings at the Admiral Benbow.

One problem children have in reading stories is a lack of familiarity with certain idiomatic usage, or modes of expression. Here the problem is obvious because the expression "took up his lodgings" is an out-of-date phrase. The child may well know, or be able to figure out, what each word is, but he may still be confused.

2. Script Instantiation

. . . lodgings at the Admiral Benbow

Adult readers now realize that the sailor has entered a kind of hotel (or inn, as we are later told). But how do we know that? We know it the same way we know that in "Sam ordered a pizza at Luigi's," "Luigi's" is a restaurant, probably an Italian restaurant.

3. Plan Assessment

"This is a handy cove," the seaman said to my father, "and a well-placed inn. Do you have much company here?"

An adult reader will recognize that the seaman has a plan to stay at the inn if it is quiet and secluded enough. We assume he is hiding, or that perhaps something even more sinister is occurring. We await the reason why. But does a child? A child must be taught to look for the plans of the characters he meets. He must learn to question their motives and see the larger picture. This is a very difficult thing for a child to learn. It involves a very new point of view for him. Young children tend to accept the people they meet at face value. They trust everybody. Moreover, they accept the world as it is. They do not see or look for sinister plans or plots.

To some extent, movies can be an aid here. Children who watch movies will learn something of plot development and sinister plans. But there is a great difference between processing text and processing pictures. In reading, many more inferences must be made about what characters actually have done. In movies, actions are spelled out in detail. Understanding that a character has a plan is facilitated by watching a movie. Inferring the details of his plan is very easy when watching a movie because we just watch the plan develop. We see every detail of a character's actions. In reading a story, we assess the plot, but we also must infer the details. Most plots depict in some way the interaction and blocking of plans and the attempt to achieve goals. Tracking such things in detail is often beyond a child's experience. He must be taught to track plans.

4. Background Knowledge of Characters

> Though his clothes and manners were coarse, he did not seem to be an ordinary seaman. . . .

Would a child recognize an ordinary seaman from an extraordinary one? What comparison is being made here? Without some knowledge of what a seaman does, looks like, wants, and so on, it is difficult to understand this sentence.

Two things are important here. First, a child should be given stories for which he has the relevant background knowledge. Second, a child must be taught to assess the traits of the characters he meets. What kind of person is being talked about?

5. Plot Development

One day he took me aside and promised me money
if I would keep me eye open for a seafaring man with
one leg.

The plot thickens. We know that, but how does a child
assess it? He must understand something of what a plot is,
how stories develop, and so on.

6. World Knowledge

His stories were what frightened people most of all.
Our plain country people were as shocked by his language as they were by the crimes he described. My
father believed that the inn would be ruined by the captain's tyranny; that people would stop coming because
he sent them shivering to their beds.

To understand this passage, one needs to know something of the values and morals of an English town in the
eighteenth century. Further, it is most important to know
about businesses—inns, in particular—and how and why
they run. A basic knowledge of commerce is needed here.
This story can be understood effectively only in the presence of the appropriate background knowledge.

7. Tracking Props and Goals

"He's a bad one, but there's worse behind him.
They're after my sea chest."

This line is the crux of the story so far. It indicates that
there will be a fair amount of plot associated with the sea
chest. Indeed, the content of the sea chest is the crucial
issue in the story. How is the child to know this? How do
we know it? We know it because we know about valuable
objects, greed, likely containers for valuable objects, and

story structure. When we see a particular prop in a story, we expect it to be used in the story. The child must be taught to look out for props and to track the goals associated with those props.

8. Inferences, Beliefs, and Reasoning

When I told my mother all I knew, she agreed we were in a difficult and dangerous position.

Why are they in a difficult position? The story makes it obvious. Our heroes possess objects of value that others know about and will want to steal. But this is not necessarily obvious to a child. A child must be taught to construct chains of reasoning based on beliefs derived from what he has heard so far and from what he knows of life. But what does the child know of life? Some of that kind of knowledge is taught by stories. Much of it must be taught when, or preferably before, a story is encountered. The child must learn to figure out what is going on.

The key point is that a child must have a well-developed sense of the world around him in order to understand stories about the world. This indicates that a great deal of what must be taught to enable reading is not so much language, per se. Rather, it is the acquisition of world knowledge, and the processes that utilize that knowledge, that constitute the key issues in reading comprehension. But how can we teach world knowledge? Should we even try? It is clear that we can enhance the child's ability to use what he already knows to help him read.

Language and knowledge are intricately entwined. There is a tendency when reading is taught to teach language, but without the knowledge part of language. What is considered significant about language and about the teaching of language is the form of language, the grammar and spelling, but not the meaning.

To see how people go about dealing with meanings in

their daily use of language, consider the sentence "John upset Mary." One of the first and most important things to realize is that this sentence is ambiguous. We can think of a number of different meanings:

> John did something to cause Mary to be upset (or anxious).
> John knocked Mary over.
> John, who should have lost his match with Mary, won.

Yet we can rule out certain of them if we hear the sentence in context, preceded by other sentences. Early in our education, we learn that "upset" is a verb. (It is also a noun and an adjective. Since it functions as a verb in our sentence, if we ask the question "What is the action going on in the sentence?" we might expect that the answer should be "upsetting.")

This answer is inadequate if we require that an action be something that an actor do to something else. We can say, "John upset Mary," but we cannot really mean it. That is to say, upsetting is not something one can do to someone. Try to picture John in your mind upsetting Mary. What do you see? Whatever you see for this sense of "upset" is liable to be quite different from what someone else sees. Because the mental pictures one forms upon hearing a sentence are analogous to what one perceives to be the meaning of a sentence, we can say here that "John upset Mary" has a very imprecise meaning. The meaning of "upset" is quite unclear for the first sense of the word given above. The action denoted by "upset" is unknown. However, the meaning of the rest of the sentence is much clearer. Whatever this unknown action was, we know that the actor was John. Do we know what the object of that action was? The temptation is to say that we do, but the object is quite dependent on the particular action. We do know something about Mary, but not whether she was the object of John's action. For example, Mary may have heard about something John did to someone else, or to himself. Rather, all we know is that Mary was upset (in the sense of anxious) as a result of John's action.

One of the more important features of the meaning of the sentence that we have just shown is what it leaves out. We know that John did something. The fact that we do not know what he did is very important. It points out the imprecision of most speech. We are quite content to leave out the actual action performed by John and speak only about the action's consequences. In fact, English has a great many words like "upset." Nearly any word that describes the mental or physical state of a person can be used as a verb or has a verb-form equivalent. Thus, we can have: *John disturbed Mary, John angered Mary, John pleased Mary,* and so on. We recognize that there has been an action left out of these statements. We don't know what John actually did in any of these cases. What do we do about it? The answer is that we often fill in the missing action by relying upon what we know about the world to help us make a good guess about what is going on. The extraction of meaning from sentences is a kind of hit-or-miss process.

Most speech, then, leaves a great deal of room for misunderstanding. Because we are left to our own devices to guess what John did, we often guess wrong and then forget which part we actually heard and which part we guessed. We may even go on to relate an inaccurate message to the next person with whom we speak.

To tell more about the action that has been left out, we can use a "by" phrase. That is, we can say, "John upset Mary by yelling at her." This informs us of the action that was missing, and we can thus replace the "did something" with "John yelled at Mary" in our present representation.

As listeners we employ rules that allow us to decide how to combine concepts that are presented in a sentence. Sometimes these rules are the grammatical rules of English, but often they are not. A sentence such as *I saw a building walking down the street* is understandable in two possible ways. However, a hearer is much more apt to assume that the speaker was walking down a street and passed a building than that a building was actually walking down the street, because we know rules of the world that tell us which possibility is more likely. Our job is not to rule out possibilities but to choose between them. Our preferences in ambiguous situations are based on what we know about the world.

In fact, understanding often means explicitly rejecting as a possibility what a sentence seems to be saying because we know better. For example, "The rock hit the boy" is a sentence that really needs to be interpreted. This sentence has an inanimate subject that seems to be doing things. A sentence such as "The rock hit the boy" is understood very differently from "The man hit the boy." We recognize that rocks never really act. We do not for a minute imagine that the rock decided to do anything. Rather, we recognize immediately that rocks are inanimate, and that ordinarily they function as objects of an action. Conceptually, then, the rock in this sentence must be an object of someone or something else's action. "What role does the boy play?" and "Who is the actor?" are two important questions to ask here. We must also concern ourselves with determining what the action in this event is. Let us think about the event a bit. What really must have happened? For a rock to have hit a boy, the rock must have been in motion. Since rocks cannot put themselves in motion, something must have put the rock in motion. Three choices seem possible: 1. a person or an animal; 2. a natural force, such as the wind, the ocean, or an earthquake; or 3. a machine.

The next question is: "Done what?" We really do not know what action set the rock in motion; it could have been pushed, swung, or thrown. We do know that the action we are concerned with is not "hit," as found in our sentence. (True, the rock may have been hit to have been set in motion, but the rock itself did no such action. When a rock is set in motion by an actor, a contact between the actor and the rock has taken place.)

Language can be highly ambiguous and imprecise. People know what they think they have heard (even though it may not correspond to what the speaker wanted them to have understood). Understanding means determining what really happened. We have had to decide on the particular meaning of the highly ambiguous word that was used, "hit." What do we know, then? It is very important to note that a lack of concrete information at any point in the understanding process is itself information. The fact that we do not know what action took place means that we may need to discover it somewhere else in the understanding process. To do this, we need to know what it is that we do not know. Since it is not possible to remedy a lack of information without recognizing that such a lack exists, the very knowledge of the lack is itself useful information.

The key to understanding is the knowledge of the nature of events. The understanding of language is a process whereby a person decodes a sentence, either read or heard, into a set of concepts that is consonant with the knowledge of the world that he has and that expresses the meaning of what was read. One must make inferences to find out what is true apart from what is just literally read.

The key issue in comprehension, we have seen, is the application of appropriate knowledge to a situation. Such knowledge helps to fill in the details behind that situation. Children cannot be expected to understand stories about which they lack background knowledge. But children can be taught to expand their background knowledge and, thus, what they can read.

The process of understanding stories relies heavily on our ability to extract what is implicitly true in a story or sequence of events. Think about what you are doing when you attempt to understand the following:

John was hungry. He went into Goldstein's and ordered a pastrami sandwich. It was served to him quickly. He left the waitress a large tip.

Suppose that after reading this, you were asked the following questions. How many of them would you have trouble answering?

What is Goldstein's?
What did John eat?
Who made the sandwich?
Who took John's order?
Who served the sandwich?
Why did John leave a large tip?

For the most part they are easy and have obvious answers. Any reading-comprehension test that contained such a story would be considered simple. But at no point are we told explicitly that Goldstein's is a restaurant (and probably a Jewish delicatessen), that John ate anything at all (let alone the pastrami sandwich), or that the waitress brought the sandwich to John.

What enables people to understand stories such as the preceding one is knowledge that is organized into structures we call scripts. Scripts organize all the information we have in memory about how a commonplace occurrence (such as going to a restaurant) usually takes place. In addition, scripts point out what behavior is appropriate for a particular situation. Knowing that you are in a restaurant script leads to knowing that if you ask a waitress for food, she is likely to bring it. On the other hand, we know that if you ask her for a pair of shoes, or if you ask her for food while she is returning home on a bus, she is likely to react as if you had done something odd.

We use our knowledge of everyday situations to help us understand stories or discourse about those situations. We need not ask why somebody wants to see our ticket when we enter a theater, or why we should be quiet, or how long it is appropriate to sit in our seat. Knowledge of specific situations, such as theater-going, allows us to interpret the remarks that people make about theaters. Consider how difficult it would be to interpret "Second aisle on your right'' without the detailed knowledge about theaters that the patron and the usher share. It would be rather odd to respond ''What about the second aisle on my right?'' or ''Where is my seat?'' or ''Is this how I get into the theater?'' The usher simply takes the ticket and, assuming you understand and have knowledge about theaters, utters his otherwise cryptic remark without your saying anything.

We often leave out the obvious connections in a story. We do this as speakers because we assume that the hearer has a script available that will make things sensible. If such a script is not available, however, the hearer (or reader) will be confused. Look at the following two stories:

> John went to a restaurant. He asked the waitress for the house special. He paid the check and left.

> John went to a park. He asked the midget for a mouse. He picked up the box and left.

In the second story we are unprepared for the reference to ''the'' midget rather than ''a'' midget and ''the'' box rather than ''a'' box. We also cannot figure out what the mouse and the box have to do with each other. The story does not refer to a standard situation; we know of none that relates midgets, mouses, boxes, and parks. The story is thus not comprehensible, because we have no world knowledge that helps us to connect the parts. If there were a standard ''mouse-buying script'' in which midgets in parks sold mice that were always packed in boxes, then we would be able to apply the script and connect the elements of the story.

What scripts do, then, is provide ''connectivity.'' In the first story, which is superficially quite similar to the second, there is a great deal of connectivity. We are not surprised when ''the'' waitress or ''the'' check are mentioned. We understand exactly the relationship between asking for the house special and paying the check. We also assume that John ate the food he was served, that he waited a while before being served, that he may have looked at a menu, and so on. All this information is brought up by the restaurant script.

Not all stories are script-dominated. That is, understanding what script one is in is useful only for setting the context. The point at which scripts cease to help is the point at which the unexpected (and thus the interesting) begins.

What scripts does a first- or second-grader know? Since scripts are cultural indicators of the purest kind, the question cannot be answered universally. It cannot even be answered for the United States. There exist many subcultures in the United States. No one reading text will suffice for all regions of the country, since few regions, and few social strata within a region, share the same script. Farmers' children, for example, will know the "working chores of the farm" script. City children will know the "playing ball in the street" script. Suburban children will know the "going shopping at the mall" script. A story about school buses requires knowledge that children who walk to school may not have. A story on zoos may be lost to children in rural areas. One on planes is lost to poor children, and one on farms to city children.

If we expect children to understand what they read, they must possess the script that the materials they are reading relies upon. Either we use the scripts that they already know in the stories we ask them to read, or we teach them new scripts. We can, of course, do both. The emphasis ought not to be on teaching reading at all, but on teaching knowledge. Reading is, in essence, a simple task. It is no more difficult than following a movie. The difficult part in following a movie is trying to make sense of a character's actions when one has had no experience with that particular kind of actor or those kinds of actions. The concept of planning to achieve a goal, whether by stereotypical plans like scripts or by novel planning techniques, must be taught to children before serious reading can or ought to be taught.

To teach children to track plans while reading, we must address ourselves to three issues:

1. teaching children to follow stories that involve plans and goals
2. teaching children how to plan to achieve a goal
3. teaching children about goal conflicts, resolutions, and other aspects of stories

In the context of reading, the first step is to accustom children to reading stories in which the relationship between sentences in the text is one of plan to goal:

A. Johnny was very hungry. He opened a cookbook.
B. Johnny was very hungry. He opened the cupboard.
C. Johnny was very hungry. He got on his bicycle.
D. Johnny was very hungry. He lit the oven.
E. Johnny was very hungry. He called to his mother.
F. Johnny was very hungry. He got some money from his piggy bank.

What is being taught here are goal–plan relationships. The relationships inherent in these sentences are as follows:

A. Gain knowledge. To achieve a goal, it is sometimes necessary to have more knowledge about how to achieve it. This is the relationship of cookbook to hunger.
B. Enablements. Often gaining control of an object requires doing something that might otherwise be seen as irrelevant. Here opening the cupboard is relevant if we assume that the cupboard contains food. This opening enables the "gain control" plan to operate.
C. Gain proximity. To satisfy a goal, it is often necessary to move to where the satisfaction can take place. Here we must assume that Johnny is going to some kind of eating place.
D. Preparation. Even when all elements are present (i.e., we know what to do, have control of the goal objects, and are in the right place), certain prepar-

atory steps must be taken. Here lighting the oven is part of that preparatory procedure.

E. Getting an agent. We need not do everything for ourselves. Sometimes others will do it for us. Of course, they are only assistants in a plan; ultimately, we will have to eat for ourselves.

F. Planning ahead. Often a plan involves multiple steps. Going to a restaurant without taking money or knowing how to get there can be a problem. Here Johnny is planning ahead for a goal that we can guess (eating ice cream?).

Quite often children don't plan, however. Usually they have a script available to help them through a situation. This is most likely to be true in common situations—when one is hungry, for example. The best way to explain sentences that indicate steps in a plan is to use stories that involve novel situations. Teaching ought to introduce the attempt to make children figure things out on their own. In this context, then, the questions that should be asked of children about the preceding stories include:

1. Why did Johnny do what he did?
2. What else could he have done?
3. How well did his actions help him get what he wants?
4. What will he do next?

I am not suggesting that the theoretical elements be taught explicitly. It makes no more sense to teach a theory of the construction of plans than it does to teach a theory of grammar. Children should not be asked to underline enablements or categorize actions in terms of planning. Knowing how to use such information, not knowing the information explicitly, is what is important here. If the child can answer the above questions, he has understood.

The next stage in reading stories based on plans and goals is helping the child to recognize that actions can enable one to put a plan into effect or to reach a goal. Here are some examples:

> Johnny wanted a new baseball glove. When Johnny's father got home, Johnny greeted him at the door with a big hug. Then he asked his father if he wanted to play catch.

> Why did Johnny greet his father in the way he did?
> Why do you think Johnny wanted to play catch?
> What do you think will happen when they play catch?
> What would you do if you wanted a new baseball glove?

> Susie was jumping rope with Jane. She was tired and she wanted to quit. But Jane hadn't had her turn yet. Suddenly, Susie yelled that her ankle hurt.

> Why couldn't Susie quit?
> Did Susie's ankle really hurt?
> Why did she say it did?
> How do you think Jane will feel?
> What kind of person is Susie?

In each of these stories, a child has a goal. In both cases the goals are stated and obvious. Children must learn to see how someone can plan a course of action to achieve a goal. In neither of these stories do the children take the most direct course of action. Children must be taught to recognize the course of action, or plan, that is being followed.

Once we find that a character has acted dishonestly, we can expect him to do so again. The following is taken from the *Treasure Island* story used earlier:

> Silver went over to talk with the pirates. They laughed together. Then he saw Jim. Jim asked who the men were that Silver had laughed with. Silver said, "What men?"

Such stories provide good opportunities to discuss issues such as guilt by association, bad traits, and so on. In stories, we are rarely told something that isn't intended to set up something else. Children must be taught to look for these clues in life, not just in texts, to guide them in their predictions about actions and their consequences.

As readers, we learn to figure out what goal is being pursued.

> Jane left the house quietly. She had all her money with her. At last she was at the store. She went in. It was a store that sold pipes. But they were all so expensive.

> What is Jane planning on doing?
> Why do you think she is doing that?
> What is the difficulty she has in achieving her goal?
> What can she do about it?

It is often a good idea to have the child answer questions like those above, and then to proceed to the rest of the story. It could continue:

> How was she going to get her father his birthday present? Then she thought that her older sister might help. She hurried home.

Understanding means learning to figure out why people do what they do. Children must learn to recognize that a story can mislead them; they can make a wrong guess and still recover.

In real life, there are times when we want what someone else also wants. Many children's stories are based on goal competition and the means of achieving a compromise or outright success. The following is from Aesop:

> Once upon a time, there was a dishonest Fox who lived in a cave, and a vain and trusting Crow who lived

in an elm tree. The Crow had gotten a piece of cheese and was holding it in his mouth. One day, the Fox walked from his cave, across the meadow, to the elm tree. He saw the Crow and the cheese and became hungry. He decided that he might get the cheese if the Crow spoke, so he told the Crow that he liked his singing very much and wanted to hear him sing. The Crow was very pleased with the Fox's request and began to sing. The cheese fell out of his mouth, down to the ground. The Fox picked up the cheese and told the Crow that he was stupid. The Crow was angry and didn't trust the Fox anymore. The Fox returned to his cave.

What did the Fox want?
What did the Crow want?
Why did the Fox ask the Crow to sing?
Why did the Crow sing?
Who won?
What would you have done if you were the Fox?
What would you have done if you were the Crow?

Here we have a series of plans and counterplans, all carried out in pursuit of the same goal. How easy is it to understand this story if you have never tried to achieve such goals yourself?

The purpose in systematically teaching children about goals and plans is to lead them to make the appropriate assumptions, create the right expectations, draw sensible conclusions, and otherwise tie together what they have read. Many of the questions I have proposed here are currently being asked of children in reading-comprehension instruction. But for the most part they are being asked randomly and unsystematically. Thus, although a child might occasionally have to speculate on some aspect of what he has read, he is not systematically learning to ask these kinds of questions of himself. And that is what he must do if he is to learn to understand.

I have attempted here to present reading as being not wholly different from other cognitive processes. If you can't read, you probably can't think, either, not because reading helps one think, but because reading entails thinking. It seems to me that the emphasis on reading instruction in this country is misplaced. To teach reading, give a child books to read, not lessons on prefixes and suffixes. To teach the thinking that reading entails, some kind of instruction is necessary. Children must be taught to reason in an inquisitive fashion, and that requires that schools encourage such behavior.

At the onset of reading, the typical child functions effectively with his language. Often the teaching of reading is confused with teaching a child about his language. Reading may be a new subject for the child, but comprehension is not. To teach a child to read requires concentrating on the problems in reading that are specific to reading. These are, for the most part, simple and straightforward and can be dispensed with after the first grade. The most significant of these problems are the association of sounds with printed words and the reliance on prediction and memory in the sight recognition of words.

The making of inferences to add facts to those explicitly mentioned and the understanding of the role of actions and characters in a story are skills critical to reading; but they are by no means specific to reading. They can, and should, be taught elsewhere. I have suggested that the movies are a good place to start. Why? Because going to the movies is fun, and good movies stimulate one's curiosity.

Of course, it should be clear what the goal is here. The goal is not to teach reading at all. It is to teach children to be able to gather information and be critical in their understanding of that information. Naturally, books are excellent sources of new information. But in the computer age they are by no means the only source. The goal is thinking, questioning, analysis, and synthesis, not reading.

How do children learn to speak well? If they are not to be instructed in their language as part of reading, should they be instructed in their language at all? The answer is complex. There is no need to instruct elementary-school children in their language. They know, and will continue to learn, how to speak and understand, and the fine points of syntax and semantics. This knowledge develops by usage, not by explicit instruction. Thus, it should be "taught" by placing children in situations that involve speaking. This is what is done by the parent. And it is what must be done by the teacher.

My suggestions are these: Have conversations with children in class. They should have to listen critically to what the teacher says. After they can read a little, have them talk about what they read and hear. We teach children to use language by making them use it. The more they use it, the more facile they will become with it. Children learn language by imitation and use. Give them good models. Do not instruct them explicitly in the use of nouns, predicates, and antonyms, and in other aspects of language that they implicitly know.

The study of language has been the focus of my professional life. I believe that the study of language—how it works, its history and development—would be a useful part of any high-school student's curriculum. Such a subject should be taught in high school, but not because it will teach the student to speak, write, or read better. It will not. Rather, it should be taught because an educated person should have knowledge of language.

Written language makes up a comparatively small part of most of our lives. Even the most educated of people spend more time speaking and hearing than reading or writing. Children understand only a small portion of what they hear. Yet they push on. Eventually, when they are ready to pay attention to a new word, they can ask about it or figure out what it means. But this happens only with a comparatively small percentage of the new words that they encounter. The same is true of reading. When a child discovers a new word in the course of reading, he usually finds it much easier to skip it than to learn its meaning. When the child completely understands the context that surrounds a word, in the sense of having predicted its meaning, he can then learn the word by reading it. On the other hand, when a new word is spoken by a friend or teacher, used a second or third time, and finally used by the child himself, it will be possible to learn the word. This is a key point. A combination of reading and usage will result in the learning of new vocabulary. But the child must be encouraged to use the new word and respond to others using it.

Can we teach new vocabulary in school? I believe we can and must. The "how" of the matter is crucial.

The watchword throughout this essay has been *knowledge*. The acquisition of knowledge about the world is the single most important part of reading. You cannot read about that which makes no sense to you. To prove this point to yourself, try reading a folk tale, in English, taken from a culture very removed from yours. A classic in this regard is "The War of the Ghosts," an Eskimo folk tale. Psychologists have demonstrated that this particular story is very hard to remember and read, as are all stories for which one does not possess the appropriate background knowledge.

One night two young men from Egulac went down to the river to hunt seals, and while they were there it became foggy and calm. Then they heard war cries, and they thought, *Maybe this is a war party*. They escaped to the shore and hid behind a log. Now canoes came up, and they heard the noise of paddles, and saw one canoe coming up to them.

There were five men in the canoe, and they said, "What do you think? We wish to take you along. We are going up the river to make war on the people."

One of the young men said, "I have no arrows. I will not go along. I might be killed. My relatives do not know where I have gone. But you," he said, turning to the other, "may go with them."

So one of the young men went, but the other returned home.

And the warriors went up the river to a town on the other side of Kalama. The people came down to the water, and they began to fight, and many were killed. But presently the young man heard one of the warriors say, "Quick, let us go home; that Indian has been hit."

Now he thought, *Oh, they are ghosts.* He did not feel sick, but they said he had been shot.

So the canoes went back to Egulac, and the young man went ashore to his house, and made a fire. And he told everybody and said, "Behold, I accompanied the ghosts, and we went to fight. Many of our fellows were killed, and many of those who attacked us were killed. They said I was hit, and I did not feel sick."

He told it all, and then he became quiet. When the sun rose he fell down. Something black came out of his mouth. His face became contorted. The people jumped up and cried.

He was dead.

The story is understandable if you "know" certain Eskimo "facts," such as: When people die, their souls, which are black, come out of their mouths. When ghosts shoot you, you do not feel it. Without these facts, the story is quite confusing.

Children face a similar situation in reading. They need to have background facts at hand, and to fill them in, so as to connect the sentences. But there is a paradox here. We use knowledge in order to read, but don't we read in order to gain knowledge? Isn't that one of the main reasons for teaching children to read?

I have attempted to treat this paradox within the progression of stages given earlier. After children learn how to fill in the implicit details of a story, and to track characters' goals and plans, they are prepared to acquire knowledge via reading. In other words, the basic background knowledge that they possess is used to help them learn to read stories that track plans and goals. The general knowledge of why people do things and how they do them can then be used to help gain knowledge about different goals and plans that are unfamiliar to them. After plans, goals, and scripts have been thoroughly learned, as they apply to reading, children must be taught to reason, draw analogies, relate one experience to another, and assess what is happening in a situation and why it is happening.

A child who can learn the language of science, and who has familiarity with its methods, can also read about science. I once brought my four-year-old son to an undergraduate class I was teaching. He happened to notice the computer terminal in the room and began to talk about how he was going to "log on," when to do a "control C," or an "SYS," how to "run a program," and so on. The students in the class were astounded. But there was nothing astounding about it. As the son of a professor of computer science, he knew all about computer terminals and had picked up the appropriate terminology from his attempts to acquire a working knowledge of how to use them. I did not present him with an elementary-school-level computer programming text. But he would have been capable of reading such a text. And that is exactly the point.

A child who sees a simple experiment in chemistry conducted in front of him, assuming his interest is excited by a good presentation, will quickly learn such words as "experiment," "procedure," "method," "instruments," "chemical," and so on. If he is allowed to participate directly in experiments, he will learn these words that much better. If this kind of firsthand experience happens frequently, then the words describing the experiment will become second nature to him. This is how to "teach" new vocabulary.

Reading is not just reading per se. It is knowledge gathering, it is entertainment, it is inquiry, it is analysis. To acquire knowledge, one must have knowledge. The reason

Johnny can't read and the reason his old man won't read is that neither of them knows much, and they don't want to know much. Teach them about something that interests them, teach them to be interested in more things, and reading will follow. As long as a child cares about what he is reading, he will happily read—if he has the requisite background knowledge. How do we get him to care about *reading*? We get him to care about *knowing* first.

A

JOURNEY OF

RELATIVITIES

▼

MARY CATHERINE BATESON
WITH
SEVANNE MARGARET KASSARJIAN

Each of us has the sense of both concurring with and differing from our respective generations, and we share a tradition of elaborating self-knowledge through observation and encounters with others, for all observation of the other is also self-observation. Less obviously, but still necessarily, all observation occurs in a Heraclitean flux in which the motion of the other is observed by the moving self; it is not only that the river flows but that the observer is in motion, stepping through the current.

In 1956 I went to Israel with my mother, Margaret Mead, who had been invited as a consultant on the assimilation of immigrants. Two days before we were supposed to leave Israel, I decided to stay and finish high school there in Hebrew. I remained for just over a year. That was the year of the Israeli campaign in Sinai and the Anglo-French invasion of Suez, the year of the Hungarian uprising. Eisenhower was President of the United States, Ben-Gurion was Prime Minister of Israel, and Khrushchev had just undertaken the de-Stalinization of the Soviet Union. I turned seventeen in the aftermath of the Sinai campaign.

In January 1988, thirty years later, I went back with my daughter, Vanni, eighteen years old and a freshman at Brown University. Together, we set out to explore the relationship between her vision and mine in the present, and between her vision now and mine at the same age, against the shifting backgrounds of time and place. Each of us has the sense of both concurring with and differing from our respective generations, and we share a tradition of elaborating self-knowledge through observation and encounters with others, for all observation of the other is also self-observation. Less obviously, but still necessarily, all observation occurs in a Heraclitean flux in which the motion of the other is observed by the moving self; it is not only that the river flows but that the observer is in motion, stepping through the current. Vanni and I had only three weeks, nearly the same time period my mother and I had in Israel before I decided to stay, but only a brief chance to test and feel the water's flow.

We are at a time of unfolding exploration of these relativities in anthropology as well as other disciplines. One dimension of this growing awareness has to do with the construction of an epistemology rooted in a renewed self-reference. For some, the exploration of self is a sufficient end. For others, the exploration of self is honed into a tool for understanding the other, through various forms of disciplined subjectivity and empathy. Perhaps because they have so often been told what they ought to think and feel, women have been pioneers in this new tuning of self-consciousness.

Underlying my curiosity about how my response and Vanni's would differ was the puzzlement I had felt in trying to unravel the curious muddle that surrounded Derek Freeman's 1983 attack[1] on my mother's book, *Coming of Age in Samoa*[2]: two different observers, one a man and one a woman, of different ages and backgrounds; two different Samoas, one American-governed and the other administered by New Zealand until 1962; fifty years' difference and therefore two different Americas. All anthropological work is rooted in comparison, all meaning in context, but Freeman's work was flawed by a stance of scientism that denied the necessary relativities. When *Coming of Age* came out in 1928, it was reviewed as highly titillating material, and Freeman apparently still finds it provocative; but if the newsmen who made such a fuss had bothered to read the book itself, where it drifts now far down the Heraclitean stream, they would have found a different book, one about young people less pressured into early sexual activity than American teen-agers today. The context for understanding sexuality has changed. Similarly, Israel gave me in 1956–57 a paradigm for something I had found lacking in my own society: commitment. Between that experience and the American present lie the impassioned sixties and the seventies, the new uncommitment of the eighties, and my own efforts to find and sustain commitments. In Israel, there has been war after war, old ambiguities have deepened, a certain innocence has been lost.

I had told Vanni a miscellany of stories about the newly founded kibbutz I had visited in the Negev, where several of my classmates planned to spend their lives. When I was there, there were only a few tentative buildings, no trees, no children. Today there are many trees, and children of all ages, but the classmates whose dedication I treasured as a model over the years have almost all left. We also visited two older kibbutzim, hearing of pervasive worry about the kibbutz-born children who want to leave, about women who point out that in spite of the ideology of equality, jobs are gender-typed and leadership positions almost exclusively given to males, about the economic problems resulting from the withdrawal of subsidies, and the competition relying on cheap labor from the refugee camps. I had told Vanni to take fresh clothes for Friday night, for surely there would be singing and dancing on the eve of the sabbath, but we were told that that hasn't happened for years. "Sometimes, though, the teen-agers have a disco." Like me, the kibbutz movement has become middle-aged and ambivalent. I commented to a friend that members seemed not to greet one another on the paths, and he said that indeed they used to do so, but eventually they became fed up. I found the kibbutzniks reminiscent of faculty at a small New England liberal-arts college, an inward-looking community with a deep conviction of virtue, locked into perpetual intimacy by economic dependency, facing daily reminders of the petty conflicts and power plays of the decades. Something like a soured marriage, with many extra faces at the breakfast table. I left Israel in 1957 with my sense of its newness, of its youth that matched my own, untarnished, just as most college students graduate before the romance of college dims.

I went to a high school in the Jerusalem area, so my friends were not the sheltered children of the kibbutz but urban children committed to the agrarian socialist ideal.

Vanni found it difficult to establish communication with the young people she met on the kibbutzim and responded with sharp skepticism and disappointment to a community that was indeed less committed and less sure of itself than it seemed to me thirty years ago. She was not doing research, of course, but recording impressions—the first impressions that give way before greater knowledge but are always valuable to record because they contain their own evanescent snatches of insight.

Ironically, in trying to express the sense of weakened commitment, Vanni drew on an image from the fifties, from the alienation of my own generation. In her notes on the trip, she wrote: "The next generation on the kibbutz is made up of kids who are not rebels without a cause. They are rebels without a clue." I know that's a harsh phrasing, grabbing for a first, quick impression. On the kibbutz I saw kids whose options had been so suddenly widened that decisions became harder to make, not easier. The fights their parents fought to establish the kibbutz have been won, and it's been built and is working, but it has nowhere else to go and can't go on as it is. To survive in the present, it finds itself undermining the ideology upon which it was based. But the contemporary options are yet to be grasped, much less accepted.

"The next generation doesn't know much about the world around them—it seems to come as a surprise," her notes continue. "The kids are forced to serve for two years in the army of a country that is constantly at war and can find itself no peace or uncontested ground on which to stand. They feel guilty if they don't want to serve in the army, and, yet, if they do they feel unsure of what they are fighting and serving for. Some have convinced themselves that they are wasting the two best and most important years of their lives for studying or seeing the world, or whatever. And yet the members of this next generation are expected to stay on the kibbutz, not to try something new, with some new knowledge they might obtain in travel or through study, but to maintain. If they don't, they are the ones corrupting and forgetting the ideology. To get the kids to stay, the kibbutz is offering them more and more bits of conveniences as inducements—they are even offering to pay for more extended trips away from the kibbutz to get people to stay. That is so fundamentally backward, it must point to a basic warping that has happened over time.

"The kibbutz seems to me to be representative of so many other things that start out idealistically—rather simple ideals, really—and inevitably fall through. But perhaps I should be congratulating them that they still exist, that they have increased and multiplied, that they are supporting their members one way or another, and some are still fighting vehemently for shreds of the original ideology. The situation's not really all that bad at this very moment; it's the future that looks dim."

Perhaps the analogy of the teen-agers I knew was closer to the group Vanni met in Tel Aviv. Less involved in ideology than the Israeli teen-agers I knew thirty years ago, burdened by the ambiguities created by Israel's repressions of protests in the occupied territories, which we heard about in each day's news, they still seemed to Vanni to have a core of commitment, mixed in with cynicism. She saw the cynicism as a strengthening element of realism. I'm not sure that in my time I would have seen it that way.

"It seemed somehow that Israel as a whole had an incredible dose of commitment. I felt as if the commitment came out of an awareness that seemed *forced on* the kibbutz kids and *adopted by* the Tel Aviv kids. The kibbutz kids seem to be fighting too hard to reconcile themselves to their future. Everything in their life has been idealistic; now, they are suddenly being given choices. They are smart and committed but they are forcing themselves into that future with this characteristic vigor and commitment, without the equipment they need to deal with it. One tool they especially seem to lack is a kind of patience that comes out of cynicism—or reality, I guess—that could keep them committed to a degree of growth and progress but hold them back from killing themselves if things don't all fall into place before they are twenty-five—if they don't make it big, shall we say, or find an ideal community. All these things like success are terribly relative, but somehow the Tel Aviv kids have a kind of perspective lacking in the kibbutz kids. The Tel Aviv kids I met are aware and intelligent and committed, too, but somehow it all is coming from different sources in a different order. They are growing up in a characteristically very committed and aware society, but without the huge doses of idealism. They are intelligent and concerned about their education and their future, but an element of their awareness reconciles them to the fact of problems like the years in the army. They seem to be taking things much more in stride, while on the kibbutz every option or change involves a decision that seems to shake their foundations.''

One of the things Vanni reacted to most strongly and negatively was the Utopian aspect of the kibbutz, the expectation that it might really be expected to achieve solutions like equality between the sexes. ''Who doesn't have that problem? Why are they acting as if it could be solved for them right away? What makes them so special, and what about the thousands who have been trying for years? The kibbutz women should be thankful that they have work and people around they can talk to and all sorts of common services. Their future is at least mappable, so they know they will be fed and clothed and will have a place for their children and a place to grow old.'' The very hopes that made possible the building of the kibbutzim and of Israel itself have some of them turned into ironies, for the Israelis have been blindsided by their own human frailty. Much as they complain that Israel is sometimes expected to meet higher standards than other nations, which it is, the occurrence of brutality in the army or corruption in the judiciary is greeted with surprised innocence. Perhaps if Judaism included a traditional belief like original sin, the founders would have taken advantage of the era of consensus to write a constitution. A friend commented to us when we visited Yad Vashem that now when she goes there with a visitor she finds herself reflecting on the potential for evil in every society.

Vanni's disappointment on the kibbutz was partly the result of multiple prisms of observation. Hearing my reminiscences as they were filtered over the years, she interpreted them against her own best models of excitement and commitment, summers of ardent effort in theater. "I couldn't help but look forward to my mother's memories. A kibbutz was going to be a small community of teeming energy, like camp or summer-stock theater. Everyone would be doing what they wanted to be doing, and because of that they would be doing it well. Everyone would be inspired by a common cause, and because of that it would be a united and self-perpetuating community of many facets and blossoming strengths. I guess in a way the romantic view of the kibbutz I had adopted from my mother's memories grew in my mind to represent Israel as a whole. Idealistically—that's how I thought everybody lived.

"But I don't think the memories that my mother helped to instill in me were the ones she left with thirty years ago. Thirty years is a long time and I'm sure her mind and heart and romantic and dramatic senses used that time to get the most out of those memories. I also don't think when she was here things were as wonderful and idyllic as my mind has conjured because things just aren't. Probably I would be more positive about the kibbutz if I hadn't thought about it beforehand. And I think her original decision to stay had more to do with not wanting to go back home to her high school than with what was in Israel. She just happened to get lucky and really blossom in the situation she found herself in. That's a difference between us—she was coming to the end of high school and wanting to do something new. I'm already into my first year at college, at the beginning of the next phase. I don't think my mom has decided yet whether she is glad that she has had no contact in thirty years or not.

"I can't even imagine thirty years.

"I'm constantly struggling with the idea of commitment.

For some reason I've happened to choose an interest or a profession or a future, whatever it turns out to be, which complicates things even more. Theater is what I care about. I can be sure that I have a degree of skill and commitment. Whether it is intrinsic in my character or something I have learned, I don't know, or how long my potential for learning will keep going. I also have no idea whether I have the kibbutz perspective or the Tel Aviv perspective. But somehow I do have something, some kind of commitment, even though it's mixed with questions and self-doubt. A lot of the people around me at college seem really lackadaisical. I have friends who have no idea where they are going or how they are going to get there, and I have grown-ups telling me that I still have to discover 'my life and my future.' Then they look at me with that glance of, 'Poor child, she really thinks she's interested in the theatre.' But I've always thought that theatre was a much better thing for me to be interested in than people gave me credit for. Besides all of my own ideals about theatre as a medium and a communicator of the human experience, a truthful art and craft, I also like to think that there are so many different tributaries to the theatre—anthropology, psychology, et cetera—that somewhere there will be room for me; it's a profession of misfits anyway. So I do have that comfort. I have the impression that my mother didn't have a comfort like that when she was my age.''

Hmm. As Vanni juxtaposes her perceptions with what she has heard from me, I have to struggle to recover and evaluate memories. I know that the question of commitment was central to my falling in love with Israel. I was cynical about any commitment to my own culture, or to any elements of nation or religion I had been exposed to. I remember quarreling with my mother in a hotel room in Athens, before we flew to Israel, about whether there was anything in America to believe in. She thought there was, was always patriotic. I know I felt like a misfit, writing poetry and coming from an odd part of town and an odd kind of family. And I know that when I left Israel to go to college I took an aching sense of loss and envy of my friends who followed their certainties into the army. But even when I daydreamed about the possibility of living on a kibbutz, I felt I would not want to raise children there. I'd be glad enough of a communal nursery and a communal kitchen, but I believe that ideal communities—or any imagined "way of perfection"—must be chosen anew by each generation, not biologically recruited. Indeed, I believe increasingly that lifetime commitments modeled on marriage, the commitment to a kibbutz as well as the commitment to a monastery, should have the same open doors that marriage has come to have—right for one phase of life, for ten years or twenty, but not necessarily binding for sixty. We are only just discovering the harvest of creativity from the departures and new commitments of the extended life cycle.

"For most of my friends at college, commitment has to do with the future. If they are like me they are committed to something because of what they see at the end of the tunnel, med school, politics, disarmament, marriage, theatre . . . but some American kids are simply committed to the future with nothing to get them there. They just have this intense belief that eventually it will come and they will have their life. It will all work itself out eventually: their hopes, their parents' expectations, the bills they will have to pay. Israeli kids are committed to the present. If they are on a kibbutz they are obsessed with reconciling their position there *now.* If they are in the army they are constantly aware of their contribution to their country *now,* if they are traveling they want to see the whole world *now.*"

I asked Vanni what she was hearing from her age mates about the trouble in the occupied territories, and whether they understood that the new round of protests and repressions represented an irreversible change. "Well, they are practical and confident but really unsure of final stands. They tend to spend a lot of time reasoning things out: 'How can we hate the Arabs . . . ? They are in a similar position to us . . . but how can they blow up innocent people . . . ? Of course they are innocent, but if I was a soldier and an Arab started throwing stones I'd want to shoot back. . . .' I asked one kid, 'Why doesn't everyone realize that nothing will be accomplished unless you at least talk it out and compromise?' And he said, 'It's easy for you to sit here, you're not on the front line,' ('You never have been and you never will be' was also in his voice.) You can hear the practicality and the commitment, but there is also this sense of helplessness, always, in people's voices. Their voices build up and then they finish their sentences on a high note, sort of questioning. But also in the voice is this confidence that life will go on—normal life seems to be what the kids want most. I'm not sure they really imagine things coming to a head.''

When fighting started in 1956, many of my friends hoped this might be the last time war would be necessary, but today conflict has become habitual as the grandchildren of Palestinian refugees face the grandchildren of pioneers.

Another way in which Vanni's view and my own first response necessarily differed was in previous knowledge of the Middle East. Israel was the first Middle Eastern country in my experience, but already when I left I was determined to learn Arabic and to understand the Arab side of the story, and much of my life since then has been involved with the Middle East. Vanni has grown up within this unfolding involvement. Her father is Armenian and she spent much of her childhood in Iran, visiting relatives in Beirut as long as it was possible to do so. In the flea market in Jaffa we found we could get better prices than our Israeli friends—because almost all the merchants are Iranian Jews. In the Old City of Jerusalem we asked our way in Arabic to the lovely serene mosques on the Temple Mount, where troops used tear gas two days later. And in the Armenian Quarter we found an official of the patriarchate who opened for us the Church of Saint James and showed us personally around the diminutive Armenian Museum, with its documentation of the Armenian diaspora and massacres in curious counterpoint to the overwhelming and superbly mounted exhibits at Yad Vashem and the Museum of the (Jewish) Diaspora in Tel Aviv. When I went to Israel I had a sense of lacking cultural roots, but Vanni could trace roots of her own there: One of the patriarchate buildings was used as an orphanage after the Armenian massacres, and there Vanni's great-uncle was brought after being rescued from the desert, and there he was trained to play in the orphanage band and carried off by Crown Prince Haile Selassie to be raised in the Ethiopian court.

In 1957 I visited the refugee camps in Jordan, and since then I have been unable to see the questions of Israel and Palestine with an undivided mind. Vanni will never see them that way and never make the mistake of singling out the Holocaust from all the sorry history of human inhumanity.

Israel has always had a complex layering of intergenerational conflict. Already when I was there, the Israeli-born sabras were visibly impatient with the Diaspora tradition and with reminders of the Holocaust, preoccupied with building something new. Today many young people who would like to emulate their parents in pioneering departures find that this means criticizing or even leaving the kibbutz or Israel rather than settling into the compromises of continuity. It is not easy for children whose parents invented their own models simply to follow in parental footsteps. No easier for Vanni launching out into the world of theater than for the children of the kibbutz.

Vanni wound up her first batch of notes, halfway through the visit, by writing: "I didn't mean to undermine so harshly my mother or the kibbutz or Israel, but I did. I guess it's just a backlash from my hopes." By the time we left she was more positive, but it seemed clear that Israel would not be for her, as it has been for me and so many others, a parable of possibility. Instead, it has become a symbol of the need to keep struggling in spite of ambiguity. Vanni seems to me far more than one year wiser than my remembered self of thirty years ago, and yet I have been accompanied in all life's compromises since that time by Israel's image of hope.

NOTES

[1] Derek Freeman, *Margaret Mead and Samoa: The Making and Unmaking of an Anthropological Myth* (Cambridge: Harvard University Press, 1983).

[2] Margaret Mead, *Coming of Age in Samoa: A Psychological Study of Primitive Youth for Western Civilization* (New York: William Morrow, 1928).

IN
DEFENSE
OF ELITISM

GERALD FEINBERG

The arguments for doing some things as well as possible are spiritual as well as pragmatic. Whatever the original reason was for doing certain activities, their continued successful performance helps to define the character of any society. One can plausibly say that what a society holds most sacred is defined by those activities that it insists be done as well as possible.

---

elitism—the leadership by the choice part or segment

In what passes for social commentary in present-day America, it is hard to find anyone who has anything favorable to say about elitism. Many writers regard it as an unanswerably devastating criticism of an institution or of a course of action to describe it as elitist. This nearly unanimous agreement on the social undesirability of elitism is unaccompanied by any sustained analysis that warrants the conclusion that elitism is universally undesirable. Indeed, an examination of some of our hallowed institutions shows that elitism is fully accepted in some circumstances, even though no one calls attention to it in those terms. No voices have been raised to condemn the Los Angeles Lakers basketball team or the Chicago Symphony Orchestra, even though those institutions are elitist according to any plausible definition of that term.

However, elitism has been attacked in many circumstances—for example, by those who object to the geographical distribution of federal scientific research grants, and the composition of the student bodies of schools like the Bronx High School of Science, whose purpose is the training of those with high ability in specific activities. A variety of criticisms has been leveled at the practice of using merit as the sole criterion in determining which universities should be given federal grants to carry out scientific research, or who should attend such schools. In many cases, including the two that I have mentioned, the criticisms have succeeded in changing the previous practice so that merit is no longer the sole criterion. These changes have been to the detriment of the institutions, and of many of their members. In the fear of being branded as elitist, we have lowered the quality of institutions devoted to socially worthwhile purposes, and by so doing, we have sacrificed both important aims of society and the welfare of some of the most talented among us.

Not only is elitism tacitly accepted in some aspects of American life, but a convincing intellectual case can be made for it, both in those places where it is unquestionably accepted and in the places where it has been under attack, such as the composition of the faculties of major universities. I will show why elitist institutions, those who choose their members on the basis of merit, are an essential means for carrying out some of the activities that we jointly consider most worthwhile. I will focus on elitist universities, such as M.I.T., and on the schools that prepare students for them. This is where most of my own experience lies, and where I have seen the follies of anti-elitism most directly. But many of my arguments would also apply elsewhere, to elite musical or athletic institutions.

I am not arguing that elitism is a desirable approach to determining who should govern society. I agree with the view that was adopted early in our society that participation in the process of government by a large part of society is a more important matter than how effective the governors are.

My defense of the proposition that elitism is a desirable attitude, at least in certain situations, is based on two simple ideas. One is that some activities are accepted as so worthwhile, both by those that do them and by society at large, that they should be done as well as they can be done. The other proposition is that some individuals are much better at doing these activities than others are, or can become by any methods now known. I will first give the arguments for these propositions, then show why they make a strong case for elitism.

There is a list of activities that any society considers to be intrinsically worthwhile. The list is usually not spelled out anywhere, but it can be inferred from the ways in which the society spends its financial and human resources. Some of these worthwhile activities, such as winning a tennis match or painting a picture, mainly involve individuals. Where these individual activities are concerned, the issue of elitism is rarely raised directly. For the most part, there is little serious argument about the positive role of elitism in individual activities, and for that reason I will not discuss that issue further in this article.

There are others among the list of worthwhile activities that are performed by groups and often require ongoing institutions through which they are carried out. In modern American society, the list of worthwhile group activities would include such diverse pursuits as musical performances, both by symphony orchestras and rock groups, team sports, such as major-league baseball, and scientific research, which is mostly now done by groups of substantial size. Sometimes, as with symphony orchestras, the groups are absolutely necessary to carry out the activities. In other cases, as with universities consisting of diverse faculties, it might be possible to do the same activities through other institutional arrangements, but the existing institutions appear to work well, and there is no reason to think that other arrangements would be more effective.

The reasons for valuing activities are, of course, varied. Furthermore, those participating in the activities often value them for reasons that differ from those of spectators or consumers. For example, scientific research is valued by many scientists mainly for the insights it gives them into the workings of the universe, while many nonscientists value it mainly for its technological by-products. Such differences in emphasis sometimes lead to disagreements over priorities, in scientific research and elsewhere. Nevertheless, it seems likely that there would be fairly general agreement on a list of group activities that our society considers worthwhile.

There might be more disagreement about the question of how important it is to perform these activities as well as possible. On this question, the main difference is likely to be between the views of people for whom the activity is peripheral and of those for whom it is central. People who are not especially interested in football might consider it an activity that can be tolerated but not consider it an important matter how well the game is played. But serious football fans would be appalled at a suggestion that the existing teams could be replaced without serious loss by players of lower ability. An illustration of this attitude occurred in 1987 during the strike of N.F.L. players. During three weeks, when the striking players were replaced by a group of substitutes, attendance at the games decreased considerably. For other activities, especially those affecting people's well-being, there is almost universal acceptance of the view that the activities should be done as well as possible. This acceptance exists both among those performing the activity and those benefiting from its results. For example, it has never to my knowledge been argued either by scientists or nonscientists that scientific research should be carried out by people who are less able than the best who can be found to do it.

The arguments for doing some things as well as possible are spiritual as well as pragmatic. Whatever the original reason was for doing certain activities, their continued successful performance helps to define the character of any society. One can plausibly say that what any society holds most sacred is defined by those activities that it insists be done as well as possible. In Periclean Athens, there were competitions for the best dramas, and the entries were performed for the whole population each year at religious festivals. In Renaissance Florence, artists competed for the right to design public exhibits, and the winner was called upon to execute his proposal. In present-day America, scientists compete for public funds to carry out their experimental investigations, and the winners get to do the experiments. In none of these cases did the system work perfectly to reward merit. Yet, in each case, it succeeded in eliciting a very high level of achievement in the chosen field. The very existence of such competitions implies that each society valued the activity enough to require that those who were best at it should be those called upon to do it. It is not accidental that these societies all attained extremely high levels of achievement at the activities that they valued so highly. In American today there are a number of group activities that we value highly, as indicated by the amount of our resources that we devote to them. Usually, as in the case of scientific research, these are the activities in which our achievements are greatest. If we use criteria in choosing those who perform those activities other than that of producing the most able performance, we sacrifice something truly distinctive about our society.

In order to avoid this, we should arrange that the members of the institutions through which these worthwhile group activities are carried out are as able as possible. Making such choices of personnel assumes that some individuals are better than others at each such activity. This proposition would be regarded as obviously true by most people, but since it is a question of fact, such agreement does not necessarily make it so. So what is the evidence for the claim that some individuals are inevitably more able than others at certain activities? There can be no doubt that when actual performances are measured, there are differences in accomplishment. Some runners consistently achieve faster times for the 100-meter dash than others. Some painters consistently produce paintings more to the liking of art collectors and critics than others. Some scientists solve problems that other scientists have failed to solve. We do not all perform the same tasks at the same level. The level of performance cannot be so easily compared for all worthwhile human activities. How does one tell who is better among two sets of parents? But the fact that such comparisons cannot always be made should not cancel out the obvious fact that they can easily be made in many cases.

Furthermore, there are directly measurable differences in the elementary physical and mental abilities that enter into the performance of any complex activity. The measured level of such qualities as muscular strength, ability to distinguish between musical tones, or facility of word memorization all vary considerably within the population. While the precise relation between these elementary abilities and successful performance of complex tasks varies from activity to activity, such relations surely exist. Someone with low muscular strength is unlikely to be a successful shotputter, however good his technique. A person who is color blind will probably not be a successful painter.

It is true that not all differences in the level of performance of complex activities are the result of intrinsic differences in ability among the individuals being compared. Performance levels also depend on the degree of training that the individual has received, and on his or her motivation to succeed, to mention just two relevant factors. For example, impressive athletic performances have been achieved by people, such as Wilma Rudolph, who had disabilities that one might have thought would make it impossible for them to compete successfully with other athletes. Beethoven composed some of his greatest works while unable to hear them played.

Some scientists, such as psychologist B. F. Skinner and population biologist Richard Lewontin, have argued that any effect on performance due to intrinsic differences of ability among people is negligible, and that with proper training, any person can achieve what anyone else can achieve. Furthermore, in much of educational philosophy, there is an unconscious bias toward the position that, with ideal training, everyone would end up with the same performance.

Evidence for these views, at least as applied to humans,

is lacking. Some animals have been trained, through the methods pioneered by Skinner, to perform activities that could not have been a part of their natural lives, such as a pigeon's being taught to play table tennis. However, this does not prove that it is possible, by means such as suitable positive reinforcement in early childhood, to train every human to perform any activity at a very high level. Such outstanding talents as Mozart, John Stuart Mill, and Norbert Weiner have been produced in this way. But it is difficult to separate the roles of heredity and training in these cases. Those three people came from families in which previous generations also had high levels of ability. Many parents have tried to imitate the achievements of the elders Mozart, Mill, or Weiner with their children and found that the effort was unsuccessful. If early training is all that is needed to produce a Mozart, then we must admit that the precise methods for such training still elude us. There are successful training programs to enhance specific abilities, such as memorization, but even these do not appear to enable everyone to reach the high levels that some people do spontaneously. We should systematically investigate the extent to which training and the stimulation of motivation can lead to high levels of performance of various activities by a randomly selected population. Until the data from such an investigation are forthcoming, one must regard the view that anyone can be trained to do anything as no more than an ideological prejudice.

In any case, even if the possibility can be realized of training anyone to do anything, this is relevant only for the future. Institutions must currently find their personnel among the existing population, who have not been subjected to hypothetical training programs that could enhance the performance of those without natural talent. There is surely a hierarchy of performance abilities in the existing population, whatever the source of these abilities. Even the most zealous advocates of training do not maintain that any methods exist by which one could take adults and train them to perform at the highest levels in activities for which they are not naturally able. Nor do we have any methods by which motivation can be consistently made to substitute for high ability. Furthermore, it seems at least probable that whatever training methods are used will be more effective for those with natural ability than those without it. Therefore, in deciding who should belong to institutions that strive for a high level of achievement, there is currently no alternative to taking the abilities of the candidates as they occur and choosing among the candidates on the basis of these abilities. I will address later a different question— How should we go about training young people who have ability to perform at high levels in different activities?

It follows from my two main propositions that for those institutions devoted to carrying out worthy activities, the principal criterion that should be used to determine who belongs to them is a likely ability to contribute to the successful performance of the main activities of the institution. The use of other criteria that lead to membership in the institution by less able people, even for such purposes as the redressing of social inequities, will result in a lower level of performance of the worthy activities that are the institution's function. When society, because of other criteria that it imposes, insists that an institution employ less able people, this amounts to a decision that success in carrying out the worthwhile activity of the institution is less important than some other aim that will be furthered by such employment. Such a decision should not be accepted without strong objection on the part of those who value the basic function of these institutions.

How should the members of the institutions that carry out the most worthwhile functions be chosen? It is implicit in my argument that it is possible to predict in advance of their employment those people who are most able to perform the worthwhile functions. For most of the activities that I have in mind, a preliminary screening of possible candidates is not difficult. By the time someone is a plausible candidate for membership in the Boston Symphony Orchestra, the Princeton mathematics department, or the Chicago Bears football team, he or she will have already demonstrated a high degree of competence, through achievement in the relevant field. Of course, there will usually be many competent candidates for any position in such institutions. The criteria by which the apparently most competent candidates can be chosen are not always precise, and not the same from one type of institution to another.

A system that is generally used to select faculty at elitist universities is a form of apprenticeship, in which candidates are chosen provisionally and given the opportunity to prove their ability through actual performance. At universities, the apprentices are usually called assistant professors, and they are given five to seven years to demonstrate their abilities. Those who perform best during this apprenticeship are then chosen as permanent members of the institution. This system has for the most part been effective at staffing these universities with able faculty members. However, it does not work perfectly for several reasons. Criteria other than able performance in teaching and research may become involved in the decisions. Furthermore, even clearly able candidates may not be chosen at a given university because no permanent positions are available there at the time when a decision must be made about them. Most universities are partly or completely dependent financially on agencies outside themselves. For example, many universities are financed in whole or part by federal or local governments. The size of university faculties is, therefore, not completely under the control of the universities.

Even for an institution of fixed size, it would be possible to use a system in which new members, when they are judged to be more able, simply replace present members. This system is used by athletic teams, for example, where a player past his prime is usually sent away, unless he is fortunate enough to have a long-term contract. Universities generally do not follow this procedure, because of a practice known as tenure. The permanent faculties of universities have what are in effect lifetime jobs, and they cannot be replaced, except in very rare circumstances, even if obviously more able candidates for their positions are available. On its face, this tenure system seems like a clear violation of the principle of maximizing the performance of the functions of the university. To the extent that tenure for the present faculty interferes with the appointment of more qualified new faculty, universities are not using the people who can best perform the scholarly functions of research and teaching. It would be more in the spirit of maximizing high achievement to give university faculty members short-term contracts, somewhat like baseball players used to have, and to replace them with other, presumably younger, faculty members when their scholarly performance begins to wane. Of course, this could produce difficulties in finding new employment for the faculty members being replaced, but the force of argument I have been making is that the successful performance of the functions of elitist institutions should take precedence over the welfare of specific individuals.

However, there are some things to be said for the tenure system even within the context of elitism. College faculty members are not evaluated solely on the basis of performance. Tenure provides some security against those inside and outside of universities who would evaluate faculty on ideological grounds unrelated to the able performance of their functions. Tenure also acts as an inertial flywheel, which keeps faculties from changing very rapidly in response to intellectual fads. The security that tenure provides allows faculty to follow the lines of investigation that they consider important for extended periods of time even when these are not showing any immediate results. It has often happened that such investigations have ultimately proven to be immensely fruitful for science or scholarship. Finally, no university can always attract whomever it wants to its faculty. Other universities, and other centers of research, such as industrial laboratories, often seem more attractive to young scientists—for financial reasons or because better facilities are available there. In this situation, the added benefit of lifelong tenure may play an important role in attracting able young researchers to university faculties. Similar considerations apply in some of the social sciences, such as economics.

The tenure system must ultimately be evaluated in the light of whether there is an alternative to it that would result in better performance of the functions of universities. At present there is no clear evidence about whether the use of tenure has a significant effect in either direction on how well university faculty perform their research and teaching functions. There have been periods, such as the 1970s, in which many highly qualified people could not be appointed to university faculties because most of the available positions were already occupied by tenured faculty. However, this is not the usual situation. My experience is that at the physics departments of leading universities, the most able candidates for faculty positions have been able to obtain appointments, even in periods when few positions were available.

In view of the positive and negative aspects of university tenure in the context of elitism, it might be interesting for some universities to try to operate outside the tenure system, with the rapid turnover of faculty that this change would allow, in order to see the effect of this change on the faculty that could be appointed and on the relative performance of these faculty.

An alternative system for choosing the members of institutions would be to give nationwide examinations to test performance in some field and award positions on the basis of performance on these examinations. While this method has been used in some European countries to choose professors at universities, it has not been used much in America to determine membership in elitist institutions, although it is sometimes used to decide which candidates will enter the training programs for these institutions. The elitist institutions in America, especially the universities, are usually independent of one another and of the central government. Therefore, even if a rank ordering of candidates could be determined, no mechanism exists for assigning these candidates among those institutions that have positions to fill. Furthermore, such examinations are not yet sufficiently accurate predictors of performance that they can effectively be used to determine membership in elitist institutions. For example, tests such as the Graduate Record Examination, given to college seniors, correlate only moderately well with performance in graduate school and even less well with eventual research or scholarly achievements.

Many universities allow the present members of their faculties to choose new members, with only moderate intervention by those outside the faculty. This system usually works well to ensure the quality of new appointments. Most faculty members wish to have colleagues who are as able as can be obtained. However, there have been serious problems with the system in a variety of circumstances. One problem that has occurred at some universities is disagreement among present faculty members about what constitutes merit on the part of prospective members of the institution. Such disagreements occur not so much over the merits of individual candidates as over the propriety of the work that they do. Often this problem exists because of fundamental disagreements among present faculty members about what aspects of their field are most important or significant. This type of conflict is likely to arise in one of two circumstances. If there has been a substantial change in the nature of the field itself, then there can be "generational" conflicts between those who practice the old and new versions. For example, in several recent situations at universities, conflicts have occurred between those who practice descriptive forms of political science or history and those who practice more mathematical forms. These conflicts sometimes paralyze the process of hiring new faculty, because the existing faculty cannot agree about the value of the new approach. This type of generational conflict usually cures itself over a period of years. If the new approach is a fad, as it often is, then it will not affect the composition of university departments for very long. On the other hand, if it really represents progress in the field, then its proponents are likely to become the dominant force at universities, as the proponents of the old practice gradually leave the scene and are replaced by those more comfortable with the new methods.

This problem is related to a general difficulty with elitism, which is the possibility that a group of leaders in some field becomes so convinced of the eternal significance of its own work that it acts to suppress, by whatever means are available to it, alternative approaches to the same subject. For example, the faculty of a department at one university may refuse to appoint new faculty members who take a different approach to their discipline than that of the existing members. This has happened many times, especially in fields where there are uncertain standards for merit, or deep disagreements about what is important in the field. It is too much to expect that fallible humans will evaluate themselves and their work so objectively that they would willingly abandon an institution they have been identified with to those they consider intellectual barbarians. However, it is a happy aspect of the organization of American society that any such control is relatively localized. Those who follow one approach to a discipline may control a department at one university or a group of universities, but there are enough other universities so that someone who is strongly motivated to follow an alternative approach can find a place to do so.

Such disagreements about the value of specific areas of a discipline may result in short-term departures from the principle of hiring and promoting people on the basis of merit but do not usually interfere with it for very long. A university faculty that holds out indefinitely against a valid new trend in some field is likely to find that it is no longer among the best departments in the field and hasten to correct its errors. A university that goes too far in filling its faculties with followers of some new intellectual fad will soon find that the students it produces are unable to make their way outside the university, and be forced to rethink its priorities.

Another, more serious, situation in which a conflict between competing schools of thought often arises occurs when the activity of the institution becomes subordinated, in the view of some of its members, to some "higher" aim, usually ideological or political in nature. This is a perennial problem in the social sciences. It is less common in the natural sciences, although some natural scientists have tried to impose their ideological views on the membership of other departments at their universities. When such ideological divisions occur, as apparently has happened recently at Harvard Law School, those on either side of the ideological divide may come to feel that it is more important to appoint members of their own faction than to find the most able candidates. Indeed, their evaluations may be determined by the views of these various candidates about whatever ideological dispute is at hand. For a long time no avowed Marxist was likely to be appointed to a professorship in economics or history at any American university. This situation was not entirely the result of government pressure, although that was a contributing factor. There was also some feeling among university social-science faculties that keeping Marxists out of universities was more important than finding the most able faculty members, or that being a Marxist was itself sufficient indication of academic incompetence.

While the exclusion of Marxists is no longer a general rule of procedure at American universities, it has in some instances been replaced by exclusions that are similarly motivated by ideology. For example, there has been systematic persecution, by ideologues inside and outside universities, of people such as educational psychologist Arthur Jensen and sociobiologist E. O. Wilson. The ideology of many of those who carry out this type of persecution is an extreme version of the view that all differences between individuals are due to upbringing or to motivation rather than to innate factors. The forms of persecution have ranged from verbal attacks to physical violence. The willingness of the ideologues to go beyond the bounds of decency in their crusade to keep universities from hearing views that contradict with those that they approve has made it highly unlikely that someone who openly advocates the view that intelligence has a strong hereditary component would be appointed to the faculty of a leading American university, either in a field such as psychology, in which the view might be relevant to an appointment, or in fields in which it would be completely irrelevant. This situation is almost entirely unrelated to any intellectual merits that the position has or lacks. Rather, it is a consequence of the willingness of some ideologues to use indefensible methods against those whose views they oppose.

This attitude of the academic ideologues is the mirror image of the exclusionary policies of an earlier time, some of which were used against the very group of people who now want to enforce a new purity of thought. Their attempt to do this is as subversive to the achievement of quality among university faculties as anti-Marxist or anti-atheist policies once were.

Ideological considerations have come to play a role in university appointments in part because in many disciplines it is difficult to determine merit. When there are real disagreements about the central core of a subject, it becomes easy to substitute other criteria for the determination of merit. When even those who are most deeply concerned with a discipline cannot agree on what is most important, elitism becomes a very difficult attitude to apply to that discipline. Happily, there are a large number of academic disciplines for which such disagreement is minimal or absent, so that it is not difficult to determine intellectual merit.

Of course, there are circumstances other than ideological crusades in which elitist institutions have failed to use the criterion of high performance in selecting their membership. Race, religion, and gender are just some of the grounds that have inappropriately been used instead of merit to choose or to exclude members of these institutions. These practices were much more prevalent in the past, when even the best universities were not so explicitly dedicated to achieving the highest standards of scholarship. But such practices still exist in some cases, with somewhat different groups being excluded. Many universities in recent years have had bitter disputes about the hiring or firing of individuals who have not been evaluated on their merits because of biases among those making the decisions.

When such exclusions happen, the institutions that practice them compromise their basic aim, which is to achieve the highest level of performance of the intellectual activities for which they were created. To the extent that elitist institutions are currently still making such arbitrary exclusions, they should be condemned as not living up to their expressed aims. Those guilty of such practices should be stripped of the power to influence future decisions.

However, the conclusion that a specific institution or university in general is biased in choosing its faculty should be based on actual practices, not on an unjustified inference that such practices exist. The fact that the members of many elitist institutions of all types do not have the same distribution as the total population with regard to race, religion, or gender is not by itself evidence for exclusion of worthy candidates. There is no reason to expect that the talents required for each worthwhile activity are distributed in the same way among different groups. Indeed, there is a good deal of evidence to the contrary. For example, in the existing population of twenty-one-year-olds, an objective evaluation of talents will show that more men than women can solve difficult mathematics problems. Given that such differences occur in the population, elitist institutions would be less effective at carrying out their designated activities if their membership did not mirror these differences in the talents required to carry out these activities.

Affirmative-action programs began as an effort toward the elimination of actual bias in hiring or promotion. However, many of them have gone beyond this and have as their goal the achievement of a distribution of members within an elitist institution, such as a college faculty, that is the same as the distribution of targeted groups in the general population. These programs have not had much direct effect on the composition of college faculties, although they have forced faculty members to do immense amounts of paperwork in order to prove that they are actually doing what they say they are—trying to hire the most qualified people to teach and do research. What is the basis of affirmative-action programs that aim toward a specific population distribution for the membership of a faculty? Their justification relies either on the explicit—and, I believe, erroneous—assumption that the talents necessary for success in each field are randomly distributed in the population, or on the implicit assumption that the activity of the institution is not worth doing as well as possible. These assumptions are not made about such elitist athletic institutions as the Los Angeles Lakers basketball team, whose membership distribution among population subgroups is also not a mirror of the distribution in the population as a whole. Those academics who, in the name of social justice, are unwilling to accept the consequences of elitism with regard to the membership of their institutions but accept it unquestioningly at athletic institutions are really saying that the academic work done at universities is less worthwhile than what is done in football stadiums. They are surely entitled to that opinion, but it should not remain unchallenged by intellectual opposition from those of us who consider it absurd.

* * *

Recently there has been discussion at universities about a different type of "affirmative action," involving not persons but ideas. Many universities teach courses, such as Columbia's Contemporary Civilization or Humanities, which require all the students to read a specific set of books, selected from those that are considered to be of special merit, or that have been extremely influential on the development of American society. This practice has been criticized by groups within the university who object to the fact that insufficient attention is paid to other works not included among those that everyone is required to read. For example, it has been argued that the literary works include too few by African, Asian, or female writers. Also, it has been argued that by emphasizing the development of European and American culture, the courses slight other cultures, making it appear to the students that these are less worthy.

Although there are some positive things to be said about this concept of affirmative action for ideas, I think that for the most part it is misguided. There are lessons to be learned from the study of other cultures, and college students should have the opportunity to do this. Also, many students who enter college have already read several of the standard works that are found in the typical Great Books course, and a case can be made that they will learn more from the study of other books than they would from a more sophisticated analysis of the same works.

However, courses of university study are necessarily limited in scope. In four years of study, a student will attend some 1,250 hours of lectures, not nearly enough time to cover the full content of human culture. Necessarily, choices must be made as to what topics or works are most worthwhile for study. There are two aspects of such choices. The specific works to be included in each course should be determined by those teaching the course, who are usually experts on that particular subject. This decision should be made solely on the grounds of the merit of the works. If the experts in a field do not believe that a work has high value according to the standards of merit prevailing in their discipline, it is a clear violation of the principles of elitist universities for others who are not experts to instruct them to believe otherwise.

The other choice concerns the decision about which topics should be included in the general requirements for education. This question is more complex, as it cuts across ordinary disciplinary lines, and must be made by the faculty as a whole. Universities vary a good deal in their general course requirements, and these requirements have changed considerably over the years, although not according to any regular pattern. A solution to this difficult problem is not the purpose of this article. Unlike such authors as Allan Bloom, I do not think that there is a unique answer that all universities should adopt to the question of how to balance the claims to a place in the curriculum among such subjects as natural science, social science, mathematics, and the humanities. However, it seems obvious that whatever the basis for such a decision, it should be made on academic grounds and should be immune to transient ideological pressures. Some universities, including my own, have considered changing their required courses of study because of actual or threatened demonstrations by groups of students who have objected to some aspects of the existing requirements. In my opinion, decisions made on this basis are an indication of academic incompetence, both on the part of the students demanding such changes and of the faculty who assent to them. It is as inappropriate for a faculty to change its curriculum in order to assuage student protesters as it would be inappropriate for the faculty to change the curriculum in order to mollify a legislature that finds the content of that curriculum subversive of public morals.

An issue related to those I have discussed is whether we should have ''schools'' devoted to the training of future members of elitist institutions. This procedure is widely followed in other countries, and to some extent is accepted in America. Institutions such as the Juilliard School for music, Stuyvesant High School for science, and the University of Oklahoma for football all play the role of preparing those who will eventually staff the various elitist institutions of America. However, this type of concentration of talented students in a few institutions has never gone as far here as in countries such as France, where, for example, almost all the future mathematicians attend one or two universities. Admission to such training schools is very important because, while innate ability is necessary, in most cases it is not sufficient to achieve the highest levels of performance without adequate training and motivation, both of which the schools can help furnish.

These training schools employ teachers or coaches who are more able than most to teach the skills needed in the activities that the students will someday perform. The curriculum to which the students are exposed is strongly focused on preparing them for these activities. Finally, students are exposed to others whose interests and abilities are similar to their own. As a product of one such school, the Bronx High School of Science, I can testify that the last of these features is in many ways the most important. The interaction with other bright students who were interested in science was one of the most important influences on my career and on those of many of my classmates.

The training schools' success in producing leaders in the various fields in which they operate has not spared them from criticism. As usual, this criticism has concentrated on schools that train intellectually able students, as opposed to those that train athletically or artistically able students. The main thrust of the criticism has been that by concentrating the able students at a few schools, we are short-changing the students who remain at other schools. The injuries that are supposedly being done to those students not at the special schools include not getting the best teachers, not getting sufficient financial support, and being deprived of beneficial exposure to the more able students who have been removed to the special schools. Many of these criticisms have been applied specifically to schools supported by some government body, but some of the criticism has been applied to any school devoted to training able students, however it is supported.

I think this type of criticism is almost entirely misdirected. When it has been taken seriously and acted upon, there has been substantial harm both to society and to the able students who have been deprived of the opportunity to reach the highest levels allowed by their talents. Of these anti-elitist criticisms, the one that is most seriously wrong both on moral and on practical grounds is the one that calls for sacrificing the welfare of the more able students in order to obtain some benefits for the less able. There is no reason to expect that a student who is talented in mathematics, for example, would choose freely to remain in a class with those less able, in the hope that his presence there would somehow stir the others to higher achievement. This practice amounts to subordinating the educational interests of some individuals to those of others, and it strongly violates a basic principle of our social organization—that no person should be regarded by society as a means to some end of another person. As Kant wrote in the *Metaphysics of Morals*: "Every man is to be respected as an absolute end in himself; and it is a crime against the dignity that belongs to him as a human being, to use him as a means for some external purpose."

This argument against special schools is also doubtful on factual grounds. There is evidence that when numbers of able students are brought together in the same class or school, it has a beneficial "cluster effect" on the performance of each student. However, there is little indication that being taught together with more able students has a similar beneficial effect on those of little talent. Indeed, there is anecdotal evidence that being in a class with much brighter students can discourage others from learning.

It has sometimes been claimed that keeping talented students in the same schools and classes as the less talented is really for their own good. The argument is that this practice allows the talented students to see what the "real world'' is like, whereas putting them in a school of their own would insulate them from contact with the majority population, with whom they will eventually have to inter-act. This argument suggests a complete lack of knowledge by those who make it of the situation of the talented in a typical school setting. To the extent that the talented have a problem in interacting with others, it is much more se-vere for children, for whom there is so much influence of peer pressure, than for adults, whose character is more fully formed. Able students have often complained about unpleasant experiences in situations in which they were the only people at a school interested in science or music or whatever their passion was, whereas it is rare to hear them complain about being at a school with other talented stu-dents.

The claim that establishing special schools for students of high ability deprives the less able students of good teach-ers is also of little merit. Anyone who has observed college teachers knows that teaching students with great talent in some field requires a different approach and different abil-ities than teaching the subject to the average student, and there is little reason to doubt that this is true at other ed-ucational levels as well. Furthermore, as I have found in my own teaching career, groups of heterogeneous ability are intrinsically more difficult to teach than more homo-geneous groups because of the problem in finding the right level at which to teach. In a group of students with widely varying ability, it is very difficult to avoid either boring the more able students or mystifying the less able ones. In many cases, teachers who are able to do one cannot do the other.

What of the argument that, by devoting financial re-sources to educating the talented, society is stinting on re-sources for the less talented? If this were valid it would indeed be a serious criticism, but it is probably not valid. Most of the recent thrust of educational concern in Amer-ica has involved those who for various reasons fall below the average of educational achievement. Such concern is indeed warranted by the sorry state of much of the education that we give to subachievers. However, this neglect of weak students has diverted us from another concern—the education we give to the best of our students. Here, also, we fall far short of what we could do. Specialized training programs for students of high ability, such as the Columbia University program for secondary-school students with talent in science and mathematics, are available only to a small fraction of the students who could benefit from them.

The truth is that in most places, there are no programs at all for educating the highly talented, and where programs do exist, the resources devoted to them are a small fraction of those used to educate those with subnormal abilities, or those who have behavioral problems. The proportion of the overall educational resources used to train the highly able is so small that, far from using too much of our educational resources on them, we err in the opposite direction, by not providing those talented students with training that would allow them to make full use of their abilities. When we neglect the needs of our best students for an appropriate education, we shortchange these students and fail to develop intellectual resources that could be of great future benefit to society.

A problem that does exist for schools that train talented students is how to determine who should be given such training. The age at which great ability can be easily recognized varies from one discipline to another. For musical performance, it can be done quite early, before the age of ten. For mathematics, it can be done in the early teens, while for less symbolic sciences, such as biology, it probably cannot be done before college. It would be a good idea to have a national testing program for those abilities—athletic, intellectual, and artistic—that can be reliably detected at an early age. If such a program were set up, youngsters who did extremely well on the tests could be identified as candidates for training to help them succeed at the activities that would make use of their abilities. This would help eliminate situations in which talented students are deprived of training because their abilities are not recognized. It is quite possible that in our present haphazard system, we are not identifying many of the children who have such abilities. It is very important to identify such students early enough to enable them to make use of their abilities. But the tests that we have available are not infallible guides to later performance. Possibly better tests to predict high achievement could be devised if we set to work on it. In the meantime we should make sure that the route to eventual membership in elitist institutions is not closed to those who did not test well when young. To the greatest extent possible, we should monitor the work of those who are not in the specialized training schools, in order to find any talented students who have been missed by the selection process. It would, for example, be foolish to foreclose the opportunity for someone to become a mathematician just because he or she did badly on a test at age twelve.

There is one objection to elitist institutions that is not usually made explicit, but which is probably the underlying reason for much of the criticism of them. Our society is committed to achieving many things. One of our aims is a form of social equality. We want to avoid having legal or social distinctions between people that are based on accidents of birth. Another aim of society is that we wish to promote those activities that are generally recognized as worthy. Some tensions exist between the accomplishment of these aims. In striving to achieve excellent results in those activities that require exceptional abilities, we must distinguish those that possess such abilities. Those who are chosen in this way often obtain financial and social advantages over those not chosen. This problem of excessive rewards for talent is most severe for those whose activities are related to some type of entertainment, who can in many cases earn hundreds of times as much for their work as the average citizen. It is this type of result that is probably the ultimate objection to elitism. If there were no social or financial advantages ensuing from membership in elite institutions, then there would probably be few objections to them.

It may not be possible to avoid completely the correlation between high achievement and social rewards. But to give up the criterion of merit because it leads to social inequalities is to raise social equality above all the other principles of our society. This could easily result in a society in which we are all equally miserable. There are surely ways to avoid a situation in which those with talents are excessively rewarded, without discouraging them from using their talent at all. For example, it is not the social and financial rewards given to faculty members of elite universities that are their prime motivation toward high achievement. The most able of the faculty whom I know are mainly internally motivated, by the desire to do as well as they can in their chosen field of work. I expect that the same is true for members of many other elite institutions, such as symphony orchestras. Convincing people that a high level of achievement is its own best reward is probably the most effective way of diminishing the social inequalities of elitism.

Perhaps if it were considered desirable, we could work toward the goal of a society in which each person could accomplish anything that anyone else can do. Alternatively, we might be able to arrange that everyone be talented in at least one of the activities that society considers worthwhile. Achieving either type of society would probably require a substantial amount of interference in personal freedom, in such matters as the raising of children. In any case, neither of these possibilities has been realized anywhere in our present world. Given that talents are not the same for everybody, and that we have limited capacity to train those without native ability to achieve high levels of performance, society must choose between two alternatives. One is to encourage strongly those who can do extremely well at the things that we consider worthwhile, accepting that this will lead to some greater financial and social rewards to those with talent for those worthwhile activities. The other is to accept a substantially lesser degree of achievement of these activities, in the name of minimizing distinctions in how different individuals fare in life. Whenever people have been given a choice between these alternative strategies, they have chosen to identify and to reward the talented, while correctly insisting that no artificial barriers should exist to determining those with real talent. There is no popular enthusiasm for anti-elitism in fields in which high achievement is possible. The weakness of the case made by the proponents of anti-elitism cannot be strengthened by appealing to the will of the people. Those of us who value high achievement wherever it is found should not allow the arguments of the anti-elitists to be used to undermine the work of the institutions whose membership they criticize. It is folly to try to further one set of worthy ends by making it impossible to carry out another equally worthy set. Elitist institutions have been responsible for some of the best achievements of our society, and it would be tragic to prevent the future extension of these achievements by destroying these institutions.

ANOTHER REALITY CLUB

▼

JOAN RICHARDSON

The collective purpose of the Arensberg circle was to change the way human beings saw themselves in the world. This was really only the age-old function of the prophet. The members of the group saw their errand into the wilderness clearly: It was to create contexts, worlds within worlds, in their works of art, in which and through which those who were willing to submit themselves to the process illustrated and demanded by these works could perceive what it meant to live on the edge of experience in an ever-transforming present.

In New York between 1914 and 1921 there was another Reality Club. While it did not bear this or any other formal name, the principle on which it was organized was the same as ours—to bring together some of the best minds of the time and create an atmosphere in which their ideas would be both stimulated and shared. Walter Arensberg, a wealthy patron of the arts who brought the group together, was himself an intellectual heir to Francis Bacon, whose *New Atlantis* first suggested to Arensberg the pattern for his "reality club."

In his *New Atlantis* Bacon conjured a Utopia where luminaries of various disciplines lived and worked together in perfect harmony. This was a fiction. In reality the best way to approach this idea, Arensberg thought, was to provide the conditions that would at least prompt imperfect harmonies on a regular basis. And so for seven years Arensberg and his wife, Louise, opened their studio apartment on West Sixty-seventh Street off Central Park West to the stars of New York's new world universe. These included, at different times, Marcel Duchamp, Francis Picabia, Albert Gleizes, William Carlos Williams, Man Ray, Mina Loy, Edgard Varèse, Walter Pach, Walt Kuhn, Arthur Davies, Carl Van Vechten, and Beatrice Wood.

As is apparent from this list of names, there was one major difference between Arensberg's "reality club" and ours—the presence and participation of scientists and mathematicians. So while the earlier group shared with us a common pursuit, the nature of the talks and activities was quite different. It must not be supposed, however, that the participants were scientifically illiterate. Quite the contrary; Arensberg, acting always as the informal director of gatherings, made certain that his ''New Atlantans'' kept current with each development that revealed something more about reality. And there was a great deal to keep up with during these years as the Great War raging across the Atlantic threatened to destroy the faith in science that had produced, together with wondrous knowledge about things seen and unseeable, the technology that was itself destroying more than eight million lives. Among the contributions and discoveries of the period were the following: Niels Bohr's formulation of atomic structure; Robert Goddard's rocketry experiments; Albert Einstein's general theory of relativity; Sir Arthur Eddington's investigations of the physical properties of stars; Max Planck's introduction of quantum theory; Harlow Shapley's determination of the dimensions of the Milky Way and Max Wolf's mapping of its true structure; Vilhjalmur Stefansson's exploration north of the Arctic Circle; Ernest Shackleton's expedition to the Antarctic; and Ernest Rutherford's uncovering of a subatomic universe. Whether in the form of readings about these events and researches prepared and assigned to the group for future discussion or from information provided by an invited speaker, Arensberg provided real food for the thoughts of the various poets, painters, musicians, and others who met regularly in his comfortable home.

At each meeting copious quantities of exquisitely prepared foods and delicacies were well balanced by constantly flowing beverages. There were games, music, readings, whispered discussions in corners, and more than occasional bizarre behavior on the parts of one, two, three, four, or more of the geniuses who happened to be present on a given evening. The Baroness Elsa von Freytag-Loringhoven, for example, who seems to have been particularly drawn to the poets in the group, was always ready to shed all her clothes and parade herself as the most successful example of a "ready-made." And then there was Mina Loy, herself a poet, who one evening together with Marcel Duchamp, Beatrice Wood, Arlene Dresser, and Charles Demuth excused herself from the larger company to enjoy group sex in Duchamp's bed, conveniently located in the adjoining studio Arensberg had generously provided for the expatriate French artist.

The games were not all this exciting, however. Most, though playful, were serious. Again following the kind of thinking implicit in Francis Bacon's program for the *New Atlantis*, Arensberg set up activities that would stretch and tone the minds of his friends. There was almost always a chess game between Arensberg and Duchamp; others could look on or play their own game on another board. The poets of the group were asked to construct poems around subtle puns and covert complex structures. On the reading of a new work, the "game" for the group was to discover the carefully hidden key. Similarly, Arensberg delighted in adding to his impressive avant-garde art collection—he had been actively involved in the presentation of the 1913 Armory Show, and many of the pieces that once hung at the show later found a home in his studio—paintings or other objects that taunted viewers with apparent nonsense. There were many pieces by Duchamp, both completed and in progress. His famous *Large Glass*, or *The Bride Stripped Bare by Her Bachelors, Even*, was worked on and completed while Duchamp lived on West Sixty-seventh Street. One of his ready-mades, his *Trébuchet* (from the French verb *trébucher*, meaning "to trip, stumble"), a coat rack with four metal hangers, was nailed to the floor of his studio. Henri Rousseau's *Merry Jesters* was another particularly intriguing puzzler. Arensberg himself was known to have stood for up to four hours before a canvas studying its meaning. He no doubt wanted his circle to enjoy a similar experience. The *Merry Jesters* depicts a family of what most closely resemble baboons, all staring out of center ground at an imagined audience. A baby bottle hangs in the place where one would expect a breast on the female baboon; the bottle squirts milk. A young baboon also looks out of the canvas, but from behind the mature animals. Two other mature animals play with what seem to be a back scratcher and a gardening tool. A cockatiel perches on a branch above, to the right of center; a sprig of fox-glove symbolically balances the bird on the left side of the canvas. These are the only interruptions to the dense green jungle foliage characteristic of Rousseau's paintings and meticulously rendered here. Members of the group spent hours trying to unlock the conundrum presented by this fanciful work.

Together with this and the Duchamps, Cézanne, Braque, Brancusi, Picasso, Matisse, Picabia, Sheeler, Derain, Joseph Stella, and Renoir were also well represented in Arensberg's collection. In addition, there were many African and pre-Columbian pieces and occasional single items from other painters like Giorgio di Chirico. Already in the second decade of the century, Arensberg was leading the avant-garde of the avant-garde. He was known in New York as the father of what would come to be called Dada, even before the movement was given its name at the Café Voltaire in Zurich in 1916.

But Arensberg and his friends had a much more serious intention than that usually attributed to the Dadaists, of shocking the bourgeoisie. While they did indeed scorn middle-class values and wholeheartedly rejected the Protestant work ethic that informed them, their purpose went beyond the specifically social aspect. The individuals who gathered regularly in the West Sixty-seventh Street apartment were acutely aware that reality as they had been educated to know it no longer existed. The impact of Darwin's discovery of our common ancestor as "a hairy quadruped, mostly arboreal in its habits," had been felt. Nietzsche had proclaimed the death of God, Freud had uncovered the unknown within each breast, and Einstein had described an unimaginable universe. In this climate, even "the absence of imagination itself had to be imagined," as Wallace Stevens, another of the members of the

Arensberg circle, put it. The poetry, music, painting, and sculpture of those who attempted to grapple with the idea of the new world they inhabited was characterized by features alien to what had come to be accepted as art until this burdened moment.

The most general and striking of these features was the apparent irreverence for the past displayed in the break from the traditional forms of representing reality. The most subtle feature was a pervasive undertone of irony that colored even what seemed to be the most purely aesthetic, abstract renderings. The most obvious of these stylistic shifts was the breaking up of surface into several planes that characterized cubism. The strongest effect of this device was to destroy the distinction between background and foreground, decentering the "subject" from the privileged position it had enjoyed in perspectival depictions. From one side this mimicked the change in the way human beings saw themselves in relationship to the historical and natural orders and to their personal, unconscious order, hidden from yet motivating them. In this sense, the decentering symbolized the actual feeling of dislocation experienced by those who allowed themselves to remain open to what the discoveries of Darwin and Freud meant. The individual could no longer be understood as something separate from the background that had produced him or her. Cubism and the other new forms reflected this breakup of an integrated identity.

Seen from another side, this reflected the aesthetic translation of Kant's perception of the indivisibility of inner and outer realms: that the understanding of reality must come not from placing inner against outer but from understanding the fused and interdependent relation between them. Since the bases of this relation are time and space, the relation constantly changes, shifts in the way cubist presentations tried to imitate. It is impossible to see all the aspects of the "subject" of a cubist canvas at once, in the same way it is impossible to see both chalice and two facing profiles in the illustration so often used to make this point about perception, the point taken as the meaning of a "relativistic" view of the pictorial plane.

In terms of cubist aesthetic and method, this was articulated in two fundamental ways, one having to do with time, the other with space. The primary apprehension concerning time was that no subject or object could be experienced fully if the subject or object was separated from past knowledge of it. The representation of reality was "truer" when the thing known was presented incorporating some record of previous experience. The various intersecting and juxtaposed spatial forms of a cubist canvas were intended to mirror this constant movement of consciousness, aware of itself as it observed something external that temporarily focused attention.

Extending this understanding to its extreme, Marcel Duchamp eventually abandoned even the canvas that created a barrier between observer and ground beyond the work. The *Large Glass*, or *The Bride Stripped Bare by Her Bachelors, Even* includes the ever-shifting present background seen through the glass but incorporated by its frame.

As early as the eighteenth century, there had been experimentation in representing a new understanding of time—in Mozart's restructuring of phrasing, for example. But not until the early twentieth century, as art became as self-conscious as consciousness itself had become with Kant and Hegel, were these aesthetic developments formalized. The philosopher who first handled these effects in a direct and practical way, examining them from various angles as if he himself were a cubist painter, was Henri Bergson, who, appropriately, wrote seminal pieces on consciousness, time, and laughter. This work was translated and published serially in Alfred Stieglitz's *Camera Work*. *Camera Work* (in which Gertrude Stein's work was first published as well), together with Freud's *Interpretation of Dreams* and certain other key texts, constituted required reading for the members of the Arensberg circle.

In translating the new understanding of time into formal artistic elements, painters, writers, and musicians focused primarily on intervals and how varying intervals could be used to approximate the distinctions between the different kinds of time that were now being discussed. The music of Erik Satie, Igor Stravinsky, Darius Milhaud, and Arthur Honegger—played by Louise Arensberg and Edgard Varèse on the piano—illustrated this clearly for the group. In poetry, too, there was an attempt to create other kinds of time intervals. By using titles that were puzzling, for example, poets hoped, in part, to force pauses or rests, spaces where the listeners or readers could try to figure out the relationship between title and poem. Oriental masters had earlier established the same kind of tension in their koans. This aspect was linked to a comic element. For Zen masters the illogicality of a koan is intended to produce the laughter accompanying the realization of reason's limits; this experience is a moment of enlightenment when, according to one of their standard texts, the individual has the experience known as the ''snow man,'' melting into a sweat at the moment of illumination—a moment when the ego dissolves.

All these innovations, including the stress on the comic element, had behind them a serious philosophical intent. In the most general terms, the aim was to dissolve the distinction between subject and object, to solve the problem Descartes had set three centuries earlier; the attempt continues today.

In his *Masters of Modern Art*, Walter Pach, another of the regular members of the circle, gave a coherent account of the historical evolution of the new forms and named the different features of these forms, all of which play around the underlying theme of the identification of inner and outer, time and space, what is and what seems. In discussing the genesis of the modernist movement, he compared the early twentieth century to the Renaissance, noting how contemporary painters went to museums to broaden their bases of reference in the same way that the fifteenth-century painters looked to the classical past. This represented an intuitive attempt to obviate the limitations derived from the eighteenth century's mannered extension of one side of the Cartesian duality, which had, then, to be compensated for by the antithetical romantic excesses of the nineteenth. The extreme separation of the thinking subject, reason's instrument, from its organic sources prompted the romantic reaction, which, when it was later empirically evidenced and argued for by Darwin, in turn prompted the disguising reaction described by the term "Victorian." Imitating the Renaissance model represented, in large part, a desire to return to a point before the disjunction between man and nature, mind and body was made, in the hope that a synthesis could be achieved. By the end of the nineteenth century this attempt had produced the symbolist aesthetic. Symbolism stressed what Charles Baudelaire popularized as a system of "correspondences," linking the individual to nature and the universe in a way that echoed the fifteenth- and sixteenth-century neo-Platonists' interest in the Cabala and Hermeticism, both of which offered, in different form, magical or mystical keys to unlock the secrets of the universe and the individual's connection with it.

Arensberg, Duchamp, and the rest of the circle were involved with the lore of the hermetic tradition. For Arensberg this interest had begun when he first became curious about Francis Bacon. In studying the literature of magic and alchemy, he learned the symbolism passed down through the centuries to characterize the processes that were necessary to the "Great Work" of finding the philosopher's stone and transmuting lead into gold. Becoming familiar with these terms helped him in his later work on the cryptography of Shakespeare (whom he, like many others around the turn of the century, believed to be identical with Francis Bacon) and Dante. He also made this arcane vocabulary available to the members of his circle so that they could make the games of their poems and paintings more challenging. Duchamp used alchemical symbols and references freely in his *Great Glass* while pointing directly to the "Great Work" with his title. Mina Loy and Wallace

Stevens, too, worked the method and iconography of the hermetic tradition into their poetry.

The original purpose of the alchemists' "Great Work" was to discover the philosopher's stone, the catalyst that would transform base metals, like lead, into gold. By the fifteenth century, after Paracelsus, this pursuit had already become a metaphor for finding the gold understood as a medicinal unguent that would cure human ills. By the time the idea itself became transmuted over the centuries, separating the early alchemists from twentieth-century initiates, the literal aspect had crystallized and been changed into chemistry, while the metaphorical aspect had sublimed into the search for a spiritual catalyst that would change the base elements of human experience into a golden rule to help individuals live their lives in a better way.

The collective purpose of the Arensberg circle was to change the way human beings saw themselves in the world. This was really only the age-old function of the prophet. The members of the group saw their errand into the wilderness clearly: It was to create contexts, worlds within worlds, in their works of art, in which and through which those who were willing to submit themselves to the process illustrated and demanded by these works could perceive what it meant to live on the edge of experience in an ever-transforming present. This meant living without the encumbrance of certainty provided by the various versions of the Western myth of progress, which for nearly two millennia had kept human beings' minds separated from their bodies. The myth had succeeded so well that the mind's technology was in the process of sacrificing the bodies of eight million young men at its altar.

The intention of those who met in Arensberg's studio was to restore to human beings what Stevens once called the "instinct of joy." Indulging this sense did not mean taking an easy step into laughing at the surface details of experience or even at the deeper, ironic condition of human life. What these individuals perceived was that the closer one could approach pure *being*, without the interference of distracting appearances—"Let be be finale of seem"—the closer one came to joy, the pleasure of merely circulating. The more often and the longer this state could be sustained, as Walter Pater had suggested in his conclusion to *The Renaissance*, the more likely it became that one could understand something about the nature of nature—by regarding it not only from outside as an object of contemplation but knowing it from inside, as one with it, experiencing the self as matter being continuously transformed into spirit, feeling the waves of energy that are the universe move in and out, pass through the temporary container of the body. The individuals of the Arensberg group were working to provide, through their carefully constructed works, an access to perceiving reality at this level.

The stress that Duchamp, for example, laid on eros is at the center of this understanding, which is not surprising, since it is usually through eros that human beings first come into mature contact with their oneness with the universe. Duchamp was not alone in having this perception. Plato and the old Chinese sages knew it, and, among Duchamp's contemporaries, D. H. Lawrence, Sigmund Freud, and Havelock Ellis began from this premise. T. S. Eliot, too, began from it, seeing the Victorians' extreme divorce of mind from body as the cause of his personal predicament and the largest single feature contributing to the conditions that gave birth to World War I.

When Marcel Duchamp—alias Rrose Sélavy (a homonymic pun for *"Eros c'est la vie"* ["Eros is life."])—arrived in New York and began presenting his work, it seemed that he had experientially understood what Freud had started to lay out abstractly and clinically in his *Three Essays on the Theory of Sexuality*, subjects he would make both broader and more specific in *Civilization and Its Discontents*. Duchamp seemed to be illustrating, with two- and three-dimensional examples, precisely the problems and consequences Freud delineated.

One of the strongest points to come through Duchamp's work is a comment on the attitude toward sex of the Western, civilized individual around the period of the First World War. This showed itself in the content of his most important works of these years. In the *Large Glass*, what was depicted was a sexual act: the beginning causes of desire described in wholly mechanical terms that are, at the same time, allegorical forms for alchemical processes. When these are considered together with his other work, the related *Nude Descending a Staircase* and *King and Queen Surrounded by Swift Nudes*, as well as with the production of his later years, it is plain that Duchamp was translating into the symbolic forms he presented his observation that the only way human beings of his generation seemed able to accept and deal with their sexual appetites was in dissociated, mechanical terms. This protected them from having to look closely at and admit, with the full range of feeling entailed, their animality.

It was not uncontrolled ribaldry alone, then, that led Mina Loy and her playmates to Duchamp's bed. There was a method to this apparent madness. A new world, another reality, was being explored. After seven years, the Arensbergs, actually quite conservative in their private manners, seem to have wearied of the expense and excitement of hosting their talented and eccentric company; they moved themselves and their by then well-noted art collection to California. (It is now part of the permanent collection of the Philadelphia Museum of Art.) The discoveries of the individuals that had been part of the circle continued, however. Almost every member of the Arensberg group went on to produce significant work or to contribute to creating contexts that made such work possible; a quick review of the names of the members attests to this. But the group did not sustain itself. Once its prime mover and presiding genius left New York, there were no more meetings, though occasionally two or three of the old circle met for lunch or dinner and shared news about their latest interests and work.

It is, I think, highly unusual and significant that almost all the members of the Arensberg circle made contributions that have in some way changed or influenced the way we experience the world around us. It was not that those who formed the group had already established their reputations—quite the opposite. What was it, then, that accounts for such a high success rate? Was it simply Arensberg's acuity in recognizing the signs of genius among those with whom he came in contact that led him to invite the chosen to his soirées? Or did the atmosphere Arensberg created trigger individual solutions to what presented itself during the early years of the century as chaotic uncertainty?

Perhaps we in 1988 have grown too comfortable with uncertainty. We no longer seem to try to come up with individual solutions to the personal, social, historical, ethical, or aesthetic problems it presents. We accept, rather, certain words about uncertainty and go about our business. In part, those of us who are not fluent in the current scientific languages feel dependent on those who can explain some of what we don't understand. Unlike Arensberg and his company, who were admittedly and actively perplexed about the crisis in belief and knowledge generated by the contributions of Darwin, Freud, and Einstein, we seem to take the facts of these contributions in stride. We assume that the scientists will provide solutions—and so we do not propose the right kinds of questions to ourselves or to others. I believe it is this situation that the present Reality Club addresses. The purpose of our gatherings is not to look simply *at* facts, but *through* them. Together we attempt to forge a common language with which questions can be posed and problems considered. With the understanding that this language can provide, we can each then go on to pursue our individual interests and make our contributions.

LIST OF CONTRIBUTORS

MARY CATHERINE BATESON is Robinson Professor of Anthropology and English, George Mason University, and author of *With A Daughter's Eye: A Memoir of Margaret Mead and Gregory Bateson* (Morrow, 1984); with Gregory Bateson, *Angels Fear: Toward an Epistemology of the Sacred* (Macmillan, 1987), and with Richard A. Goldsby, *Thinking AIDS* (Addison Wesley, 1988). SEVANNE MARGARET KASSARJIAN is a student at Brown University.

MORRIS BERMAN is an author, lecturer, and social critic. His published works include *Social Change and Scientific Organization* (Cornell University Press) and *The Reenchantment of the World* (Bantam). His article in this issue is adapted from his forthcoming book, *Coming to Our Senses* (Simon & Schuster).

WILLIAM CALVIN is a neurophysiologist at the University of Washington in Seattle, and author of *The Throwing Madonna: Essays on the Brain* (McGraw-Hill, 1983) and *The River That Flows Uphill: A Journey from the Big Bang to the Big Brain* (Macmillan, 1986). His article in this issue is adapted from his forthcoming book *Conscious Machines: Seashore Speculations on Darwinian Designs* (Bantam) and from his recent article in *Nature*, entitled "The Brain as a Darwin Machine."

MIHALY CSIKSZENTMIHALYI, a research psychologist who studies "flow states," is Chairman, Department of Behavioral Sciences, University of Chicago, and author of the forthcoming *The Psychology of Optimal Experience* (Harper & Row).

K. ERIC DREXLER is a researcher at M.I.T. and Stanford who is concerned with emerging technologies and their consequences for the future. He is the author of *Engines of Creation* (Anchor, 1986).

GERALD FEINBERG is a particle physicist, Professor of Physics, Columbia University, and author of *Life Beyond Earth* (with Robert Shapiro; Morrow, 1980) and *Solid Clues* (Simon & Schuster, 1985).

JULIUS KOREIN, M.D., is a neurobiologist who studies brain states of death, vegetation, and life. He is professor of Neurology, New York University Medical Center.

ROBERT LANGS, M.D., is a clinically trained psychoanalyst and author of twenty books on psychotherapeutic interaction, including *A Primer of Psychotherapy* (Gardner Press, 1988) and the forthcoming *Decoding Your Dreams* (Henry Holt). He is chief, Center for Communicative Research, Beth Israel Medical Center, New York.

LYNN MARGULIS is a biologist, Distinguished Professor (Department of Botany) at University of Massachusetts at Amherst, and author of *Symbiosis in Cell Evolution* (W. H. Freeman, 1981); *Origins of Sex* (with Dorion Sagan; Yale, 1986); *Microcosmos* (with Dorion Sagan; Summit, 1986); and the forthcoming *Mystery Dance* (with Dorion Sagan; Summit).

JOAN RICHARDSON is a biographer, professor of English at City University of New York, and author of *Wallace Stevens: The Early Years 1879–1923* (Morrow, 1986) and *Wallace Stevens: The Later Years 1923–1955* (Morrow, 1988).

DORION SAGAN is a writer, author of *Origins of Sex* (with Lynn Margulis; Yale, 1986); *Microcosmos* (with Lynn Margulis; Summit, 1986); and the forthcoming *Biospheres* (McGraw-Hill) and *Mystery Dance* (with Lynn Margulis; Summit).

ROGER SCHANK is professor of Psychology and of Computer Science, Yale University, and author of *The Cognitive Computer* (with Peter Childers; Addison-Wesley, 1984) and *The Creative Attitude: Learning To Ask and Answer the Right Questions* (Scribners).

ROBERT STERNBERG is IBM professor of Psychology and Education, Yale University, and author of several books: *The Triarchic Mind: A New Theory of Human Intelligence* (Viking); *The Triangle of Love* (Basic, 1988); and the forthcoming *Love the Way You Want It* (Bantam).

JOHN BROCKMAN, Editor
KATINKA MATSON, Associate Editor

REALITY CLUB TALKS

JOHN ALLEN: "Space Biospheres: Creation of Networked Evolutionary Entities." John Allen is executive chairman of Space Biospheres, a founder of Institute of Ecotechnics, and dramaturge to the Caravan of Dreams Theater.

MICHAEL ANDRE: "Untitled Reading." Michael Andre is a poet and the publisher of *Unmuzzled Ox*.

ISAAC ASIMOV: "The Interplay of Imagination and Reality." Isaac Asimov, author of hundreds of science and science fiction books, is one of the world's most prolific writers.

RICHARD BAKER-ROSHI: "Zen and World Survival." Richard Baker-Roshi is a Zen master and the founder and former abbot of the San Francisco Zen Center.

EDWIN BARBER: "The Future of the Book." Edwin Barber is vice-president of W. W. Norton and Co.

MARY CATHERINE BATESON: "Privacy and Biography." (*See* List of Contributors, page 317.)

PETER BERG: "Bioregionalism." Peter Berg is an environmentalist and the editor of *Planet/Drum*.

MORRIS BERMAN: "The Body as History." (*See* List of Contributors, page 317.)

STEWART BRAND: "Doing Good"; "The Media Lab." Stewart Brand, publisher and editor of Point Foundation, is author of *II Cybernetic Frontiers* and *The Media Lab: Inventing the Future at M.I.T.*, and editor of *The Whole Earth Catalog* and *The Whole Earth Software Catalog*.

JOHN BROCKMAN: "The Reality Club." John Brockman, founder of The Reality Club, is a writer and literary agent. He is the author of *By the Late John Brockman*, *37*, and *Afterwords*, editor of *About Bateson*, and co-author of *The Philosopher's Game*.

ELLEN BURSTYN: "On Acting." Ellen Burstyn is an actor, and star of *Alice Doesn't Live Here Anymore*, *The Exorcist*, and *Twice in a Lifetime*.

WILLIAM CALVIN: "Throwing and Brain Evolution." (*See* List of Contributors, page 317.)

FRITJOF CAPRA: "The Turning Point." Fritjof Capra is a physicist, founder of The Elmwood Institute, and author of *The Tao of Physics*, *The Turning Point*, and *Uncommon Wisdom*.

DOUGLAS CASEY: "Anarchy." Douglas Casey is a libertarian, financial expert, and author of *Crisis Investing* and *The International Man*.

SIDNEY COLEMAN: "How Unified Theory Happened." Sidney Coleman is a cosmologist and professor of physics at Harvard University.

RON COOPER: "Voids and Volumes." Ron Cooper, "the king of downtown," is one of the original artists in the L.A. downtown loft scene.

MIHALY CSIKSZENTMIHALYI: "The Psychology of Optimal Experience." (*See* List of Contributors, page 317.)

ANNIE DILLARD: "Total Eclipse." Annie Dillard is the Pulitzer Prize-winning author of *Pilgrim at Tinker Creek*. Her other works include *Holy the Firm*, *Living by Fiction*, and *Teaching a Stone to Talk*.

HUGH DOWNS: "Celebrity and Visibility." Hugh Downs is the co-host of ABC News's "20/20" and a social commentator.

K. ERIC DREXLER: "Nanotechnology: Beyond Genetic Engineering." (*See* List of Contributors, page 317.)

ESTHER DYSON: "Communing Computers." Esther Dyson is editor and publisher of *Release 1.0*, a newsletter about the computer industry and the transformation of artificial intelligence into a commercial technology.

FREEMAN DYSON: "Engineer's Dreams." Freeman Dyson is professor of physics at The Institute of Advanced Study, Princeton, and author of *Disturbing the Universe* and *Weapons and Hope*.

EDWARD A. FEIGENBAUM: "Expert Systems." Edward A. Feigenbaum is professor of computer science, Stanford University, and co-author of *The Fifth Generation*.

GERALD FEINBERG: "The Future of Science"; "What is Life." (*See* List of Contributors, page 317.)

TOM FERGUSON, M.D.: "Medical Self-Care." Tom Ferguson, M.D., is the editor of *Medical Self-Care* and co-author of *The People's Book of Medical Tests*.

BARBARA FLYNN: "Art Galaxy." Barbara Flynn is an art critic and dealer and the founder and director of Art Galaxy, a non-profit gallery.

RICHARD FOREMAN: "Ontologic-Hysterical Theatre." Richard Foreman is a playwright and director and founder of The Ontologic-Hysterical Theatre, whose productions have been staged throughout Europe and the United States.

BETTY FRIEDAN: "The Second Stage." Betty Friedan is a feminist and the author of *The Feminine Mystique* and *The Second Sex*.

FRANK GILLETTE: "Art, Certainty, and Consensus." Frank Gillette is an artist who has shown his work at the Museum of Modern Art, the Whitney Museum, and the Leo Castelli Gallery.

DANIEL GOLEMAN: "The Social Trance." Daniel Goleman is the behavioral science writer of *The New York Times*. A psychologist, he is the author of *Vital Lies, Simple Truths: The Psychology of Self-Deception*.

ALAN GUTH: "The Birth of the Cosmos." Alan Guth, particle physicist at M.I.T., is the father of "the inflationary scenario" of the beginning of the universe.

CHARLES HAMPDEN-TURNER: "The Management of Dilemma." Charles Hampden-Turner is a psychologist and the author of *Radical Man* and *Maps of the Mind*.

MICHAEL HARNER: "Shamanic Healing." Michael Harner is an anthropologist and the author of *The Jivaro* and *The Way of the Shaman*.

ERICH HARTH: "Objects and Their Neural Images." Erich Harth is professor of physics at Syracuse University and author of *Windows on the Mind*.

NICK HERBERT: "Bell's Theorem." Nick Herbert is a research physicist and the author of *Quantum Reality*.

DANNY HILLIS: "Why My Company Is Called 'Thinking Machines.'" Danny Hillis is a computer scientist specializing in parallel programming. He is a founder of Thinking Machines Corporation.

ABBIE HOFFMAN: "Reality Club Banquet Speech"; "Notes from Nicaragua." Abbie Hoffman is a political activist, and author of *Woodstock Nation* and *Soon to Be a Major Motion Picture*.

MITCHELL KAPOR: "On Electronic Media and Information." Mitchell Kapor is the founder of Lotus Development Corporation. He is a visiting scientist at the Center for Cognitive Science at M.I.T.

JULIUS KOREIN, M.D.: "The Onset of Brain Life." (*See* List of Contributors, page 318.)

ROBERT LANGS: "The Two Sciences of Psychoanalysis." (*See* List of Contributors, page 318.)

LAWRENCE LeSHAN: "Domains of Science." Lawrence LeShan is a research psychologist, co-author of *Einstein's Space and Van Gogh's Sky*, and author of *The Mechanic and the Gardener*.

STEVEN LEVY: "Why Should I Talk to You?" Steven Levy is the author of *Hackers: Heroes of the Computer Revolution* and *The Unicorn's Secret: Murder in the Age of Aquarius*.

AMORY LOVINS and L. HUNTER LOVINS: "The Future of Energy." Amory Lovins is a physicist and L. Hunter Lovins is an attorney. They are co-authors of *Soft Energy Paths* and *Brittle Power*.

BENOIT MANDELBROT: "The Fractal Geometry of Nature." Benoit Mandelbrot, mathematician and father of "fractals," is an IBM Fellow at the IBM Research Center, and Abraham Robinson professor at Yale.

LYNN MARGULIS: "The Origins of Sex." (*See* List of Contributors, page 318.)

PAUL MARIANI: "John Berryman's Dream Songs." Paul Mariani is a biographer, critic, and poet, and the author of seven books, including *William Carlos Williams: A New World Naked*.

JOHN MARKS: "Intelligence and National Security." John Marks is a journalist, co-author of *The C.I.A. and the Cult of Intelligence*, and author of *In Search of the Manchurian Candidate*.

TOBY MAROTTA: "The Politics of Homosexuality." Toby Marotta is a gay activist and the author of *Sons of Harvard* and *The Politics of Homosexuality*.

KATINKA MATSON: "Short Lives." Katinka Matson, writer and literary agent, is the author of *The Encyclopedia of Reality* and *Short Lives*.

ROLLO MAY: "Psychology and Mythology"; "The Crisis in Psychotherapy." Rollo May is a psychologist and the author of *Love and Will* and *Freedom and Destiny*.

MICHAEL McCLURE: "The Shape of Energy: Biology and Poetry." Michael McClure is a poet and playwright, and author of *The Beard*.

PAMELA McCORDUCK: "Science and Meaning in Art." Pamela McCorduck, a writer, is the author of *Machines Who Think* and *The Universal Machine*, and co-author of *The Fifth Generation*.

RICHARD MULLER: "Nemesis: The Death Star." Richard Muller is professor of physics, University of California, Berkeley, and author of *Nemesis*.

DAN OGILVIE: "Dreaded States and Outcomes: Beliefs About Satisfaction Across the Life Span." Dan Ogilvie is a psychologist at Rutgers University.

RICHARD OGUST: "Reconceptualizing the Book." Richard Ogust is an artist and the author of *IBHR*, *IBHR-1*, and *IBHR-4*.

ROBERT PACK: "A Packet of Poems for Professor Pagels." Robert Pack is a poet, the director of the Breadloaf Writers' Conference, professor of English at Middlebury College, and author of *The Irony of Joy* and *Faces in a Single Tree*.

ELAINE PAGELS: "Adam, Eve, and the Serpent"; "The Politics of Paradise." Elaine Pagels is a professor of religious history, Princeton University, and author of *The Gnostic Gospels*, and *Adam, Eve, and the Serpent*.

HEINZ R. PAGELS: (1939–1988): "The Cosmic Code"; "Perfect Symmetry." Heinz R. Pagels was a high-energy physicist and executive director, The New York Academy of Sciences. He was the author of *The Cosmic Code*, *Perfect Symmetry*, and *The Dreams of Reason*.

GILLES QUISPEL: "The Black Madonna." Gilles Quispel is professor of religious history, Utrecht University, and author of *The Gospel of Thomas* and *The Secret Book of Revelation*.

RICHARD RABKIN, M.D.: "Brief Psychotherapy." Richard Rabkin, M.D., is a psychiatrist and the author of *Strategic Psychotherapy*.

JOAN RICHARDSON: "Wallace Stevens's Reality Club." (*See* List of Contributors, page 318.)

RICHARD RUOPP: "New Technology Initiatives in Education." Richard Ruopp, educator, is the former president of Bank Street College of Education.

PAUL RYAN: "A Triadic Logic"; "Human Triadic Relationships"; "Ecochannel for the Hudson Estuary." Paul Ryan is a cyberneticist and the author of *Cybernetics of the Sacred*.

DORION SAGAN: "The Origins of Sex." (*See* List of Contributors, page 318.)

RABBI ZALMAN SCHACTER: "Judaic Reality." Rabbi Zalman Schachter is professor of religion, Temple University, and author of *The First Step*.

ROGER SCHANK: "Explanation, Learning, and Creativity." (*See* List of Contributors, page 318.)

CAROLEE SCHNEEMANN: "Fresh Blood—A Dream Morphology." Carolee Schneemann, painter, film maker, performance artist, and writer, is the creator of the erotic film *Fuses*, and the kinetic performance *Meat Joy*.

EUGENE SCHWARTZ: "Post-Abstract Abstraction." Eugene Schwartz is a writer, publisher, and software developer. He has been collecting art since 1962; selections from his collection have been shown in almost every major museum in the world.

SEKA: "On Sexuality and Reality." Seka, "The Platinum Princess of Porn," is an adult-film actor, and star of *Inside Seka* and *Rockin' with Seka*.

JACOB SHAHEM: "The Neutron Star." Jacob Shahem is an astrophysicist, and professor of physics, Columbia University.

ROBERT SHAPIRO: "What Is Life?"; "Origins." Robert Shapiro, biochemist, is co-author of *Life Beyond Earth*, and author of *Origins: A Skeptic's Guide to the Creation of Life on Earth*.

DAVID SHAW: "Massive Parallelism." David Shaw is managing general partner of D.E. Shaw & Co., a securities firm.

RUPERT SHELDRAKE: "Morphogenetic Fields." Rupert Sheldrake is a plant physiologist, and author of *A New Science of Life* and *The Presence of the Past*.

DIMITRI SIMES: "The Gorbachev Revolution." Dimitri Simes, Sovietologist, is senior associate and director of the U.S.-Soviet Relations Program at the Carnegie Endowment for International Peace.

MORTON SMITH: "The Historical Jesus." Morton Smith is professor emeritus of ancient history at Columbia University, and author of *The Secret Gospel* and *Jesus the Magician*.

PAGE SMITH: "What Is History?" Page Smith is a historian, former provost of Cowell College, University of California, Santa Cruz, and author of *John Adams* and *A People's History of the United States* (8 volumes).

KENNETH SNELSON: "An Artist Views the Atom." Kenneth Snelson is a sculptor who is interested in the subject of structure.

GERD STERN: "Recent Poems." Gerd Stern is a poet and artist, co-founder of USCO, and author of *First Poems and Others* and *Afterimages*.

ROBERT STERNBERG: "On Love." (*See* List of Contributors, page 318.)

DONALD STRAUS: "Decision-Making in the Year 2000 and Beyond." Donald Straus, decision theorist, is the former president of the American Arbitration Association.

DAVID SUDNOW: "Ways of the Hand." David Sudnow is a sociologist, and author of *Ways of the Hand* and *Pilgrim in the Microworld*.

WILLIAM IRWIN THOMPSON: "Imagination and the Construction of Objects." William Irwin Thompson, cultural historian and journalist, is the author of *At the Edge of History* and *Pacific Shift*, and the founder and director of The Lindisfarne Association.

HANNE TIERNEY: "On the History and Evolution of Nonrepresentational Theater." Hanne Tierney is a theater artist.

JOSEPH TRAUB: "Complexity and Information." Joseph Traub is professor of computer science and chairman of the computer science department, Columbia University.

SHERRY TURKLE: "Computer Holding Power." Sherry Turkle is a sociologist and psychologist in M.I.T.'s Program in Science, Technology, and Society, and author of *The Second Self: Computers and the Human Spirit*.

JERE VAN DYK: "The Mujahidin." Jere Van Dyk is an adventurer, and author of *In Afghanistan*.

ROY L. WALFORD, M.D.: "Life Extension"; "Maximum Life Span." Roy L. Walford, M.D., is a biogerontologist and immunologist, professor of pathology, UCLA Medical School, and author of *Maximum Life Span* and *The 120-Year Diet*.

MARTHA WELCH, M.D.: "Holding Time." Martha Welch, M.D., is a psychiatrist and creator of the "Welch Method."

FRANK WILCZEK: "The Dark Matter in the Universe." Frank Wilczek is a cosmologist, professor of physics, Institute for Theoretical Physics, and coauthor of *Longing For the Harmonies*.

STEPHAN WOLFRAM: "Cellular Automata and Complexity in Nature." Stephen Wolfram is professor of physics, CCSR, University of Illinois, and a computer software entrepreneur.

ROGER WOOLGER: "Past Lives Therapy." Roger Woolger is Jungian analyst, and author of *Other Lives, Other Selves: A Jungian Psychotherapist Discovers Past Lives*.

RUDOLF WURLITZER: "Lightning Bob." Rudolf Wurlitzer is a novelist and screenwriter, and author of *Nog* and *Flats*.

DAVID and PHYLLIS YORK: "Tough Love." David and Phyllis York are psychologists, founders of Toughlove, and coauthors of *Toughlove* and *ToughLove Solutions*.

ABOUT THE EDITOR

JOHN BROCKMAN, founder of The Reality Club and editor of *The Reality Club*, is a writer and literary agent. He is the author of *By The Late John Brockman* (Macmillan, 1969), *37* (Holt, Rinehart and Winston, 1970), *Afterwords* (Anchor, 1973), *The Philosopher's Game* (with Edwin Schlossberg; St. Martin's Press, 1975), and editor of *About Bateson* (E. P. Dutton, 1977).